COGNITION:
AN INTRODUCTION

COGNITION:
AN INTRODUCTION

MICHAEL I. POSNER
The University of Oregon

Scott, Foresman and Company
Glenview, Illinois   Brighton, England

ACKNOWLEDGMENT

The quote on pages 62–63 from E. Hanfmann and J. Kasanin's *Conceptual Thinking in Schizophrenia*, a Nervous and Mental Disease Monograph, 1942, *67*, is reprinted by permission of the Smith Ely Jelliffe Trust.

To Sharon, O and A

Foreword

Both the content and the format of the beginning course in psychology vary widely today, not only between institutions and departments but also between instructors within the same department. There is a range of acceptable possibilities for organizing the course and considerable freedom for the instructor to select and emphasize those aspects of modern psychology which he considers most important and useful. One of the major reasons for course differences is the variety of subject matter and topics that are grouped under psychology. It is impossible to give adequate treatment to all the relevant topics within the time limitations typically imposed on the introductory course. To make matters more complicated, the accumulation of knowledge is proceeding at such a rapid pace in the different areas of psychology that it is virtually impossible for anyone to keep pace with new developments in all these fields. Thus, an instructor often rightfully limits his treatment to those topics which he feels competent to present with knowledge and understanding. Finally, the current emphasis, in response largely to student and public demand, on the uses of psychology, on its relevance, must be noted. To be sure, not all instructors are convinced of the appropriateness of teaching the application of psychology in the beginning course, pointing to the potential dangers of a little knowledge and of premature attempts to use information not well tested or standardized. In contrast, however, many who teach the introductory course give considerable time and attention to the application and the meaning of what is known.

With this variety in content, technique, and orientation among instructors, there is need for a corresponding variety of textual material. The Scott, Foresman Basic Psychological Concepts Series has been prepared in response to that need. Each title within the Series addresses a single topic. While the volumes are relatively brief, each gives a more intensified development of the topic than is available in any omnibus introductory textbook. Each volume has been prepared by an expert, who presents not only full knowledge of the current substantive and methodological state of his field, but who also provides an original and creative treatment of this material. The books are more than the typical cut-and-dried survey of a topic. There is room in each for the kind of original analysis of the problem heretofore unavailable in introductory reading.

Each title in the Series is independent of the others. They all have been written as a whole so as to maximize the coverage of psychology with minimal overlap and redundancy. No single title is a prerequisite to any

other in the Series. At the same time, we should note that there is considerable cross-referencing among the volumes and a general attempt at integrating facts and theories that are pertinent to several topics. While the titles are independent and may be used alone, they are also part of a larger, coordinated, comprehensive survey and interpretation of psychology.

The purpose of the Series is to provide both flexibility and expertise for the instructor and the student in the beginning course. The Series is adaptable to a variety of educational goals. The teacher can select and construct a set of reading units, with the content, emphasis, and sequence he desires, that will fit the general purpose and orientation of this course. He may, for example, base his course on several selected topics, each of which is developed in a separate volume. Alternatively, he might use only a single volume to fill a void or to further develop a topic of special importance. Volumes from the Series may be used in conjunction with most general textbooks. It is furthermore conceivable that one or another of the volumes would be useful in advanced courses, as preliminary reading for the student ill-prepared to contend with a topic on that level or as a supplement developing the background in a related topic. Because of the distinguished authorship of this Series, the teacher can feel confident in his selection without fear of uneven quality, superficiality, or duplication. This Series has a variety of uses at different educational levels, depending upon the needs of the student, the purpose of the course, and the creativity and imagination of the instructor.

In *Cognition: An Introduction,* Michael Posner takes a new and refreshing look at an ancient set of questions about the things people can do with their minds. These questions concern the competences and cognitions of human beings that permit them to retain their experiences, to integrate this knowledge with information from their present circumstances, to generate ways of behaving which are appropriate to those circumstances, and to move beyond both existing knowledge and present circumstances to inferences and to the production of truly creative acts. In psychology, research on these questions has been limited, until recently, by the S-R orthodoxy which dominated during the first half of this century. Because of the kind of data it would accept as scientific and the kind of theorizing it would allow as legitimate, behaviorism suppressed the scientific search into cognitive processes. The dominance of S-R psychology began to wane in the early 1950s, partly as a response to the obvious fact that not all behavior could be so rigidly construed, and partly because methodological innovations began to reveal important and interesting facts about human mental life. The growth of cognitive psychology has proceeded at an accelerated pace over the last decade.

Cognition: An Introduction reflects this growth. Professor Posner reviews the literature in cognitive psychology, mostly as it has developed over the last fifteen years. He organizes this body of knowledge according

to fruitful pretheoretic notions which center around the living organism as an information-processing system. And he speculates about the future of cognitive psychology, the directions it will take, the important problems and issues that remain to be addressed.

Just as cognitive psychology is a new and exciting area, so *Cognition: An Introduction* is an exciting, challenging book to read. The ideas discussed are not always easy, but a true understanding of them promises significant rewards. A new way of looking at human beings and their behavior is set forth, and new insights into how and why people are able to do the fantastic things they do in their heads are described. In short, *Cognition: An Introduction* provides the most comprehensive review presently available of this modern topic in psychology.

Lyle E. Bourne, Jr., Series Editor, University of Colorado
Leonard Berkowitz, Series Editor, University of Wisconsin

The study of how we think is both old and new. It is old because it raises questions which have played a prominent role in the two-thousand-year history of Western philosophy. It is new because recent laboratory experiments and psychological theories have shed some light upon these questions. *Cognition: An Introduction* is an attempt to place old questions within the framework provided by new studies.

Some of the best investigations into human thinking have used animals, children, brain-damaged patients, computers, or very creative individuals as subjects. We all have an interest in the new and the unusual, and the workings of organisms or machines different from us can reveal fascinating insights about thinking. At times this book uses such information, but in general the emphasis is upon more familiar insights obtained from the study of people who are like most of us. The idea is that the results obtained from unusual populations and machines are better understood when evaluated within a general framework drawn from studies of more typical human cognition. This book is an effort to abstract such a framework.

I have tried to select information that relates to central questions concerning human thought. Questions about the use of visual images, the nature of consciousness, and the bias introduced by past experiences have arisen repeatedly in philosophical speculation. However, not all the questions which might be asked can be answered. Thus it is important not only that questions be central, but also that some experimental analysis be available. Chapter 1 traces the central questions about thought that have puzzled mankind, and summarizes the history of various approaches to answering them.

To answer questions about mental images, memory structures, and mental operations requires us to study entirely internal events. At the beginning of experimental psychology this was attempted by means of introspection. Trained individuals tried to observe their own mental processes and draw inferences about them. Later psychologists reacted to the failure of the introspective method to provide consistent results by emphasizing overt behavior, and avoiding or deferring questions about internal events. The approach in *Cognition: An Introduction* is to raise questions about internal events, and to use objective experimental techniques, rather than introspection, as the basic means of exploration. The terms for internal processes are often borrowed from the older, introspective psychology *(consciousness, attention)* or from computer theory

(*processing capacity*), but their exact meaning depends on the experimental operations being discussed. Thus the material is objective in the sense of being based upon experiments which can be repeated freely and openly. It is subjective only in the sense that *inferences* are drawn about processes inside the organism. By the end of the book, it should be clear that only certain kinds of mental operations are available to conscious analysis.

It is doubtful that any reader will be entirely satisfied with the kinds of answers experiments have provided. Indeed, psychologists themselves are not. What I hope is clear is that experimental psychologists are working to understand the basic questions about the nature of human thought, questions which arise whenever the human mind turns to speculation about itself. Moreover, I hope the feeling is conveyed that psychologists are making some progress in developing answers and in formulating new questions. While it is disturbing not to find easy or definitive answers, the quest is both pleasant and at times fruitful.

This book has benefited greatly from my discussions with many colleagues and students. Much of the research described here has been supported by the National Science Foundation and by the National Institute of Education through grants provided to the University of Oregon. My colleague Ray Hyman, who knows more about thinking in all its forms than anyone else I have met, has given me very valuable help. I am also grateful to my colleagues and students who have participated in the research studies and read part or all of the manuscript, particularly Stephen Boies, Lyle Bourne, Robyn Dawes, Steven Keele, Joe Lewis, Robert Leeper, Sharon Posner, Gerald Reicher, and Paul Slovic.

Michael I. Posner
Eugene, Oregon

Table of Contents

1

A History of
Memory and Thought

Philosophy begins in wonder.
Alfred North Whitehead

Human thought in every era has led inevitably to some consideration of itself. With typically human self-regard, philosophers and scientists have given central importance to the activity in which they purport to engage. What is the nature of human thinking and what is its content? A carpenter knows that his task is to shape wood. At a superficial level, at least, the properties of the wood are simple to grasp. But what is the object with which the thinker deals and how does he alter its form?

The student of modern experimental psychology may only dimly realize the relationship of current studies in pattern recognition, visual memory codes, and decision making to the classical issues of abstract ideas and the laws of thought. When today's psychologist measures the time taken to press a key indicating that two visual objects are identical, he may do so without being aware of the seventeenth-century philosopher John Locke's third mental operation ("the clear perception by which we determine if two ideas are the same or different"). Nevertheless both men, in their own way, see the recognition of identity as basic to thinking.

In one sense Plato's quest for an object of thought still goes on, with the tools of clock, electrode, and mathematics supplementing, not replacing, the reflection upon which the natural philosophers relied. It is true that the exact questions asked by philosophers of antiquity and of our own time have not been answered and perhaps can never be answered. Experimental analysis brings its own problems and ways of asking questions, as well as its own methods and standards of answering them. A brief historical survey may provide a framework for judging the contribu-

tions of experimental analysis both in altering questions and in providing answers.

The historical development of the study of human thinking reveals two major strands which have combined to form the current field. The first strand has been concerned with the materials out of which thoughts are constituted. These constructions, whether called ideas, images, concepts, motor programs, engrams, traces, or a dozen other names, constitute the material stored in human memory. Some theories have viewed memories, like imprints on a wax block, as static duplications of perceived experience. Others have regarded memories as active and continuously changing, like the weaver's loom. Despite such vast differences in emphasis, some concept of the storage of information within the human nervous system is a necessary component for any understanding of cognition.

Memories alone are not sufficient, however. The second strand in the study of human thinking deals with the active reorganization of memory and its combination with new information. Cognitive acts of recognition, understanding, and judgment require the *use* of memories, together with mental operations. The study of mental operations in the form of the "laws of association" goes back to Greek times, and these laws continue to form a part of experimental psychology.

There is no strict separation between these two strands, either historically or in experimental analysis. Nevertheless, both the history of cognitive speculation and the current experimental scene are easier to organize and review if one tries to separate the stored representations or structures which people bring to a situation from the processes of search and computation which take place during the course of a task. The remainder of this chapter will outline some of the major questions concerning memory and thought which arose from and were developed in speculative philosophy.

GREEK THOUGHT

In pre-Socratic (fifth century B.C.) philosophy, the role of psychological theory was confined primarily to the analysis of the nature of sense organs (Stratton, 1917). For the most part this psychology was a natural extension of physical theory. Indeed, the name *natural philosophy* did not distinguish between physics and psychology. There was, for example, no separation between the study of light (physics) and of vision (psychology).

Diogenes of Appalonia (Beare, 1906) was the first to postulate mechanisms for the integration of sensory information which could serve as the seat for higher intellectual performance. Diogenes had notions both of memory and of the "common sense" which deals with information from the individual senses of vision, audition, touch, etc. He suggested that

memory was related to the natural physical element air. He observed that we breathe more easily after recall of a forgotten fact and that the process of remembering is frequently accompanied by catching one's breath. Diogenes built his model of intellectual processes upon the theories of the sense organs which had been worked out previously. Thus thinking was understood as a "central sense" related to the information presented by the specific senses in the same way that the sensations of vision and touch were related to the physical phenomena of the external world.

Plato also attempted to develop a theory of thought based upon the operation of the individual senses. For just as each sense organ is designed to apprehend a particular aspect of the environment, Plato held that human thought must also apprehend something in the real world. The object of thought, according to Plato, was the timeless, unchanging universal which lies behind the shifting impressions of sense. For example, the universal "man" was the true or ideal form of which each individual "man" is no more than a pale reflection. When we think about "man" in general, our central sense experiences this universal. This solution was not only consistent with the sensory bias of pre-Socratic psychology, but it also allowed Plato to propose a solution to the problem of truth in a world of shifting impressions.

Plato considered a theory of memory which made an analogy between memory and a wax impression. He said, "Imagine, then, for the sake of argument, that our minds contain a block of wax, which in this or that individual may be larger or smaller, and composed of wax that is comparatively pure or muddy, and harder in some, softer in others, and sometimes of just the right consistency." He went on to suggest, "Whenever we wish to remember something we see or hear or conceive in our own minds, we hold this wax under the perceptions or ideas and imprint them on it as we might stamp the impression of a seal ring. Whatever is so imprinted we remember and know so long as the image remains; whatever is rubbed out or has not succeeded in leaving an impression we have forgotten and do not know [p. 897]." Although Plato later dismissed the analogy as inadequate, the underlying view has persisted.

Two thousand years later, William James was still impressed with the efficacy of such a physical model of memory when he suggested, "Some minds are like wax under a seal—no impression, however disconnected with others, is wiped out. Others, like a jelly, vibrate to every touch but under usual conditions retain no permanent mark. These latter minds, before they can recollect a fact, must weave it into their permanent stores of knowledge. They have no *desultory* memory [p. 293]."

Aristotle rejected Plato's idea that universals existed as physical entities. Instead, the universal was *in* things, not separate from things. This required a theory of cognition which would allow the human mind to act upon objects to separate the universal. In some way the mind had to extract from many individual tables the concept or principle of "table."

Aristotle argued that the sense organ cannot itself apprehend the universal, but that we come to know the universal only through the active intellect. This view seemed to require that the universal be constructed by the intellect through an active process. It was in the description of this process that the major psychological questions of universals were embedded. However, Aristotle was almost totally obscure in describing the means by which the active intellect produces the universal. Thus Aristotle did not offer any real solution to the question of universals at the psychological level, although his doctrines clearly provided for such an account.

Aristotle made at least two other major contributions to the psychology of thought. The more important was the doctrine of *association.* Plato had observed the tendency of thought to run from one idea to another related idea. Aristotle proposed three laws of association which determined the course of thought. Ideas were associated by contiguity (i.e., had occurred together previously in time), similarity, or contrast. With minor modification, these laws have continued to be used down to the present. Aristotle also discussed mental operations which were not associational, by dealing with the processes of human reason closely related to logic. He did not distinguish between psychology and logic, so we do not know how much of his doctrine was meant to describe actual human behavior. Aristotle introduced a theory of the use of evidence as a method of arriving at truth *(induction),* and he discussed the rules of reasoning from a premise to a conclusion *(deduction).* These mental operations have also played a role in the development of the psychology of thinking, but until recently they have been overshadowed by the laws of association.

THE MEDIEVAL PERIOD

The long centuries between the decline of Greek science and the start of the Renaissance have not usually been thought of as fruitful in regard to scientific activity. However, modern historians have begun pointing to important developments which took place in the attitudes of scholars before the development of modern science. Mathematician and philosopher A. N. Whitehead suggested the role of medieval philosophy in generating the proper intellectual atmosphere for science:

> I do not think, however, that I have even yet brought out the greatest contribution of medievalism to the formation of the scientific movement. I mean the inexpugnable belief that every detailed occurrence can be correlated with its antecedents in a perfectly definite manner, exemplifying general principles. Without this belief the incredible labors of scientists would be without hope. It is this instinctive conviction, vividly poised before the imagination, which is the motive power of research: that there is a secret, a

secret which can be unveiled. How has this conviction been so vividly implanted on the European mind? My explanation is that the faith in the possibility of science, generated antecedently to the development of modern scientific theory, is an unconscious derivative from medieval theology [pp. 18–19].

The restricted information on the teachings of Aristotle during the tenth and eleventh centuries and the importance of theological consideration led to an emphasis upon the question of whether or not universals existed in nature. The view of *exaggerated realism* held that universals existed in nature and were apprehended or sensed by people. Two other doctrines were more closely related to how people obtained and used universals. The simpler was *nominalism,* which held, in its purest form, that universals were merely words. According to this view, all general statements referred only to the relationship between words. Thus thinking operated in an entirely linguistic domain. A more complicated view was *conceptualism.* According to this view, people constructed universals through a process of abstraction. The conceptualist view was much closer to the doctrine of the active reason which Aristotle had suggested. It viewed the universal as a mental entity, not one present in the external world.

In the eleventh century Peter Abelard outlined a psychological doctrine of how the mind comes to abstract universal qualities from individual objects. He described the mind as being able to attend to one aspect of the individual object, ignoring other aspects, and thus isolating those dimensions which relate differing objects. For example, a ball and an apple, though different, are identical in that both are round. It is important to note that his was purely a descriptive account, a theory of how the mind operates, and not a prescription for how a person ought to think, nor still less an analysis of a socially approved method for obtaining knowledge.

In the later Middle Ages the psychological theory of universals became closely related to the study of methods for correct induction. Recent scholarship has traced the development of the scientific method to the Oxford School, which flourished from the thirteenth to the fifteenth centuries (Crombie, 1953). The founder of the Oxford School and, according to historian of science Crombie, the first to understand and use the new theory of experimental science was Robert Grosseteste. Grosseteste united in his own work the experimental and the rational traditions of the twelfth century and set forth a systematic theory of experimental science. Grosseteste, more clearly than Aristotle, rested the inductive aspects of his new science upon an analysis of the psychological process underlying the abstraction of universals.

The evolution of the scientific method continued within the Oxford School, with the work of Roger Bacon being particularly important. Bacon proposed an experimental science and is often credited with being the

founder of the scientific method. His work represented a clear tendency away from psychological description, and toward a set of rules about how to find the true state of affairs.

In the centuries following the end of the medieval period, philosophers and logicians continued to develop theories which would provide methods of obtaining true inference from the evidence at hand. Much of this work on the scientific method was separated from consideration of descriptions of human thinking. However, such classics of philosophy as J. S. Mill's *A System of Logic* (1843) and G. Boole's *Laws of Thought* (1862) clearly indicate the close relationship between psychological theory and the development of logic and of the scientific method. The current psychology of thinking reflects these important historical ties. For example, modern work in the learning of concepts by human subjects (Bruner, Goodnow, & Austin, 1956) has shown that, under some circumstances, people untrained in logic will use methods quite similar to those which Mill proposed as logical rules for induction. Other investigators have used the mathematics of probability theory to form a baseline against which to test human performance in the use of evidence (Edwards, 1962). Thus there has been a long historical relationship between psychological theories of how people think and logical systems concerned with how one should think, such as the scientific method.

THE MODERN PERIOD

Since the seventeenth century, questions of representation of information in memory and of mental operations for using such representations have been developed in many fields of inquiry. What follows is an attempt to trace the main influences upon current experimental research in psychology without doing undue violence to the historical tradition from which these ideas rose.

Memory Representation

The wax-impression theories discussed earlier placed heavy emphasis upon representation in the form of direct copies of external reality. Memory traces were considered primarily duplications of what was perceived by the senses. This basic concept of memory traces has been carried over into the modern experimental period. There is an acute problem for philosophy only when the physical object to which the memory refers is not readily apparent. This is clearly the case for the representation of universals. What is the object to which the idea "triangle" refers? We have experienced only individual triangles; how do we get the notion of "triangle" in general?

In the seventeenth century, John Locke proposed that we store a *concept* which is abstracted from our individual experience, but which

has its own separate representation in memory. It is not entirely clear what Locke meant by a concept, but in attempting to refute his view, George Berkeley supposed that Locke intended that we had an image or picture of the universal (e.g., a universal triangle), which was separate from each individual triangle.

The idea that images were the main representations involved in thought led to the earliest experiments in the psychology of thinking. At the end of the nineteenth century a group of German psychologists (the Wurzburg School) began to set up simple problems under carefully controlled conditions (see Mandler & Mandler, 1964). They found no evidence to support the view that people were conscious of an image of a dog between hearing the word "dog" and being able to produce a category of which that word was a member (e.g., "animal").

Despite the inability of these experiments to show the involvement of images in thinking, the analysis of images was still a subject of much interest. In 1932, F. C. Bartlett published an extensive experimental study on memory. Bartlett (1932) pointed out that the basic fallacy in the study of images throughout the early history of experimental psychology was its emphasis upon the descriptive and subjective aspects of images, rather than upon the functions they performed in the mental processes of the subject. Thus Bartlett said,

> It is often held that, since images are generally vague, fleeting, and variable from person to person and from time to time, hardly any statement can be made about them which will not be im-mediately contradicted on very good authority. This view has arisen because most statements that have been made about images in traditional psychology concern their nature rather than their functions, what they are rather than what they make it possible to do; and many of the controversies that have been raised about them have been concerned primarily with their epistemological status [p. 215].

During the period from 1910 to 1940, relatively little experimental or theoretical analysis was concerned with the question of imagery. Quite recently, however, the analysis of imagery has begun to play a more important role in psychological theory (Neisser, 1967). This time the emphasis is upon objective methods of identifying images and upon analysis of how they enter into the thought processes, rather than upon a static description of them. Within this new framework, the idea of composite or abstract representations as a means of storing certain types of visual information is again being tested in the laboratory.

All theories of thinking have been very concerned with the use of language (Slobin, 1971). The earliest laboratory studies of learning (Ebbinghaus, 1913) investigated the development of associations between

verbal items. Words are extremely flexible vehicles for thought because they have no necessary resemblance to the objects that they represent. Moreover, the combination of words into sentences provides one means for the expression and comprehension of universals. Indeed, the philosophical view called nominalism held that universals were identical to abstract words. Nevertheless, it still appears important to posit nonlinguistic memory systems which can lead to our recognition of a new visual item as an instance of a particular word. The study of language is a part of the subject of thinking, but not the whole of it.

There is still a third tradition of representation in memory, the retention of motor skills. The process by which one ties a knot is represented neither as an image nor as a series of words, but rather as a motor program which allows recall only by doing (Bruner, Oliver, & Greenfield, 1966). Some philosophers have suggested that all concepts are best thought of as high-level skills for performing certain types of recognition, grouping, or classifying (Aaron, 1952). Philosopher Gilbert Ryle (1949) suggests a crucial difference between remembering based upon words and images ("remembering that") and remembering based upon motor skills ("remembering how"). He points out that while a person is performing a skill (e.g., tying a knot), he may be thinking about something else. But in dealing with visual or verbal recall, one's conscious attention is given to the act of remembering itself. Ryle's view raises the issue of how skills are represented in memory and what role they play in thought.

Many complex memory representations appear to have a dual character. On the one hand, they can be brought to consciousness and inspected like an image. On the other, they can produce a particular behavior. In recent years psychologists have begun to develop objective methods for distinguishing between skill memories and memories based upon visual and verbal codes. These methods can be used to help unravel the complex combination of memory codes which comprise many of our concepts. Moreover, such distinctions reduce the tendency, so common among philosophers, to choose one coding system as the basis for thought. In this way, debate about whether the elements of thought are images, skills, or logical propositions is being replaced by an analysis of the role of each kind of code in thinking.

It should be apparent that many of the traditional questions about thinking concern the form in which past experience is represented in memory. Philosopher H. H. Price (1946) summarized the crucial importance of this information very well:

> For our present purpose, however, the most important point is this: that if we ignore these standing features of the mind, these persistent cognitive states, and concentrate all our attention on mental acts—then we can give no adequate account of thinking and particularly of thinking in absence. No theory of thinking in

absence can possibly be adequate unless it takes into account three sorts of acquired but persistent mental states: first, our permanent familiarity with certain universals; secondly, our permanent capacity to utter or image certain symbols; and lastly, the permanent associative linkage between these two [p. 122].

In Chapters 2 through 4 our goal will be to understand the experimental analysis of the features represented in memory over long periods of time.

Mental Operations

Memory, however important to thinking, is not the entire story. Two other concepts first introduced by Aristotle still play an important role in the modern theory of thought. First are the laws of association, which continue to be used as a means of accounting for how one thought leads to another. All theorists of thinking have remarked on the importance of contiguity between events as a means of developing associations or connections between internal representations (Reeves, 1965). In particular, psychologists have been concerned with the relationship between the frequency with which items are paired and the probability (strength) of their association. Laws of association other than contiguity have been disputed; some authors view contiguity alone as fundamental, while others hold that laws of similarity and contrast are also needed.

Laws of association are not sufficient as a basis for thinking. The early German experiments on thinking posed a difficult problem for such laws (e.g., Otto Selz, as cited in Mandler & Mandler, 1964). Suppose that a subject is instructed to respond with a category to a word he hears. He is then given the stimulus word "dog." How does he arrive at the common response of "animal"? According to a strict associational account, the instruction "category" activates certain associations which include not only the word "animal," but also "cat" (which is a category for such words as "Persian" or "Siamese"). The word "dog" then activates its associations, which include "animal" and "cat," among others. Because certain words are associates both of the instruction "category" and of the word "dog," they receive a double activation and are likely to be elicited. However, associational theory cannot explain why the word "animal," which is a category to which "dog" belongs, is usually given as the response rather than the word "cat," which is a close associate to "dog" and also a category (though not one to which "dog" belongs). In other words, how does the double instruction "category" and "dog" lead inevitably to a word which is not only associated with "dog," but which is also associated by a particular relationship (namely, category)?

To explain this, Otto Selz proposed that, in addition to the strength of association, thought must involve the use of specific relationships (e.g., superordinate). The fact that a word is included within a superordinate

category must be explained by a theory of thought. Selz's view emphasized the importance of the relationship between ideas. The results of early experiments on thinking indicated that such relationships were needed to explain even the most simple judgments.

As one moves from very simple to complex human tasks, the laws of association become even less adequate as a complete basis for thought. Aristotle also emphasized the importance of *abstraction, induction,* and *deduction* as possible principles on which to base human thinking. In the seventeenth century, John Locke proposed *perception, retention, distinguishing, comparison,* and *composition* as fundamental mental acts. These efforts at defining the basic operations of human reason were not particularly successful, but they did provide the basis for a school of psychology which stressed mental operations or acts as the basis of thought.

By the late nineteenth century there were two rival theories concerning thought. One placed primary emphasis on the structures or representations which entered into thinking. This structural psychology was expounded by Wilhelm Wundt in Germany and was heir to the tradition of memory representation that we have sketched. Its rival was a psychology which placed primary emphasis on operations or cognitive acts, and was represented by the German psychologist Franz Brentano. Brentano thought of memory representations as static entities which had little importance for psychology. Rather, he felt, it was the cognitive acts of comparing, judging, and feeling which were the primary study of psychology. In many ways the current experimental psychology of thought can be seen as an effort to find methods for relating the more static representational structures created by learning to the dynamic changes which occur in mental acts.

It has been difficult to design and execute experiments which reveal the basic mental operations underlying the myriad different kinds of thinking. As early as 1869, the Dutch physiologist F. C. Donders attempted to measure the time for simple mental operations such as discrimination and choice. Others tried to develop measures for more complex operations. However, the methods used were not entirely adequate and the enterprise was largely abandoned until recently. Perhaps the major effort to study mental operations during the early twentieth century was contained in the developmental psychology of Jean Piaget. Piaget developed a theoretical framework for the growth of thinking in the child by tracing the maturation of certain logical operations. At the same time, but in a somewhat less systematic way, experimental psychologists were studying the operations of abstraction and judgment in the adult. Laboratory tasks required subjects to isolate aspects or features of objects (e.g., color or number) from complex displays. More recently, the study of rule learning has focused on the ability to combine information in recognition and judgment.

The study of mental operations has often required psychologists to import from mathematics, logic, and philosophy ideas concerning correct or optimal ways of making judgments or decisions. These prescriptions for correct thought had their historical origins in the development of the scientific method and, as has been pointed out, they were heavily influenced by early psychological theory. It is not surprising that these ideas have considerable relevance to psychological problems.

Chapters 5 through 7 of this book will focus on current efforts in the study of mental operations. An attempt will be made to study performance of such operations within simple tasks and to illustrate the role of these same operations in more complex judgmental and problem-solving situations.

INNATE IDEAS AND CONSCIOUSNESS

One doctrine which has played a prominent role in philosophy is difficult to classify in terms of memory and mental operations. It is the notion that there are inborn structures and organizing principles in thought. Emanuel Kant viewed the categories of time and space as innate operations which organized an otherwise chaotic world. For many years the controversy between innate and learned factors raged within the area of perception (Hochberg, 1964). Careful experimental studies of color, depth, and form perception have worked out many of the ways in which innate structures and learning are coordinated to bring about mature perception. Recently the same issue has emerged in the area of language and thought. The linguist Noam Chomsky (1968) has stressed the importance of innate factors in the development of language in the child. He has held that the speed and efficiency with which the child develops grammar from the small number of utterances which he experiences suggest the importance of innate language universals which are basic to the learning of particular languages. A fuller discussion of Chomsky's ideas is available elsewhere in this series (Slobin, 1971).

There is as yet little empirical evidence which would allow a detailed account of innate and learned factors in language development, and still less in thought in general. Moreover, since this book is focused on adult thinking, it is even more difficult to tease apart learned and innate factors. Time and space are clearly important organizers of human experience, whether one holds these principles to be innate categories or categories derived from earlier experience.

The nature of consciousness has also been a central problem in Western philosophy, but if one were to judge by the indexes of books on experimental psychology, it might be supposed that psychology had little interest in the functions of consciousness. Most modern experimental textbooks make no reference at all to consciousness, and treat its functions only under various disguises.

Philosophers have long been concerned with the supposed separation between consciousness (mind) and matter (body or brain). The mind-body or mind-brain problem refers to the difficulty which various philosophers have had in developing a unified theory which would encompass the seemingly different worlds of mental and physical phenomena.

Philosophers have presented many reasons for separating matter and mind. Seventeenth-century philosopher René Descartes suggested that matter was subject to analysis by formal mathematics, and thus to the development of a sophisticated natural law. Mind, on the other hand, was not amenable to quantitative analysis. Descartes wrote,"Though one thing can be said to be more or less white than another or a sound sharper or flatter and so on, it is impossible to determine exactly whether the greater exceeds the less in the proportion of two to one or three to one, etc. [Burtt, 1954, p. 44]." The success of psychologists in measuring sensations (Stevens, 1966) and in otherwise extending the use of mathematics in the formulation of psychological laws (Luce, Bush, & Galanter, 1963) raises many problems for this Cartesian position.

A more important reason for separating mind and body has been the notion that, although body is extended and requires space, mental operations do not and are therefore fundamentally different from matter (Kant, 1909). The ability of electronic computers to perform mental operations suggests that such operations can be handled within the context of physical law. As will be suggested in Chapters 5 and 6, the measurement of human mental operations by their requirements for time and space within the central nervous system raises further difficulties for this rationale for separating mental and physical events. Thus developments which have taken place within experimental psychology have cast some new light on these old problems.

As long as psychology consisted primarily of the introspective method, the subject was of necessity restricted to processes which were conscious. No others were amenable to introspection, and therefore they were by definition outside the scope of psychology. It was usual to consider nonconscious processes to be in the domain of physiology. There were disputes about which aspects of thought could be revealed by introspection and which were outside conscious analysis. For example, Wundt held that introspection could reveal the structures or elements out of which consciousness was composed, but that the processes by which these structures were combined were not preserved in consciousness and were thus a part of physiology. On the opposite side, Brentano held that only these processes or mental acts were conscious and that the structures on which such acts operated were not conscious and were therefore part of physiology.

Sigmund Freud was probably the first to popularize the idea that mental processes might be either conscious or unconscious and still be within the realm of psychological theory. While others prior to Freud had proposed

the idea of unconscious thought processes (see Reeves, 1965, for a review), Freud's theory was the most detailed psychological analysis. Freud suggested that unconscious processes were capable of at least the full range of complexity of cognitive operations which were available to consciousness.

Experimental psychology in the first half of the twentieth century did not attempt an analysis of the functions of consciousness. Most experimental theories failed to distinguish between conscious and unconscious processing, and thus were able to ignore the questions of the functional utility of consciousness. However, the problem of consciousness continued to enter into the analysis of problem solving and thought, if only by the back door. As was noted earlier, the distinction between skill and image involves the degree of conscious attention required. There were reports both anecdotal (Poincaré, 1929) and experimental (Patrick, 1935, 1937) of the phenomenon of incubation. The idea was that, following a period of intense work, the solution to a problem was likely to pop into mind spontaneously after the problem had been set aside for awhile. The implication was that the solution was produced by an unconscious thought process.

In the presence of a theoretical framework that excluded the idea of consciousness and methods for its investigation, it has not been easy to evaluate the idea of incubation. However, several recent developments within experimental psychology are providing a framework in which a new experimental analysis of consciousness might be possible. This analysis is outlined in Chapters 5 and 6, and applied to problem solving and the question of incubation in Chapter 7.

SUMMARY

This chapter has reviewed the history of questions which are currently being analyzed in laboratories devoted to the psychology of the thought processes. The historical analysis has concerned: (1) memory structures used to represent information; (2) mental operations performed upon these memory structures. These two areas taken together form the basis for modern views of human thought.

The history of memory representations has been concerned primarily with how people are able to understand universals (e.g, "man"), having only experienced particulars. The attempts to solve this question have had implications both for logic and for psychology.

Efforts to understand the types of mental operations which people perform go back to the laws of association first formulated by Aristotle. However, the idea that all thought is based on connections or associations between ideas has proved inadequate to handle even simple problems.

Somehow the ability to use different types of relationships between internal representations must be taken into account.

Two issues of special interest to psychology are innate ideas and consciousness. These problems have received a great deal of attention in philosophy, which is now being carried over into experimental psychology studies.

Section I

STATICS OF COGNITION

2

Representation in Memory

The understanding once stored with these simple ideas has the power to repeat, compare and unite them to an almost infinite variety and so can make at pleasure new complex ideas.

John Locke

All authors who have been concerned with the study of thinking have realized the importance of memory. Only in recent years, however, has the theory of memory become sufficiently rich to contribute to an understanding of the limitations and characteristics of human cognition (see, for example, Norman, 1970). This development has been due mainly to the distinction psychologists have begun to make between the characteristics of different memory systems and the codes which these systems employ. A *memory system* is a set of common mechanisms for storing information. We infer a common mechanism from such features as the rate at which information is lost. *Memory codes* refer to qualitative differences in the format of items within a memory system. This chapter will deal with two different memory systems and three general types of qualitative codes.

The distinctions between systems and codes will be based upon properties determined by experiments, and not by introspective accounts. The use of experimental data to make these distinctions has two advantages. First, it insures that different investigators have the same distinctions in mind. Second, it provides a technique for producing the phenomenon and observing its properties. In general, the experimental

distinctions correspond to many of our introspections, but experimental methods allow us to go beyond properties which can be reported verbally, to explore characteristics of the system or code of which we may not be aware.

MEMORY SYSTEMS

Human memory can be roughly divided into two vastly unequal systems. The first contains all items which are in an active state. There are few items in this state because the capacity to maintain active items is quite limited (Broadbent, 1958). This limitation is familiar if you have ever tried to dial a new phone number after a momentary interruption or if you have been interrupted in a conversation only to find that you now do not know what you were discussing. The remainder of the human memory capacity not presently in an active state is called long-term memory.

While the distinction between active and long-term memory is not absolute or precise, it is of enormous importance in the study of thinking because active memory provides a system within which incoming information can be related to previously stored information.

The classical doctrine of association (p. 4) held that contiguous items were associated with each other. Do such associations depend upon the information's occurring together in the external world? If so, the associations would be fixed entirely by the ordering of external-stimulus events. Active memory permits external information and information already in long-term memory to become associated, thus providing a means of reorganizing and updating long-term memory.

It is possible to view the function of active memory as somewhat analogous to that of a desk top (Broadbent, 1971). When working on a problem, an individual may assemble materials related to the topic from various files and books and place them on the desk top. When he is finished, he may stuff the materials placed on the desk into a drawer and keep them as a unit. Or he may return the items to their original locations, perhaps storing the problem solution. Of course, active memory works somewhat differently, since we do not remove items from long-term memory in the course of activating them. Nor do we have perfect control over which aspects of the desk-top organization are remembered and which forgotten. Nevertheless, the analogy provides a useful picture of the role of active memory.

Active memory also allows us to readjust associations on a trial basis without changing the underlying associational structure of long-term memory. An example of an organized sequence in long-term memory is the digits from zero to nine. If someone says the number "three," you are more likely to respond with "four" than with any other number. This is because you have stored in your memory a list of numbers in the order corresponding to their numerical magnitude. This can be shown experi-

mentally in the following way. If someone asked you to respond as quickly as possible whether a digit belonged to the set of digits from one to four, you would be quite fast in responding "no" to "nine," but much slower in responding "no" to "five" (Morin, DeRosa, & Stultz, 1967). This illustrates that the digit five is more closely linked or associated with the set one to four than is the digit nine. Other lists, such as the alphabet, also have an ordered character, as can be demonstrated by trying to recall the letter before J. To do this task, it is often necessary to go back several letters and name them in the forward order.

The basic list organization of the number series in long-term memory can be reprogrammed in active memory with great ease. Suppose you were asked to try to remember the series eight-six-three. Immediately after the presentation of these three numbers, the probability of your being able to recall them correctly would be virtually 1. However, if your attention was distracted for even a brief period of time, the probability of your recalling the numbers in the correct order would decline. The new order (eight-six-three) is temporary and it is quickly lost from its active state. This rapid loss restores the dominance of the long-term associative links. This is not to suggest that a given digit may be in only one list in long-term memory. The digit three may appear in different orders in such lists as your telephone number and your address. However, using a memory system which is strictly temporary allows us to try out new combinations of ideas without fear that they will later interfere with our more habitual organizations.

Active memories are of two kinds. Either they are new items presented to one of the senses (vision, audition, etc.) or they come from our own long-term memory. Psychologists interested in the study of memory have been more concerned with the first of these, often called *short-term memory*. A striking aspect of items in short-term memory is that they have a very brief life in the absence of sustained attention. If, for example, someone provided you with a list of random digits, the maximum number you could repeat after a single trial would be about eight. This number is called the *memory span*. As was suggested earlier, even within this span, exact retention can be very limited. If you were presented with three unrelated letters and your attention was diverted for a period of time by a task such as counting backwards, your probability of recall would drop from nearly 1 to about .2 within a few seconds (Peterson & Peterson, 1959). The more thoroughly attention is controlled during the interval, the more dramatic will be the rate of loss (Posner & Rossman, 1965). When the incoming list is slow and you are free to rehearse, or when the material is novel, long-term retention is better.

Material can also be activated from our own long-term memory. Such items are then said to be in *operational memory*. Suppose you are asked to think about your own telephone number. You can assemble the ordering of digits which corresponds to that number. These digits will then be in a

state of active memory that has many similarities to the state which accompanies the presentation of new information. For example, the rate at which information can be examined is the same whether it is new information or information activated from long-term memory (Sternberg, 1969).

There are, however, ways in which retention of new input and retention of material activated from long-term memory are different. If rehearsal of new information is disrupted, recall is lowered. However, if you are interrupted after activating items from your own long-term memory, you can still recall the items. It may be that it will require more time to do so, but since the material is present in long-term memory, you will probably be able to find it.

Many psychologists (Hebb, 1949) and physiologists (Konorski, 1967) have proposed that the mechanism underlying active memory is a continuing electrical process within the brain. In contrast, long-term memory is thought to involve a more permanent structural change in the properties of brain cells. This view argues for the distinction between two memory systems and also suggests that items in operational memory are simultaneously located in both systems, while items in short-term memory are represented only by the active process. If this view is accepted, the same limitation of six to eight unrelated items (memory span) applies to material in short-term memory and to material in operational memory (Hunter, 1964). The general limitation of active memory represents an important constraint upon our ability to solve problems.

MEMORY CODES

Imagery

One of the most important aspects of memory is the coding of items. *Coding* refers to the qualitative form of the information. The term *image* refers to an internal representation which bears a close correspondence to the sensory experience which gave rise to it. *Iconic codes* refers to images in the visual modality, and they have been the most widely studied. Auditory images have sometimes been termed *echoic codes.*

Active memories can sometimes be shown to involve the same mechanisms used by the sensory systems. For example, certain icons can be shown to involve use of the brain's visual system. Another way in which an iconic code resembles the experience may be in the preservation of certain relationships present in the physical stimulus. For example, when you think about a friend, you may describe him in a purely verbal way as having a long nose, blue eyes, etc. Many people report that they can construct a kind of visual representation which includes more information than they can verbalize. Reitman (1965) proposes the following

demonstration of this phenomenon. Suppose you think about a walrus with a cigar and a top hat. Try to hold such a picture in your mind's eye. Can you say where the cigar and the top hat are? In most cases the constructive representation will have the cigar in the mouth and the top hat on the head, although no instruction of this sort was given in the verbal description. Psychologists are rarely happy with introspective reports as a means of assessing the coding of stimuli. The language of such reports differs greatly with each subject and it is easy to suggest inadvertently the type of report which you want the person to give. Instead, a number of tests have been constructed to provide objective methods of observing the coding of memories.

Active memories tend to have a code associated with one or another of the sensory modalities. This is especially true of short-term memory for new information. If a single letter is briefly flashed, there is a period of time during which it can be erased by a subsequent visual flash (Kahneman, 1968). This backward masking of prior input by subsequent visual information suggests that the prior information is in a store which is highly visual. A single letter can be named so quickly that backward erasure of this type can be obtained for only about a tenth of a second after the stimulus. Somewhat longer masking effects can be obtained in the visual modality if such a large number of letters are shown that a subject has difficulty naming them all. Even with this technique, the period of time during which a visual trace is subject to erasure by subsequent visual information is rather short (less than a second).

A similar phenomenon can be obtained with auditory material (Crowder & Morton, 1969). A series of digits followed by a speech sound yields a lower probability of the listener's recalling the last item than does the same series followed by silence or a tone. You may demonstrate this rather easily. Prepare a number of eight-digit lists. Read them aloud to your subject, following half of them by the word "recall" and half by a pencil tap. As soon as you say "recall" or tap the pencil, have your subject repeat the list in the order presented. The results may be plotted as in Figure 1. Note that recall of the last item or two is much worse when you say "recall" than when you tap the pencil. Careful experimental work suggests that this effect is due to masking of the final digit by the subsequent sound in a way which appears analogous to that found in vision. The brief life of memory codes which can be erased by modality-specific input suggests that these codes have relatively little importance for thinking.

Items in long-term memory can also be activated in a way which illustrates their iconic character. Figure 2 shows a pattern which subjects were asked to imagine (Brooks, 1968). Most people can do this satisfactorily, although the language they use to describe the experience differs. The subjects were then asked to go around their image of the F, starting in a given position and responding if each corner was either on

FIGURE 1   ERRORS IN RECALL OF EIGHT DIGITS AS A FUNCTION OF ITEM POSI-
TION

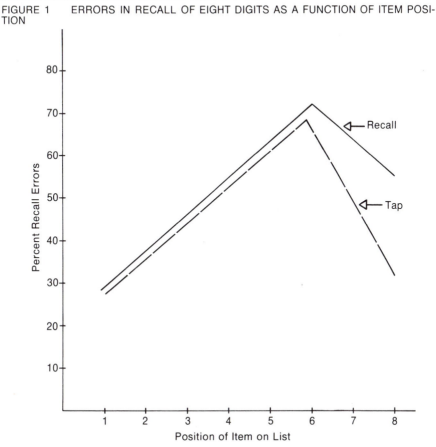

Hypothetical data patterned after Crowder, R. G., and Morton, J. Precategorical acoustic
storage. *Perception and Psychophysics,* 1969, *5,* 365–373.

the top or bottom of the figure ("yes") or not ("no"). In three conditions
subjects indicated their responses by either (1) saying "yes" or "no," (2)
tapping their left or right fingers, or (3) pointing to "yes" or "no" in a
pattern of symbols like those shown in the right half of Figure 2. It took
longer when subjects were required to use new visual input in pointing
out their answers.

By itself this result may not be too meaningful, but Brooks was careful
to eliminate the possibility that pointing to the visual Y or N was itself
more difficult than the other two means of indicating the response. He did
this by a second condition in which subjects had to memorize a sentence
(e.g., "A bird in the hand is not in the bush"). They were then required to
think through the sentence and classify each word as either a noun or not.

FIGURE 2   DOTTED FIGURE OF THE LETTER F

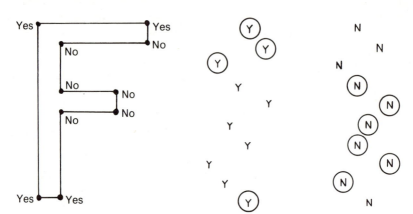

Subjects were asked to imagine this figure (left panel) and indicate whether or not each dot was a corner dot either orally or by pointing to the correct letter in a column of Y's and N's (right panel). Adapted from Brooks, L. R. Spatial and verbal components of the act of recall. *Canadian Journal of Psychology*, 1968, *22*, 349–368.

The response was to be made in each of the three ways described previously. For this task the verbal response (saying "yes" or "no") took longer than the other two conditions. Taken together, these findings indicate that dealing with new visual information interferes with visual imagery, while verbal output interferes with auditory (verbal) imaging. It has also been shown that instructions to image reduce the probability of detecting new input presented in the modality of the image (Segal & Gordon, 1969; Segal & Fusella, 1970). Notice that in these studies there is no erasure, but merely competition between the imaging and new information, as if they required access to the same mechanism.

Another good example of the iconic character of constructed images is shown in a study by Atwood (1971), in which subjects were given short sentences such as "The nude devoured the bird." They were then asked to try to construct a visual image which represented the scene. After receiving each sentence they performed a simple mental calculation with either a visually presented digit or an auditory digit. It was found that the presentation of a visual digit reduced the number of sentences which could be reproduced later by the subject. When the sentences were abstract so that it was difficult to construct images (e.g., "Einstein was a brilliant physicist"), the auditory-digit task produced as much interference as the visual digit.

One must be careful to point out that the mechanisms used by imaging are not identical to those used to perceive information. If they were identical, it would not be possible for a subject to tell the difference

between perception and imaging. In fact, it is usually quite simple to do so, although there are reports of confusions between weak signals and images (Perky, 1910; Segal & Gordon, 1969). The simplicity of such discrimination may depend in part upon the sensory modality. Imagining the feeling of an insect or spider crawling on the skin may be much more difficult to discriminate from the actual perception than is the case for visual imagery (Konorski, 1967). In the tactile modality, imaging can frequently become so vivid that the subject becomes very uncomfortable.

A less severe criterion for a visual code than those discussed above is that it preserves information which would be lost by a verbal description. It seems doubtful that our verbal descriptions of a face would be sufficient for us to recognize the face again. Yet our ability to recognize faces and pictures is much greater than our ability to recognize words (Shepard, 1967). In one sense the memories which serve to recognize such purely visual experiences may be said to be visual, even though there is as yet little evidence that such memories necessarily involve the visual system.

It is possible to distinguish experimentally between the visual and verbal code of a letter. The following experiment illustrates the existence of such separate visual and verbal codes. A subject is shown a single letter long enough to see and name it. He is instructed to press a key as quickly as possible if a second letter which follows has the same name. It is found that when the second letter matches the first in both name and case (e.g., AA), the key is pressed more rapidly than if the case is switched (e.g., Aa). This faster response when the letters are physically identical is present for only one or two seconds, after which both cases have the same latency. Presumably, during this period the visual representation of the first letter is in an active state and can be used in a very efficient way. After that period, matching based on the visual code is no longer more efficient than matching based upon the name. However, by use of other techniques it is possible to show that the visual code is still present even after many minutes.

Unfortunately, we are still far from a detailed knowledge of the ways in which sensory memory codes resemble actual perception. Simon (1969) reports an experiment in which subjects imaged a 3-×-3 matrix of digits. It was found that they took much longer to scan the image along a diagonal than in a left-to-right order. Simon suggests that scanning an image is more like remembering a series of words than it is like looking at a picture. There may be difficulties with this conclusion, since left-to-right scan is usually easier even if the actual matrix is presented in the visual field. However, the suggestion that images are limited to a few simultaneous items and are scanned in a definite order corresponds closely to careful subjective reports obtained by Sir Francis Galton (1907). You can determine this for yourself quite easily. Imagine the word "pumpkin." Most people can get a moderately clear picture of the word. If you can, try

spelling the word backwards. It is more difficult to do than one would expect if a picture of the word were present. That images are not identical in all ways to perception should not obscure the fact that both subjective reports and objective experiments (Atwood, 1971; Brooks, 1968) testify to their intimate relationship to particular sensory modalities.

Visual imagination, as inferred from experiments, may not turn out to be identical with subjective reports. Still, in the absence of experimental results using objective techniques, it is useful to turn to such reports to get a feeling of the variety of visual imagination. Galton (1907) conducted extensive surveys of imagery. Some of the subjects reported far more complex forms of imagery than those which are studied in the laboratory. Several of Galton's reports included detailed accounts of the visual forms which came to mind when his subjects thought about dates or made numerical calculations. Although the visual forms were often quite elaborate, the reports suggested that they were scanned with only a few items coming into view at any one time.

A vivid form of imagery present in some people is called *eidetic.* In these cases the detail of the visualization is much greater than in the average person. This form of imagery is popularly called *photographic memory.* While it appears to occur more frequently in children, relatively little is known about its cause. There appears to be little reason to doubt that complex imagery, such as in the number forms described by Galton's subjects, or in detailed eidetic images, is similar in kind to normal imagery. For example, studies have shown that eidetic imagers, like normals, have greater difficulty obtaining images with materials which contain a large number of items (Leask, Haber, & Haber, 1969). However, the detail and complexity may be far beyond the normal range (Stromeyer & Psotka, 1970). Whether the presence of eidetic and other forms of complex imagery in certain people is mainly a matter of practice or is due to differences in basic capacity, or both, is not known.

At the time of the Wurzburg School (see Chapter 1), imagery was widely accepted as the memory code most related to thought. The failure of the Wurzburg experiments to obtain accounts of imagery in solving simple association problems contributed to a rejection of its use as a means of understanding all aspects of thinking. The experiments cited in this section show that imagery can be studied and analyzed experimentally. Moreover, there are clear reasons to accept the importance of iconic and other modality-specific codes in some types of learning and thinking. For example, it would hardly be possible to recognize a face or picture without some form of visual memory. The utility of visual codes in improving the rate of learning associations has been demonstrated by a number of investigators (Paivio, 1969). It is also possible to show the importance of visual codes in some types of problem solving (see Chapter 7).

Motor Codes

When Gilbert Ryle distinguished between "remembering that" and "remembering how" (see Chapter 1), he was referring to the fact that motor skills, such as riding a bicycle, can be performed while our conscious attention is on another task. Since riding a bicycle is taken as evidence that one remembers how to ride, it appeared to Ryle that remembering a motor act was rather special in that it was not connected with actively attending to the memory. More directly, D. E. Broadbent (1958) suggested that memories for skills do not usually give rise to the same reports of conscious imagery which tend to accompany visual or verbal memories.

It is possible to demonstrate experimentally differences between motor codes and images. If a subject is provided with visual input such as the position of a point on a line, he can accurately reproduce the position after a short interval. The length of the retention interval does not by itself affect the accuracy of reproduction, at least in the range from zero to thirty seconds (Posner & Konick, 1966). Moreover, in such an experiment most subjects give vivid reports of visual imagery. They will discuss their retention in terms of a visual line which they can inspect even when the objective stimulus is removed. The ability to actively rehearse information stored in this form is similar to what occurs with verbal material (e.g., digits). For digits, rehearsal seems to be related to silent speech which allows the material to be rehearsed by silently repeating it over and over again. Apparently visual information can be recycled in somewhat the same way, but within the visual system.

When a movement is to be reproduced, the experimental results are quite different. A delay in recall will lead to forgetting (reduction in accuracy), regardless of whether one is free to think about the movement in the delay interval or not (Adams & Dijkstra, 1966; Posner & Konick, 1966). If the subject's attention is distracted during the interval, retention of verbal and visual material is further reduced, while motor retention is not much affected (Posner & Konick, 1966). Furthermore, brain damage known to make learning of verbal and visual information virtually impossible has been shown to have relatively little effect upon learning motor sequences (Milner, 1965; Starr & Phillips, 1970). In the case of one patient, the motor skill improved regularly over successive days even though he could not remember having ever practiced it before (Milner, 1965). These findings suggest that motor codes are different in their functional characteristics, and that this difference is related to the reduced involvement of attention in their storage and performance.

Memory codes which preserve motor activity have been called *enactive codes* (Bruner, Oliver, & Greenfield, 1966) or motor programs (Keele, 1968). Does much of our thinking rely upon enactive codes? Develop-

mental psychologists (Bruner, 1968; Piaget & Inhelder, 1969) have suggested that these codes are important in the genesis of thought in the
child. Piaget argues for a sensorimotor period of child development
during which mental operations are closely tied to motor activity. Bruner
believes that many of the properties of images and symbolic codes arise
out of and are attributable to enactive codes. He has studied the operations babies perform upon objects which they hold in their hands. He
proposes a fundamental relationship between the motor operations of
holding and acting upon what is held, the perceptual experience of a
background upon which a figure emerges, and the linguistic idea of
sentences containing a topic and a comment upon that topic. Thus the
same fundamental relationship may be exhibited within three different
memory codes.

It is difficult to isolate enactive from other types of codes in adult
thinking. Typing, however, provides an example of how such codes can
be separated. If a skilled typist is asked to type the alphabet, he can do so
in a few seconds and with a very low probability of error. If, however, he
is given a diagram of his keyboard and asked to fill in the letters in
alphabetic order, he finds the task difficult. It requires several minutes to
perform and the likelihood of error is high. Moreover, the typist often
reports that he can only obtain the visual location of some letters by trying
to type the letter and then determining where his finger would be. These
observations indicate that experience with typing produces a motor code
which may exist in the absence of any visual code.

A more general example is the difference between two ways of knowing
how to get from one place to another. In one way you may mentally
construct something like a map, so that if asked, you could draw the route.
In another sense of knowing your way, you may be completely unable to
produce a map, but perfectly capable of making the correct turns which
would get you to the intended place. Thus people may know something in
the sense of a motor code without being able to translate that knowledge
into another type of code.

In most discussions of thinking and problem solving, verbal and visual
codes are given much more emphasis than are motor programs. However,
Fitts (1964) has pointed out that the movements used in hitting a baseball
are so complex that it would require as many operations to program a
computer to play baseball as it does to program it to play chess. Another
prominent theory of thinking (Bartlett, 1958) proposes that all thought can
be conceived of as a high-level skill. The reduced involvement of
conscious attention in motor performance has tended to isolate activity
based upon enactive codes from the study of thinking. Nonetheless, it is
probably going to be necessary for us to understand both images and skills
if we are to develop a complete analysis of thinking. The more abstract
mental structures which underlie our complex concepts have some

characteristics of an image and some of a skill. Clearly both kinds of codes are involved in the study of symbols, to which we now turn.

Symbolic Codes

A symbol is something which stands for or suggests something else by reason of an arbitrary relationship rather than by reason of resemblance. Thus symbols are in some ways the opposite of images. Language is a striking example of symbolic representation in man. Of course, words can themselves be images, as when we attempt to remember or reproduce an accent. Moreover, language is one of our most highly developed skills. There are also other symbol systems beside natural language, as, for example, the visual ☮ as a symbol for peace. However, words are one of our main ways of representing the outside world to ourselves, and we will confine our analysis of symbolic memories to verbal material.

Once we have learned a language, we often describe our experience in terms of words, regardless of how the experience took place. If we are shown a picture of a dog we may store a visual code, but we are also likely to remember the word "dog" as a description of the picture. Thus much of our experience is recoded into words.

It can be shown that the process of naming is rather different when the stimulus material itself is verbal (letter or word) than when the subject must find a word to describe a nonverbal stimulus. It is much easier and quicker for an adult to read a word than it is for him to obtain even a highly familiar name. For example, Fraisse (1969) exposed subjects to the visual form "O" in the context of other letters or, alternately, in the context of geometrical forms. In the letter condition they were to respond orally "o," while in the forms condition they were to say "circle." Even after much practice, it always took longer to call the stimulus a "circle" than to call it an "o." This result reflects the general advantage which reading has over naming.

Another good example of this advantage is the Stroop test (Jensen & Rohwer, 1966). In this test, color names (e.g., "yellow") are written in different-colored ink (e.g., blue). If the subject is required to read the word, he has little interference from the ink color, but if he is required to name the ink color, he has great difficulty because of interference from the color name. Again this suggests that the relationship between a verbal stimulus and its name is much more direct than the description of a nonverbal stimulus in words. It is not clear why reading should be easier than naming in literate adults when, in fact, children learn to read after they learn many picture names. Perhaps amount of practice is the answer; or this result may be due to the one-to-one relationship between a visual word and its name, while most visual patterns other than words have many nearly equivalent names. Another reason might be because much of

our experience with color or forms does not involve naming. When a light turns green, we go; we do not say "go" or "green." In any case, it is well to keep in mind that the process of naming a picture is not identical to that of reading a word.

Once information is stored in long-term memory, the source of the word is of relatively little importance. Since more is known about the organization and retention of verbal material than any other kind, the remainder of this chapter will concentrate upon long-term memory for verbal material.

ORGANIZATION OF LONG-TERM MEMORY

In Chapter 1 the history of the laws of association was briefly outlined. These laws concern how and why we pass from one idea to another. The results of past associations are organized within long-term memory, and this section is concerned with current studies on the organization of long-term memory.

In nearly all theories of association, contiguity was considered primary. That is, things which occurred closely together in time became associated. However, theories differed as to the form of contiguity required for association. Contiguity between ideas or thoughts was primary in early philosophical theories. During the early twentieth century, in an effort to make psychological theory more objective, contiguity between stimuli and/or responses was considered the crucial factor in association. In *classical conditioning* (Pavlov, 1927), for example, two stimuli are presented closely together in time. The first, a relatively neutral stimulus *(conditioned stimulus),* such as a bell or a light, comes to evoke the response usually produced by the more intense second stimulus *(unconditioned stimulus),* such as a shock or puff of air. This view of association allows the experimenter to control the elements of the association. Many felt that classical conditioning could serve as an experimental model for the study of all association.

Since thinking often consists of activating structures within long-term memory, classical conditioning cannot be a sufficient guide for its study. Active memories may occur either from the external world or from long-term memory. It seems reasonable to suppose that items from both sources become associated when they are activated at the same time. This principle of contiguity is like the older idea of association of ideas, but it can be made more explicit since new techniques allow psychologists to identify the characteristics and limitations of active memory.

It may seem surprising at first that associations should be relatively unaffected by whether the items come from external stimulation or long-term memory, since we often can discriminate between events which took place and our thoughts at the time. However, such discriminations are not entirely reliable. Tea-leaf readers and fortune-tellers fre-

quently take advantage of this characteristic. They manipulate the conversation so that the client thinks about a particular person or event. When recalling the situation later, the clients have a high likelihood of believing that they were told about the person or event, whereas actually they had merely thought of it themselves in the course of the conversation.

What experimental evidence is there that internal and external perceptual events and the memories they activate are associated together? Actually, there is strong evidence for this, since the principle is involved in many practical memory systems. For example, if you were asked to associate "fly" and "crane," a common means of learning the association would be to develop some internal idea which connects them. You might try to combine the two words by imaging a fly being lifted by a crane, or you might think of a word series which links the two, such as "fly"-"airplane"-"train"-"crane." When "fly" is then presented on the next trial, the internal mediator ("airplane"-"train") is activated, as well as the associated external event. There are many studies which indicate that such internal mediation leads to efficient learning (Adams, 1967; Paivio, 1969). This could be the case only if words activated from long-term memory were easily associated with new input.

Indeed, Underwood (1965) has shown that this process can occur quite automatically, even in situations in which it is not advantageous for performance. In his experiment, subjects were presented with a long list of several hundred words. When each word was shown, the subject had to identify it as "old" if it had been presented previously in the list. Following the first presentation of some of the words (e.g., "table"), a high associate to that word (e.g., "chair") was tested. There was a greater tendency to identify "chair" as "old" than there would have been if "table" had not been presented. There are two reasons this could occur. Perhaps on the original presentation of the word "table," other associated words tend to become active within the operational memory of the subject and acquire some strength within the memory system representing the total experience of the list. Another possibility is that there is no activation of associations at the time of the original presentation, but when the subject is given the test ("chair"), he tends to think of other associated words ("table"). According to this view, the confusion occurs during the time the subject is tested for the item.

One experimental result (Anisfeld & Knapp, 1968) points to the first explanation as the correct one. Some words have associations in only one direction. For example, "bitter" usually elicits the word "sweet," but "sweet" does not usually produce "bitter." If a word like "bitter" was used in the list of words, the probability of saying "old" to "sweet" was increased, but if "sweet" was used, there was no increased likelihood of saying "old" to "bitter." Of course, many different word pairs having this one-way relationship were used to make sure that the finding was not limited to only one pair. The results suggest that when words are

presented, they tend to elicit their associates, and these associates acquire some strength as members of the list even though they were not actually presented.

Memory Cells and Storage of Episodes

We shall use the term *memory cell* to refer to a set of memories which are activated and then stored together within the long-term memory of the subject. The items within a memory cell may include those which have been presented to the subject from the external world and those associated thoughts which are activated from the subject's own long-term memory. By a memory cell we do not necessarily mean a particular location within the central nervous system, but a network of associated items which have a high probability of producing each other. Thus when one thinks about any single item within the memory cell, other items and experiences tend also to be activated.

The idea of a memory cell as an organized structure within long-term memory is similar to the proposal of Gestalt psychologists that memories are stored in a *trace column* (Koffka, 1935). The memory of past experience, according to Koffka, is recorded as a temporal sequence of events within the trace column. The memory cell is similar to the trace column, but it adds the idea that temporal organization is maintained by successive orderings of material in active memory. The memory cells provide a means of storing the temporal order of our personal episodes (Tulving, 1972). However, the record is not of the order of external happenings, but rather of the order of our own thoughts at the time.

Perhaps the best experimental analyses of the episodes stored in the memory-cell structure are in the studies of rote learning. Suppose a subject is given ten pairs of words to memorize so that he can give the proper response each time one item of the pair is presented. It may take him twenty to thirty trials to be able to make the proper response each time. This process can be analyzed into two stages (Underwood & Schulz, 1960). In one stage the subject isolates the set of responses which might be used within the list. Underwood has called this the *selector mechanism.* This activity seems to take place rapidly when the items are meaningful units, such as words. After this stage the subject makes no intrusions; that is, he makes no responses not actually included within the list of selected items. It may then take him many additional trials in order to learn exactly which response goes with each item. The learning of exact associations between items is rather slow, but the ability to isolate the list of responses which are appropriate to a given situation occurs very quickly.

The efficiency of the selector mechanism, in comparison with the slow and painful way in which the individual pairs are learned, suggests that isolation of a network of associations (memory cell) is basic, and that the

formation of associations between specific pairs is a derivative and more difficult process. The selector mechanism makes it possible to take familiar items used in many different contexts and isolate them in a particular temporal situation so that, at least for a time, they enjoy a high mutual association.

The isolation of such associations can be shown experimentally. In one study (Slamecka, 1966), subjects were required to learn new associations to words which already had very strong associations with other words. For example, the word "queen" might be taught as an associate to "table." After learning was complete, the investigator measured the speed of habitual associations by presenting the experimental word ("table") and measuring the time needed to produce a frequent associate (e.g., "chair"). The time for habitual association was unaffected by the extensive learning process used to teach the subject to say "queen" to "table." Thus new memory cells may be kept isolated from old associations.

In later chapters we shall see how the ability to fill memory cells with items from external and internal sources plays an important role in developing the internal representations which allow rapid access to the information needed to solve problems.

Organization at Input

Perhaps the most crucial time for the retention of information is the moment at which the information is received. The way in which information is organized and filed at that moment governs the uses for which it will be most readily available in later thinking. Suppose you make a new acquaintance. You may observe that the person is a psychology student and that you share a common interest. Later, if you choose to review people with whom you might discuss psychology, his name and/or face might come effortlessly to mind. There are many bases upon which such classifications can be made. You might classify the person as tall, red-shirted, or rude. All of these observations might serve as the cue for rapid retrieval of the person whom you have met. On the other hand, there are other facts about the person which may be stored but not used as a means of classification at the time of input. You may not be reminded of the person by the description "scar on the right cheek," but if you are thinking about him for some other reason, you may remember that he has such a scar. Part of the experimental study of thinking requires an effort to distinguish between cues used to organize information when it is presented and cues which are available only after the memory is retrieved later.

How can we determine whether a particular classification is made at the time of input? Normally, short strings of items are best recalled in the order in which they are received. This suggests that they are filed in temporal order. In some cases the material is sorted so efficiently on a

basis other than temporal order that even immediately following presentation it is easier to recall on that basis. For example, Broadbent and Gregory (1961) presented pairs of digits simultaneously to eye and ear. It was easier to report all the items presented to one modality followed by all those presented to the other modality, rather than reporting them in temporal order. At the time of input the items appear to be separated by modality, and the use of this classification is easier than the use of temporal order. Content classification may also have this characteristic. For example, if a list contains grossly different contents, such as a mixture of letters and light flashes (for which one reports the spatial locations), it is easier to recall by content than by temporal order. Mixtures of letters and digits provide about equal recall by temporal order or by content, while mixtures of odd and even numbers are better recalled in temporal order (Sanders & Schroots, 1968). These results suggest that gross distinctions between items are made at input, and that the items are filed in the appropriate portion of the memory.

The tendency of subjects to group information by content is not confined to physical differences. For example, many studies have shown that words of similar meaning tend to be grouped in recall (Cofer, 1965). In these experiments, long series of words were given in which preexisting concepts such as automobile names, tree names, or animal names were embedded. Results indicated strongly that words which have the same meaning tend to be clustered together within the recall of the subject.

Under certain circumstances this clustering of information can lead to great increases in the amount recalled. Normally, a single presentation of a list of words, at a rate of approximately one word per second, will lead to recall of less than ten words. If, however, the experimenter uses easily identified categories, each of which consists of highly overlearned clusters of words, such as the directions (north, east, south, west), then the number of words recalled may be dramatically increased (Cohen, 1963). In such cases the memory experiment becomes closely related to thinking, since one may hear a word from a given category, infer the category name, and may then use knowledge of the category to aid in generating the correct words.

Unfortunately, with long lists of words it is difficult to tell whether the subject is performing the organization when the words are presented or during recall. Perhaps he does some of each. It seems likely that the complex flood of information available in everyday life often forces subjects to make detailed classifications at the time of input. In order to determine the likelihood of their making such classifications, it is important to have an experimental method which does not force subjects to make classifications. It may then be possible to infer which classifications of stimulus content are habitually used by the subjects. With very short lists and a brief period of time in store, it is possible to keep

difficulty relatively low and to observe how retention is influenced by input classification.

One effort to do this (Peterson & Peterson, 1959) presents three items to a subject and then distracts his attention for a brief period of time (up to twenty seconds). On the first trial of such an experiment, the subject loses very little of the information and recall is nearly perfect (Keppel & Underwood, 1962). After a few trials, however, recall dips quite rapidly. It is thought that the decline depends upon the items stored in previous trials being confused with, or somehow disturbing, the retention of the items in the current trial. The effect of prior items upon retention of a given item is called *proactive interference.*

It is possible to tell something about how subjects are handling the new items by the effect previous trials have upon recall. It has been shown that the interfering effects of prior items dissipate with a delay of about two minutes (Loess & Waugh, 1967). Items presented within a two-minute period appear to be stored in the same memory cell. As that memory cell fills, it becomes increasingly difficult to discriminate the proper order of the items and the subject makes errors. If more than two minutes elapse, the subject seems to classify the material in a new memory cell. Since successive trials two minutes apart appear to be relatively independent of the previous context, this experiment gives us some idea of the temporal span of information contained within one memory cell, at least under conditions of brief retention intervals.

The similarity of items received prior to a given item also influences retention of the item. This fact suggests that classification by content is also important. If subjects are presented with digit triples for a number of trials and then switched to consonant triples, the probability of recalling the consonants will be very high on the first few trials after the switch (Wickens, Born, & Allen, 1963). This is true even when the time between trials is small (twenty seconds or so), and it can be observed over and over again in a single session. The tendency for recall to improve for several trials after a switch has been called *release from proactive interference.* This tendency has been observed not only with switches between digits and letters, but also with switches between semantic categories, such as from animal names to trees.

This method tells us something about the types of cues which subjects can use to distinguish between old and new items. Moreover, some of the cues which produce release from proactive interference do not give rise to any reports by the subjects that they are aware of a switch in the type of words presented. Two kinds of interpretations of these data are possible. The first suggests that the words are sorted at the time they arrive and are stored in different locations of the memory system, depending upon their meaning. Thus, when the category is switched, subjects go to a different memory location for retrieval and have no interference from previous

items. If this view is true, this method might be able to tell us all the categories which subjects use when they sort words (Wickens, 1970). A second view is that subjects store the words in temporal order. However, at the time of recall they use the differences between word lists as a means of avoiding confusion. For example, if they have received several sets of digits and are then switched to letters, they can easily avoid recalling any digits, thus avoiding interfering effects from them. It is possible that some combination of the two theories is correct.

In later chapters we shall return to the question of the kinds of classifications which are made at input. This is an extremely important question in trying to clarify how subjects build up memory structures. At present, no single method allows us to determine the range of input classifications which subjects do make.

How do input classifications affect what we remember about our previous experience? One classical study which illustrates the consequences of classification involves the retention of visual shapes (Carmichael, Hogan, & Walter, 1932). The subjects were shown shapes which could fit either of two verbal categories. Separate groups of subjects were supplied with different labels. When required to reproduce the forms, the subjects distorted them to fit the verbal label with which they had been supplied. This study suggests that the same stimulus (0─0), when filed with memories of one kind (e.g., spectacles), takes on different properties than when filed with stimuli of another kind (e.g., barbells). Unfortunately, it is not possible to attribute the effects in this study to input classification as distinct from distortions which are introduced at the time of reproduction.

Another study (Funkhouser, 1968) does a better job of showing that input classification affects retention. The stimuli were pictures of simple objects such as apples, trucks, etc. Separate groups of subjects were instructed to classify them by color or shape, or to make no classification. After a brief distracting task, subjects were required to recall the names of the items they had seen. Some were allowed to use the same categories as at input, while for others the categories were shifted. It was found that subjects who were allowed to recall the items in the same categories which they had used at input were superior in speed and accuracy to those who had to impose a new order on the items. This study suggests that a classification system imposed upon material at input limits the ways in which the material can be used at retrieval. If subjects are allowed to use their input categories, recall can be relatively effortless and effective. Otherwise, recall is slow and less accurate.

The organization of information during learning has consequences for the ease with which it can be used later. However, this does not rule out the subject's ability to sort through stored material on the basis of new categories given him at the time of retrieval.

Limits of Organization

The basic limit on the organization of material at input is the time available for the subject to perform such organizations (Broadbent, 1958). The more complex the network of associations to which a given word is tied, the more time is required. The close relationship between amount of material stored and time is suggested by the finding that a relatively fixed total time is required to store an item, regardless of how the time is divided. If subjects have twenty seconds to learn a particular item, it makes relatively little difference whether that twenty seconds is divided into ten two-second trials, five four-second trials, two ten-second trials, or one twenty-second trial (Bugelski, 1962).

At fast rates of presentation, insufficient time is available for storage, and the number and complexity of organizations to which a stimulus word is tied is therefore limited. This can be observed in the following experiment, in which the presentation of eight different visual letters is compared with aural presentation of these same letters. At relatively slow speeds the subject who receives visual information has no trouble extracting and storing the letter names. This can be demonstrated by the presence of acoustic (e.g., "V" for "P") confusion errors in his recall (Conrad, 1964). At slow rates of presentation, visual items lead to at least as good recall as auditory presentation. However, the mental operations which produce the letter names require time. Thus, as the rate of presentation is increased, auditory presentation often becomes superior to visual presentation (Aaronson, 1967). Similarly, interference between words which sound alike predominates when fast presentation is used, but with slower presentation interference by meaning is more important (Shulman, 1970). Structures related to meaning are contacted more slowly than those related to sound.

A more complex example of this same type of difference in coding may be illustrated by presenting strings of binary (zero and one) digits. A subject might try to store these directly as strings of zeros and ones or, with appropriate learning, he might recode the information into equivalent decimal digits (for example, $100 = 4$). If the subject has adequate time, the strategy of recoding into decimal digits is very efficient. In one study (Miller, 1956), a subject skilled in recoding was able to obtain the equivalent of thirty binary digits, rather than the usual ten. However, if the rate of presentation of the binary digits is increased so that there is not sufficient time for the recoding process, the subject is better off storing the raw binary digits.

The same thing occurs with mnemonic devices designed to help in the storage of information. For example, Bugelski, Kidd, and Segman (1968) trained people to develop a picture of a stimulus object which would relate it to the response. The subjects were able to use the device at

presentation rates of four and eight seconds per item, but they could not do so at a two-second rate. Thus the usefulness of complex mnemonic devices depends upon the time available for the subject to make the necessary recoding.

There may be structural as well as temporal limitations to the classifications subjects make on input items. Everyone is familiar with such structural limitations in trying to outline lectures or readings. The outline represents a compromise between preserving sufficient detail and preventing the number of categories at a given level from becoming overly complex. Most experimental studies of structural limitations have been concerned with the organization subjects impose upon lists of words. You will remember that subjects can recall only about seven to ten unrelated items from a single presentation of a word list. With long lists, the subjects often categorize the words (Mandler, 1967). In recalling categorized lists, the limitation tends to be the number of categories which can be represented in the recall, rather than the number of words. Some studies indicate that subjects will recall items from three to seven different categories and that each category may contain from three to seven items, allowing recall of twenty-five or more items from a single, efficiently categorized list. This led Mandler (1967) to suppose that the basic structures for organizing lists of words were hierarchical, with a limit of about five items at any one level. This kind of structure suggests that subjects reorganize long-term memory in such a way that as any particular topic becomes elaborated, concepts of higher and higher generality are evolved. These concepts contain, as elements, simpler structures which have evolved previously. Much of Chapters 3 and 4 will be concerned with how subjects develop such structures.

Consider a concrete case to illustrate the types of organization implied by these ideas. Suppose a person begins to memorize the various states of the United States to understand basic factors in economic geography. He may decide to develop an overall list of the fifty states. However, as he begins to work on an economic problem, he finds that limitations on active memory make it too difficult to search back through all fifty states. A useful breakdown of the fifty states may be made by considering such regional groupings as the Far West, Middle West, Southwest, Southeast, East, New England, etc. While considering the question of unemployment, for example, he may mentally calculate its impact on each of the regions, bringing to mind the names of each. The names of the states are present only implicitly as parts of the region. If more detailed information is needed concerning a particular product, he may then consider only the Far West and bring to mind the states within that region. This is the kind of hierarchical organization of long-term memory which will be described in later chapters. The experimental results of Mandler and others do not require that memory be organized exactly like this, but such an organiza-

tion does help in understanding the way in which subjects search their memory in the process of problem solving.

There are important cognitive consequences of such an organization. Many things known to be true of a region may be considered true of all member states of that region. This structure is economical, since not all information about the region as a whole needs to be stored with each state, but it can lead to important kinds of errors which will be considered in Chapter 4.

Parallel Storage

Perhaps no concept is more important for an understanding of memory than that of *parallel memory codes.* New input is always embedded within the context of contiguous external and internal events which are active in memory. These form the basis for the temporal memory cells of our personal experience. When time is available, considerable cross-filing and referencing of stimulus information may take place. Thus new input can be incorporated in the hierarchical structures which were discussed earlier.

Parallel storage implies that filing of information in hierarchical structures does not replace memory cells based upon temporal order, but rather both are simultaneously represented. Suppose subjects were given a list of mixed digits and consonants (e.g., 7 B 6 9 J 8 R 5) and were told that at the end of the list they would be asked to recall the digits, followed by the consonants. The rate of presentation would be slow, so the subjects could do their best to separate the items at input into a consonant set and a digit set. If asked to recall, they would respond by type of material more easily than by temporal order, suggesting that the sorting had taken place at the time of presentation.

Now suppose the subjects were given four lists with the same order within each class, but with differences between class sequences (e.g., 7 6 9 B J 8 5 R or 7 6 B 9 J R 8 5), and were required to pick out the particular list with which they had been presented earlier. With short delays, the subjects would probably do quite well in recognizing the correct list. This would suggest that they had available some representation of the temporal information, as well as the recoded material. This temporal information would probably be forgotten rather rapidly, since it was not rehearsed.

While this experiment has not been carried out, a less satisfactory experimental test of the notion of parallel storage has been performed. Series of eight digits were presented to subjects at a rate of one item per second (Posner & Rossman, 1965). The subjects were expected to recode specified digit pairs by adding and remembering the sum. At the end of the series of digits, the subjects were required to recall the input information. Recoding reduced recall of the digits immediately prior to

the recoded pair. However, the pairs which the subjects recoded were actually somewhat better retained than those pairs on which no recoding was performed. This suggests that recoding or filing of information does not obliterate the basic temporal structure within the memory cell.

Recoding of information from iconic to symbolic form also produces parallel storage. When introduced to a new person, you may store his name under his profession, his friends, the type of people who were present when you met him, etc. None of these particular operations need obliterate some visual representation of the subject's face. The parallel storage of different levels of information is very important for understanding thinking. At a later time information can be activated from many different sources, including both the temporal verbal record and the iconic or visual representation of the face. If you had filed the name of the person under his profession, you might still be able to locate the temporal record and thus find out who was present at the time you met him. If the color of the subject's eyes becomes important, there is some probability that the original iconic coding of the subject's face will preserve that information, even though it was not verbally coded at the time.

Much of what we call thought refers to efforts to relate different representations. The next two sections will be concerned with two important constraints upon our ability to locate stored information: first, the dynamics of change within the long-term memory system; and second, the problem of retrieval from long-term memory.

Dynamics of Long-Term Memory

One view of memory is to regard it as spontaneously active and changing (Koffka, 1935). This view regards memory representations as evolving in accordance with their own dynamic laws, independent of the mental operations at the time of input and retrieval. Gestalt psychologists suggest that laws of perceptual organization continue to operate upon information stored in long-term memory. Freudian psychologists have also held that complicated manipulations of information, in accordance with unconscious motives, take place in the memory system. The opposite view is that memory traces are essentially inert except when reorganized by an active process involving conscious attention.

At several points we shall return to the complex question of what kinds of operations may take place outside conscious attention. It will not be possible to provide any complete answer to this question, since the controversy which attends it has by no means been settled by experimentation. Nonetheless, the principles discussed so far suggest that memory would *appear* to be dynamic, even if one considers the long-term memory system itself as inert.

In order to illustrate these principles, we shall consider two areas of

change within long-term memory. The first of these is the reduction in memory which occurs over time *(forgetting)*. The second involves changes in the structure of memory, which may be called *reorganization.*

Forgetting.   It has been noted several times that material is lost from active memory if the subject is distracted. Presumably this applies not only to new input information, but also to new organizations of old items assembled in operational memory. This allows new organizations to be tried out on a provisional basis without being encoded into long-term memory.

Once a given organization is successfully encoded into long-term memory, there is still evidence of changes which may lead to the subject's inability to recall that material. These changes appear to be a function of the relationship between new learning and previous learning, and have been summarized under the title *interference theory of forgetting.* The principle which underlies the interference theory of forgetting is captured by the story of a professor of fisheries who complained that each time he learned the name of a new student, he forgot the name of a fish. This suggests that the very act of learning new information reduces the likelihood of our being able to retrieve old information. The memory is not necessarily obliterated forever. Rather, the information may become more difficult to retrieve because memory cells have merged, making it necessary to search a larger area of memory.

This explanation is suggested by studies of retention of word lists (Ceraso, 1967). In one experiment, subjects were repeatedly shown lists of ten nouns. When they could recite a list by heart, they were shown a second list of nouns and memorized it in the same way. The subjects were then asked to recall words from both lists in whichever order they came to mind. The recall task was given to separate groups either immediately or twenty-four hours after training. The expectation was that because the words had been organized into two separate lists, they would emerge in clusters representing the two lists. Immediately after learning, the words were clustered by separate lists. After twenty-four hours, however, the subjects' orders of recall were almost completely independent of the lists.

Were any of the items actually lost? Another experiment was addressed to this question. Subjects were required to learn two lists of ten nonsense-syllable-word pairs. Immediately, or twenty-four hours later, subjects were confronted with one of two tests. In one test they were presented with all the material which they had learned and were required to match which nonsense syllable went with which word. The second test involved trying to recall the words. In the first test there was little loss in performance over the twenty-four hours. The recall test, however, did show a sharp decline. The main effect of the twenty-four-hour delay was to cause the two lists of material to lose their separate identities and to

merge within a longer list. This inability to maintain the boundaries of learned information underlies much of the decrement in recall observed over time.

There is evidence to suggest that when a memory is isolated because of the unique quality of the information, there is very little loss in the ability to recognize it, even over long periods of time. For example, one study (Rock & Englestein, 1959) had subjects view a peculiar nonsense form in a situation in which there was no incentive to learn or memorize it. It was found that subjects were able to select the shape from a large variety of similarly shaped objects even a month later.

An account of a man with greater than usual memory capacity (Luria, 1968) suggests that he experienced each particular event as a unique instance. The subject was able to report tactual, kinesthetic, olfactory, and taste experiences from each verbal word presented. The constellation of memory codes laid down by the occurrence of each word made it unique. This protected the particular word from interference from other items and, therefore, from difficulties of retrieval.

Reorganization.   Forgetting from active memory and interference occurring in long-term memory are but two examples of the dynamics of memory. The principles we have been discussing in this chapter give rise to a number of methods by which the organization of long-term memory changes continually. When new information is presented, a subject interprets it in the light of information from his own long-term memory. Thus the new information and the stored items are within active memory at the same time. These items tend to be organized together. If the subject then gives sufficient attention to the activated structure, it becomes a memory cell within the long-term memory system. New structures continually combine present information with information taken from previous experience. These structures are organized not upon the basis of temporal experience as it occurred in the real world, but upon the basis of relationships which the subject makes between presented material and material taken from his own long-term memory.

A second feature of storage which leads to the continual reorganization of memory is filing new incoming information under a variety of categories. We discussed this idea earlier as organization at input. As the interests and activities of the subject change, the particular files under which new items are represented also change. A striking example of such a change in the characteristic filing of information occurs in the tendency of children to associate words which sound alike (Luria & Vinogradova, 1959), while adults make associations based upon meaning. This suggests that the characteristic filing categories change from those which emphasize the physical characteristics of words to those which represent the meaning of words.

Memory appears to be spontaneously changing because the principles by which it is organized allow structures to combine old ideas in new ways.

Retrieval

The process of retrieval is crucial in all aspects of memory and thought. Retrieval is the process by which information stored in long-term memory is activated to recognize new input or to solve a problem. Most of the chapters of this book are concerned with questions of retrieval. This section will develop only certain broad principles of retrieval, which will be expanded as we take up various aspects of the formation of concepts and the dynamics of solving problems.

Retrieval from memory can be a rapid and effortless process on those occasions when the context of the present information fits the organization of memory exactly. Perhaps the recognition of words in normal print is the best example of an *effortless retrieval.* When the new input presented to a subject is not identical with information in memory, the retrieval process may become *effortful.* It is still likely, even in such cases, that effortless retrieval plays a part in the overall process. That is, when a subject sees a familiar face which he has not seen in a long time, the task of producing the proper name or the situation in which the face was last seen may take considerable time and effort.

This process can be broken down into two stages. The first stage resembles the effortless retrieval we have just been discussing. In this stage, the subject's attention is directed to parts of his memory in which it is likely that more information about the particular face is stored. The subject may be able to say immediately, and without effort, that he recognizes the face in the sense that it is familiar or that he has seen it somewhere. Or the subject may be able to say that he knows the face is someone he saw in his childhood or someone he was familiar with in a particular class. This initial portion of the retrieval process resembles effortless retrieval, except that the information is sufficient only to reach a given area in memory rather than a specific association.

Indeed, it is possible to isolate experimentally this phase of the retrieval process. One study (Hart, 1967) used questions like "Which planet is the largest in our solar system?" or "Who wrote *The Tempest?*" If the subject was unable to produce the answer to such a question, he was asked to rate whether or not he knew the answer well enough to recognize it. Following the rating, he was given a recognition test such as: (a) Mars, (b) Venus, (c) Earth, (d) Jupiter. It was found that subjects were able to correctly state whether or not they would recognize the answer even though they could not produce it. Presumably their ability to know that they could recognize the answer had to do with their finding an area of memory in which they knew the answer would be located. If this area was well stocked, that is, if

it had a dense structure, the subject could be fairly sure that he would be able to recognize the correct answer. If, however, he knew nothing about astronomy or nothing about plays, he might say rather definitely that he would be unable to recognize the answer.

Another example of effortful retrieval in which effortless retrieval plays a role has been called the *"tip of the tongue" phenomenon.* To investigate this, Brown and McNeill (1966) provided subjects with definitions of unfamiliar words. The "tip of the tongue" state was defined as occurring when subjects were unable to produce the word, but were able to recall words of similar form and meaning. That is, they had a general idea of the proper word, but were unable to recall it exactly. For example, when faced with a definition of "sampan," the subjects would recall either words which sounded similar, like "sipan," "siann," or "sarong," or words which were similar in meaning, such as "barge," "houseboat," and "junk." Subjects in the "tip of the tongue" state were often able to give the number of syllables in the correct word or its initial letter.

The authors proposed that the definition might start an effortless-retrieval process, similar to a key-sort card system in which the cards are notched at the time of entry. When a rod is inserted into the cards, it catches all those with a particular notching. Suppose the definition had been "navigation instrument having to do with geometry." The rods pushed into the holes for each of these features might produce a single retrieved word, such as "sextant." If this word was satisfactory, the subject would then report that he had the answer. The rods might also produce a series of entries, such as "astrolabe," "compass," "divider," "sextant," and "protractor." In this case the subject might search the items which had been put into his operational memory, one by one, and decide that "sextant" was the most reasonable of the answers and thus again be correct. Notice here that the effortless retrieval was supplemented by an effortful search of the operational memory store. Another possibility is that "sextant" would not be among the words retrieved. In this case the subject might search the words retrieved and conclude either that one of the words was sufficiently close to the definition and report it, in which case he would make an error, or he might decide that none of the words was adequate and say that he did not know the answer.

All of these possibilities require effortless retrieval, followed by a slower effortful search of the retrieved (activated) information. The "tip of the tongue" phenomenon represents a more complex process. Suppose the subject retrieved only part of a word. Instead of retrieving a clear notion of "sextant," suppose he only retrieved "s"-blank-"t"-blank. In this case the subject would know the initial letter and the number of syllables, but would be unable to produce the word because he did not have sufficient cues. When dealing with that situation, a slow and effortful retrieval process would be required to attempt to fill in the gap. The process might take advantage of the subject's information about the

normal serial order of the English language, such as the fact that the letter "e" has a high probability of following "s." Through this process the subject might be able to provide the information Brown and McNeill found in the "tip of the tongue" state. Is it reasonable to infer that only part of the correct word is retrieved in such cases? Our vocabulary for producing items is known to be more limited than our vocabulary for recognizing them. Thus one may recognize "sextant" easily, but be unable to produce it because of partial representation in memory.

So far we have considered effortless retrieval as the ability to reach some area in long-term memory which might contain one or more items which could then be placed in an activated form. Effortful retrieval, on the other hand, has been confined to a search among items or parts of items already activated by an effortless retrieval process. It is also possible for a search of long-term memory to be effortful. For example, the presentation of three animal names and three mineral names might cause subjects to file each in a separate location by content. These input categorizations would correspond to the notches placed in the cards in a key-sort file. When the context of the new input matched the classifications made during storage, the items would become activated in an effortless manner. However, suppose the context at retrieval were different from when the items were stored. For example, suppose you were given the list "February," "June," "July," "December," "Mary," "Alice," "Martha," and then told to recall the four girls' names. Three would come to mind effortlessly, but the fourth might require some thought because "June" was probably filed as a month.

Long-term memory can be searched effortlessly provided that the context at the time of retrieval matches the classifications made at input. A memory of this type has been called *content addressable* (Shiffrin & Atkinson, 1969). When, however, the context at retrieval calls for a new classification, the process of searching long-term memory may be difficult. Indeed, much of what we call thinking appears to be just this difficult sort of a retrieval process. Difficult here may be thought of as highly conscious and demanding. In Chapter 6 a more detailed experimental analysis of such conscious operations will be made.

SUMMARY

Memory can be divided into two systems: first, the small number of items which are in active memory at any time; and second, the remainder of memory, which is called *long-term store.* It is also possible to distinguish between three qualitatively different memory codes: imagery, enactive, and symbolic. These codes provide different kinds of information to the subject.

Active memory is used both to try out new organizations of thoughts on a temporary basis and to organize the storage of information in long-term

memory by relating incoming and retrieved experience within the same temporal memory cells. Active memory is also used to sustain experience long enough to allow various mental operations to code or file experience within different categories. Long-term memory appears to be dynamic, at least in part, because it is subject both to forgetting and to reorganization by the creation of new memory cells.

The process of retrieving information can be divided for analysis into two components. Effortless retrieval occurs when the input contacts its address in memory without any conscious search. Effortful retrieval occurs when the subject is forced to search the items retrieved into active memory, or when he does not have sufficient content to locate the items in long-term memory unambiguously.

3

Abstraction and
Iconic Concepts

*Its essential tenet is that thinking has a special sort of
object, which are variously called universals, concepts
or abstract ideas.*

H. H. Price

The material reviewed in the last chapter emphasized retrieval of exact
information from long-term memory. It has long been known (Bartlett,
1932; Neisser, 1967) that human memory is not designed for exact
reproduction of previous events, but has rather evolved for the purpose of
abstracting the general form of events and representing them in a way
which allows us to act reasonably intelligently in the future.

Experiments which concern learning frequently involve presenting the
same item on successive occasions. The only difference between successive presentations is the time when they occur. In real life, events are
never the same twice. The Greek philosopher Heraclitus suggested that it
is impossible to step into the same river twice. Life is a swiftly changing
flow of events. We see familiar faces, but not an identical face. Thus
human memory requires us to recognize new stimuli, not from a single
stored trace which has grown in strength through successive experiences,
but from a trace system which stores different events within the same
memory cell. It is this abstractive nature of memory which provides the
subtle flexibility necessary for participation in the changing tapestry of
human thinking.

Indeed, too exact a memory can be very harmful. Remember the man
studied by the psychologist Luria whose retention of events was so exact
that he made his living demonstrating his memory? Luria explained that
the man's ability was partly owing to his experiencing each event in a

completely unique way. Every word he heard was accompanied by a range of colors, smells, and tastes. This, together with an unusual number of mnemonic devices, allowed the man to preserve events in unity and isolation, and thus to be little influenced by the crowding and interference discussed in the last chapter. A consequence of such isolation was that his memory was not abstractive. A normal person's memory of a familiar scene is a kind of composite of different experiences at that place. For Luria's subject, each experience was kept so separate that it was not combined with previous ones. As a result, Luria found that the thought processes of his fantastic memorizer were not superior, but rather inferior to those of most people. The subject's concepts were in terms of the concrete and individual, rather than the abstract and general. A memory system which is designed to combine and abstract, rather than isolate and preserve, has disadvantages for exact recall, but it serves as the basis for intellectual performance.

This abstractive quality of human memory has been variously labelled in different areas of psychological research. Consider a specific experimental example. Imagine that you are presented with a series of different tones which range between 1000 and 3000 cycles. After a delay, you are asked which of a particular pair (e.g., a 2200 or 2500 cps) was presented. It should be clear that the number of tones in the stored list would affect the likelihood of a correct choice. The more tones, the more difficult it would be to say which of the two stimuli had actually been in the series. The difficulty would increase with delay. It would be reasonable to say that the forgetting was due at least in part to an inability to keep separate the properties of the individual tones. Suppose, however, that the choice is between tones of 2500 and 5000 cycles. In this case you would be asked to discriminate between one tone which was in the correct range of the previously presented tones and one which was not. The more tones presented to you, the better you would probably do, since the 5000-cycles tone would stand out more. In the study of perception, this adjustment to the range of stimuli is called the *adaptation level* (Helson, 1964). The same tone will seem to have a high pitch after a series of low tones and a low pitch after a series of high tones. Adaptation level for any dimension is most heavily influenced by immediately previous experiences. The point is that the loss of specific information about individual tones has disadvantages for exact recall, but it allows us to build up a concept against which to judge new tones as relatively high or low.

This principle is illustrated by a study of memory for words (Reicher, Ligon, & Conrad, 1969) which shows both the advantages and the disadvantages of abstraction. In this experiment subjects were presented with long series of words. Within each series was a critical word which had to be recognized after the series was over. In some conditions there were a number of different words which rhymed with the critical word. The idea was that the critical word, in the presence of words similar in

sound, would have less chance of being recognized. Indeed, some evidence was found for this decremental effect of rhyming materials. A more important effect, however, was that the subjects who were exposed to the series of rhyming words always remembered something about the rhyming class to which the correct word belonged. That is, their retention of a specific word was slightly reduced by additional rhyming words, but they always selected words belonging to the same rhyming class as the word presented in the list. One thing the subjects clearly had learned was to abstract the particular rhyming pattern of the words. It is just these general relations among events which form the conceptual basis for understanding the world around us. The phenomena of proactive interference and crowding are destructive in the sense of reducing our ability to retain the exact ordering of past experience; however, they are conditions necessary for us to sense invariance and commonality in a world which is constantly changing.

ICONIC ABSTRACTIONS

Chapter 1 reviewed some of the traditional philosophical distinctions concerning human ability to abstract. In modern psychology this topic has been pursued under the name of *concept formation.* Despite the bewildering complexity of operations and experimental techniques which have been applied to the study of concepts, the idea underlying their study is quite simple and closely related to the philosophical disputes we have discussed. A concept has been formed when a human subject shows the ability to respond to a series of different events with the same label or action (Bourne, 1966).

For example, we learn to call a large number of two-dimensional forms "letters." We also learn to respond to differently shaped two- and three-dimensional objects with the label "dog." Finally, we are able to give the label "revolution" to events as different as those which engulfed Russia in 1917 and those which occasioned the development of the factory system in modern England. In each case we have learned to identify or abstract the commonalities among things we could easily tell apart.

Rote Concepts

These three examples should suggest the diverse psychological processes involved in different types of concept formation. Learning to label various forms as "letters of the alphabet" involves processes better treated in a book on memorization rather than in a book on thinking. While letters have some common properties (e.g., relatively simple, two-dimensional forms), there is no known rule for specifying them. There is nothing in common among instances of the category "letter" which allows them to

be separated from many other simple forms. In order to know that "3" is not an instance of "letter," one need simply know it is not. In this sense, the visual category "letters of the alphabet" is an arbitrary one. The child learns it as he might learn another long series of visual forms. The term "letter" bears only an arbitrary relation to the individual forms. Nevertheless, we do hold in memory the letters of the alphabet, the digits, and many other lists which we have learned. These lists play important roles in the dynamics of the thought processes.

Common Elements

A concept often involves a common element which characterizes the instances. One of the earliest systematic studies of such concepts was that of Clark Hull (1920). Hull used a large number of Chinese letters, some of which are shown in Figure 3. Each group had a particular visual sign in common. In some of the forms the sign was obvious and isolated from the rest of the figure, while in other forms it was deeply embedded in the

FIGURE 3   CHINESE LETTERS USED TO STUDY THE GROWTH OF CONCEPTS

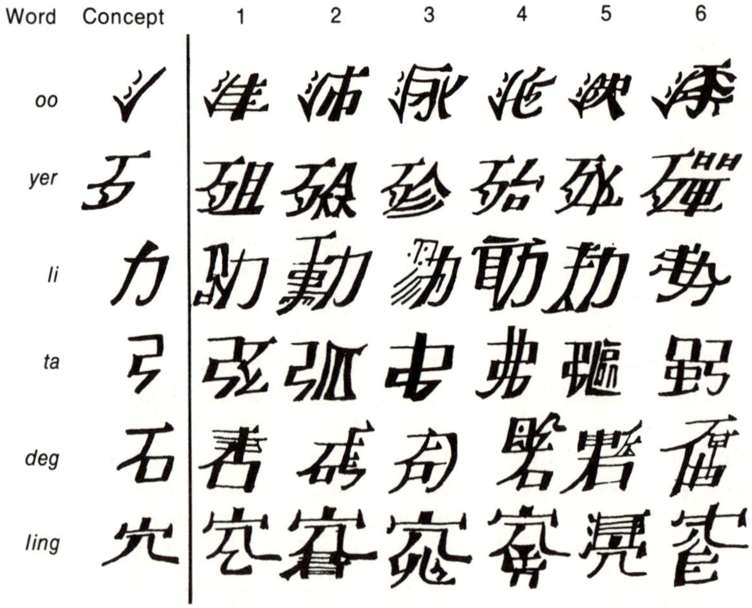

Each row was given the name shown in the first column. Each pattern within a row contained the sign shown in the second column. Adapted from Hull, C. L. Quantitative aspects of the evolution of concepts: An experimental study. *Psychological Monographs,* 1920, *28* (1, Whole No. 123). Copyright © 1920 by the American Psychological Association. Adapted by permission.

network of strokes. Subjects were given the task of memorizing long lists of these letters so that they could produce a particular name each time a letter appeared. Unknown to the subject, the lists were arranged so that all forms with one particular sign were given the same name. Slowly, over many trials, the subjects were able to classify correctly new letters as well as ones they had seen before.

In this task the subject's attention was focused on learning, and not on a search for the particular common element. Thus the ability of subjects to draw or to point out the sign which typified each response category emerged slowly. In many cases the subjects were able to show by their behavior that they could classify the letters before they could point out the basis of the classification. In fact, Hull trained some subjects directly on the signs which were common to a particular class. He found that although these subjects could reproduce the signs virtually perfectly, they did no better in recognition than subjects who were trained without seeing the common signs isolated from the letters. However, if the crucial sign was painted in red so that the subjects' attention was attracted to it while they viewed the entire form, learning was better than if they had to learn by repetition of the individual letters. Finally, Hull found that it was important for subjects to see a variety of forms. Experiencing more instances of the same class improved recognition, despite a reduction of training on each individual form.

It is possible to conclude from Hull's study some important ideas about the ability of people to abstract the common aspect of different visual experiences. In the first place, Hull's task did not instruct the subjects to look for common elements. In fact, the common element seemed to emerge from the act of seeing the different letters and classifying them. Second, knowing the common element did not lead to particularly good performance unless the common element was shown in the context of the individual forms which had to be recognized. Third, variability of experience was important; that is, the subjects did better when they saw more different patterns.

Hull's subjects could classify new forms because they looked as if they belonged to the proper categories, even though the subjects could not define the property which made the patterns look alike. Since recognition depended upon learning a variety of instances, it seems likely that it did not rest upon any single stored form, but upon a trace system which summarized the set of individual instances given a common label.

How is such a trace system formed? Earlier we saw that a word may automatically activate its associates, which then obtain strength within the same memory cell. In the same way, one might expect a new form to activate forms with a similar configuration and then be stored together with them. The common label provided by the experimenter provides a cue for retrieval of the trace system developed by this process. In this way a memory cell consisting of forms from a given category could be built up.

This structure would represent the category at the visual level and would in turn be tied to the name of the concept. All this might be done without the subject's having to verbalize anything about the common properties of the concept. A new pattern would tend to activate the memory cell of forms similar to it, thus giving rise to the name and the correct classification.

The Hull experiment goes a small way toward helping us understand how one represents past experience in trying to recognize a new pattern. One limitation of his study is that Hull chose to base the classifications on a single common element for each concept. This is by no means typical of real pattern recognition. When a person recognizes a hand-written letter as an "A" or a four-footed animal as a "dog," there is no single common characteristic he can point to as the crucial identifying sign.

Schema Formation

In the late nineteenth century, Galton experimented with composite photographs produced by superimposing several faces. He found that the composite photographs of a particular group (e.g., members of the same family) served as a particularly good example of the group as a whole. Some writers have suggested that such composite photographs might serve as a physical analogue of the processes involved in the learning of visual concepts (Woodworth, 1938).

Recent studies concerned with this question have used simple visual patterns. The basic pattern can be called a *prototype* or *schema*. Transformations of the prototype are constructed either by applying some systematic operation (rotation, reversal) or by some form of random distortion which allows the components of the original figure to move haphazardly to new positions. Figure 4 shows what happens when dots constituting the digit 4 are moved about randomly. In a case of random distortion, the prototype represents the average of the set of distortions.

Some studies have attempted to show that the prototype or central tendency of a set of patterns plays an important role in allowing subjects to learn to identify distortions. Attneave (1957) demonstrated that pretraining on the prototype of a set of patterns could facilitate the subject's learning to name new distortions of the same patterns. It has also been shown (Hinsey, 1963) that pretraining on the prototype pattern is superior to pretraining on one of the peripheral patterns.

One set of studies (Posner & Keele, 1968, 1970) sought to investigate whether the prototype could be abstracted from a set of distortions. Stimuli were nonsense patterns consisting of nine dots, similar to those in Figure 5. The subjects learned to associate four different distortions of each prototype with a single name, but were never shown the prototypes. The subjects were then presented a list of patterns which they had to classify based upon their learning. The new list consisted of prototypes

which had never been seen before, old distortions which they had just finished learning, and control patterns which were distortions of the same prototypes. The similarity of the control patterns to the individual, stored distortions was equal to the similarity of the prototypes to the stored patterns. If the stored distortions were viewed as lying on the circumference of a circle, the prototypes would be the center. The control patterns would also lie within the circle, but not precisely at its center. The difference between the control patterns and the prototypes was that the prototypes shared the particular features which most clearly represented the set of patterns.

Classification of the prototypes was quite good. In some experiments the prototypes were as accurately classified as the patterns which the subjects had just finished memorizing. In all cases the prototype patterns were classified more accurately than the control patterns. Moreover, with a week's delay following the learning task, retention of the memorized distortions declined, while the prototype patterns showed no decline.

FIGURE 4   DIGIT 4 BEING DISTORTED BY A RANDOM PROCESS WHICH MOVES EACH DOT BY SUCCESSIVELY GREATER DISTANCES

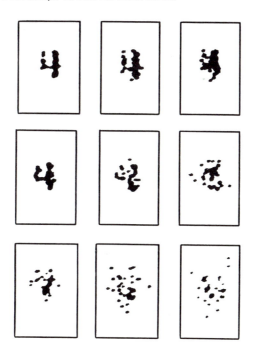

Reprinted from White, B. W. Recognition of familiar characters under an unfamiliar transformation. *Perceptual and Motor Skills*, 1962, *15*, 107–116. Reprinted with permission of author and publisher.

FIGURE 5   DISTORTIONS OF A RANDOM-DOT PROTOTYPE

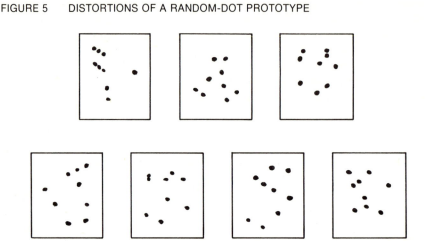

The top row consists of three random-dot prototypes. The bottom row shows four distortions of the right prototype. Reprinted from Posner, M. I. Abstraction and the process of recognition. In G. H. Bower and J. T. Spence (Eds.), *The psychology of learning and motivation.* New York: Academic Press, Inc., 1969. Pp. 44–96.

Does the subject really "recognize" the prototype, or is he merely able to classify it? That is, when he sees a prototype, does he think that he has seen it before, or is he merely able to put it into the right category? One experiment (Posner, 1969) involved a recognition memory test. Subjects were asked to classify a list of patterns as either seen before in the list ("old") or seen for the first time ("new"). After viewing a number of distortions of the same prototype, subjects were shown the prototype pattern which they had never seen before. The subjects tended to classify the prototype pattern as "old," as if they had actually experienced it in the list. The experience of seeing different distortions produced a trace system which misled the subjects into thinking they had seen the prototype of that series when they had not.

The automatic nature of the development of the prototype is emphasized by other experiments which, like Hull's, do not tell the subject to learn a concept. In one series of such experiments, subjects were shown cards which had simple geometric figures (Franks & Bransford, 1971). They were instructed to remember each card so as to reproduce it later. After seeing a number of cards, the subjects were given tests which included cards they had seen and prototype cards which represented the commonalities among those actually presented, but which had not actually been shown. Subjects "recognized" the prototype forms with a greater probability than patterns seen before. In related studies (Evans, 1967), subjects were instructed to determine which of three simultaneous

patterns was "different" from the other two. Two of the patterns came from one prototype and one from another. Subjects learned to identify the odd pattern with increasing accuracy, even when they were given no special information on the correctness of their performance and no special set to learn the common characteristics.

Although most of this work has involved random forms or simple geometrical figures, there are experiments using pictures of faces which have obtained similar results (Reed, 1972). Reed had subjects classify schematic faces into one of two categories shown in Figure 6. He tested several models which could describe how this classification took place. The strategy which best fit his results and which was also equivalent to the introspections of most of his subjects was to form an abstract image of a prototype to represent each category and to classify test patterns on the basis of their similarity to the two prototypes.

It is important to recognize that, unlike a composite photograph, the trace system underlying schema formation involves storage of more than the prototype. Subjects are able to recognize the patterns which they memorized much better than they would have if *only* the prototype pattern were stored. The trace system does reflect the prototype, but it contains information relevant to the individual instances as well. In order to understand how the trace system reflects the individual patterns which have been presented, it is necessary to turn to studies which manipulate the variety of experiences subjects are given.

FIGURE 6   EACH ROW OF FACES REPRESENTS ONE CATEGORY INTO WHICH PEOPLE HAD TO SORT FACES

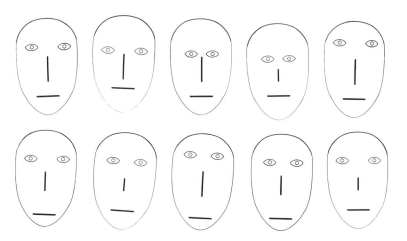

Reprinted from Reed, S. K. Pattern recognition and categorization. *Cognitive Psychology,* 1972, *3*, 382–407.

Variability

Hull found that merely showing the subject the crucial sign was not a good way to insure future recognition. Rather, the subject had to see the crucial feature embedded in different concrete instances. This appears to be a general feature of experiments on schema formation.

Dukes and Bevan (1967) compared a group that was given four repetitions of a single facial pose with one that saw four different poses of the same face. They found that the repetition fostered recognition of the particular pose, but that the group seeing the four poses did better in recognizing new poses. This study, like Hull's, suggests that variability aids in pattern recognition. The Dukes and Bevan study did not control the distance of new poses from the ones learned. Variability could be effective simply by increasing the likelihood that a learned pose would be close to the one shown in the recognition test. Posner and Keele (1968) manipulated variety by choosing instances at varying distances from a prototype. Subjects were taught either a low-variety (tight) concept or a high-variety (loose) concept. A low-variety concept involved patterns which looked alike, while the high-variety set had little apparent similarity. After learning, subjects were required to classify new, severely distorted patterns into one of the previously learned categories. The results of the study suggested that subjects learning the high-variety (loose) concept did significantly better in classifying severely distorted patterns than those learning the low-variety (tight) concept.

This need not always be the case. Some experiments, using photographs of random shapes (Bregman & Charness, 1970), have shown that at low levels of training, subjects learning a tight concept, or seeing only the prototype pattern itself, did better in later transfer than those learning a loose concept. At high levels of training, the results favored a loose concept. Perhaps the reason for this discrepancy is that two processes are involved in the development of the trace system which summarizes past experience with patterns. One involves learning the central tendency or prototype, and would be expected to occur more rapidly with small distortions. However, the ability to abstract the common element does not itself guarantee successful pattern recognition. A second process involves representing the boundaries of instances to which the concept might apply. Highly variable instances probably increase the difficulty of extracting a prototype, but if learning is sufficient to allow such extraction, the variability eases recognition of distorted patterns.

If subjects are taught a tight concept, they tend to be very careful about classifying any particular pattern as an instance of that concept. They tend to reject a relatively small distortion of the prototype as an instance, and they rarely classify a pattern as a member of the concept when it is not. On the other hand, subjects learning high-variability concepts often falsely classify patterns as members of the concept, but rarely reject a

member of the concept incorrectly. Thus tight concepts tend to get subjects to say "no," while loose concepts tend to get subjects to say "yes." The situation largely determines which type of learning will be superior.

The importance of variability of experience is illustrated by an experiment on the recognition of photographs of white and black students (Malpass & Kravitz, 1969). It was found that the ability to learn to recognize a photograph was better when the photograph was of a member of a subject's own racial group. The effect was greater for white subjects than for black subjects. Presumably familiarity with one's own racial group fosters learning of new faces of the same type. The lack of experience with other races appears to reduce our ability to distinguish between individuals who share relatively unfamiliar features.

The trace system which underlies the recognition of patterns can be characterized by a central tendency and a boundary. This system is a type of mental structure which can be stored in memory. It is a relatively primitive type of mental structure in that other animals share with humans the ability to recognize objects despite distortions.

It may well be that this type of memory structure provides an answer to the debate between Locke and Berkeley about the existence of abstract ideas. Perhaps when one imagines a face or a triangle, he activates the central tendency of a trace system such as the ones we have been discussing. Thus a prototype serves as an internal representation of a whole set of individual patterns. D. O. Hebb (1968) has proposed something of this sort. He says, "The object is perceived both as a specific thing in a specific place with specific properties, and as generalized and abstracted from—but not all of this simultaneously. In imagery, only part of this activity may be reinstated . . . . A memory image, that is, may consist only of second- and higher-order assemblies, without the first-order ones that would give it the completeness and vividness of perception [p. 473]." It remains for future studies to develop more details about the relationship between the trace system underlying pattern recognition and the subjective experience of imagining the same object.

Transformation Rules

When one deals with random distortions of nonsense patterns, there is little one can learn about the distortions themselves. Amount of distortion, rather than kind, is the important thing. In real life, however, we learn that there are many kinds of distortions, some of which are of little importance in discriminating among patterns. For example, changes in size and inclination occur as an object moves closer or further away without indicating a new object.

Pick (1965) found that children will often classify as identical patterns which differ in rotation, or size, or degree of curvature. When the children

were trained on these types of distortions with one set of patterns, they were able to avoid similar errors when dealing with a new set of patterns. Apparently the subjects were able to learn what kinds of transformations were considered relevant to discriminating objects (Caldwell & Hall, 1970).

It is obvious that people can attend to separate attributes of visual objects such as form, color, and size. The study of perception is concerned with how these attributes lead to our ability to perceive objects (Gibson, 1969; Neisser, 1967; Uhr, 1966). Our concern in studying thinking is less with the basic perceptual processes which allow us to see objects than with our ability to combine such percepts in learning concepts. Taking the perceived object as the starting place, a person's analysis of it into attributes is a cognitive achievement of considerable complexity. Indeed, the ability to describe the difference between objects by reference to a set of attributes is more difficult to acquire than the ability to discriminate the objects. It is easier to distinguish between dogs and cats than to say why they are different.

Hyman and Frost (1974) set out to show that subjects pass from a knowledge of individual patterns, through abstraction of prototypes, and finally to a realization of the attributes upon which the patterns differ. They used random-dot patterns like those shown in Figure 5. The patterns were systematically distorted by stretching them along either the vertical (height) or horizontal (width) dimensions (Figure 7). A total of eight patterns were shown to the subjects during learning. The "A" patterns tended to be tall and narrow, while the "B" patterns were short and wide. Hyman and Frost tried to infer the structure by which the subjects represented the patterns by their speed and accuracy in classifying the patterns they had learned and new patterns which were similar. The experimenters reasoned that if the subjects had stored a list of the learned

---

FIGURE 7   DIAGRAM OF THE DISTORTIONS USED BY HYMAN AND FROST IN THEIR STUDY OF ATTRIBUTE LEARNING

Tall	D	A	x	x	x
	A	C	A	x	x
Height	x	A	x	B	x
	x	x	B	C′	B
Short	x	x	x	B	D′

Narrow   Wide

Width

Each letter indicates a particular pattern having a particular degree of distortion of height and width. Adapted from Hyman, R., and Frost, N. Gradients and schema in pattern recognition. In P. M. A. Rabbitt (Ed.), *Attention and performance*. Vol. V. New York: Academic Press, Inc., 1974.

patterns, they would be fast on them, but slow on any new patterns. If, however, they had abstracted a prototype for the "A" and "B" patterns, they would be best on the central tendencies of the two categories (patterns "C" and "C¹" in Figure 7). If, however, they had learned the attributes on which the patterns differed (e.g., height and width), they would do best on "D" and "D¹," which were the most extreme examples of these attributes.

The authors speculated that the list organization would be dominant early in training and would be replaced by the prototype organization. They found evidence for both types of organization by different subjects. The data did not show that the two forms of organization were related to degree of training. It was clear, however, that few subjects achieved a representation of the attributes. Knowing the attributes would greatly enhance the value of learning, since such knowledge could be transferred to any set of patterns which varied in height and width. Moreover, a knowledge of the attributes would allow subjects not only to recognize, but also to construct new patterns. More studies of the development of representations with practice are clearly needed.

In Chapter 4 we will discuss in greater detail the process by which subjects pass from iconic representation to symbolic concepts based upon the underlying attributes.

LONG-TERM ICONIC MEMORY

It is easy to show that the retention of visual information in memory undergoes distortions from many sources. For example, it was suggested previously (p. 33) that visual information stored at the same time as a verbal label tends to be distorted in the direction of the verbal label (Carmichael et al., 1932). In the same way, Bartlett (1932) found that visual retention of an unconventional sphynx-like figure was distorted in memory toward a more conventional pattern of a cat.

A study by Bahrick and Boucher (1968) is particularly instructive in this regard. They exposed separate groups of subjects to lists of visual patterns, one from each of several familiar categories (e.g., teacups). Some groups were required to name each object at the time of learning, and others learned without being required to name the objects. Subjects were tested either immediately or after six weeks' delay. They first tried to recall the object's name (e.g.,"teacup"), and then they attempted to recognize the particular object from a list of similar objects of the same category. The recognition test was carried out by showing the subjects ten different teacups, for example, and having them try to identify the particular one they had seen at the time of original learning.

Several aspects of this study were striking. When tested immediately after learning, the group instructed to verbalize the names during learning showed superior recall of the object names. After six weeks, however, the

verbalization condition did not affect recall of the names. This finding supported unsolicited statements by the subjects which suggested that they depended heavily upon visual information as a means of recall. The authors concluded from their subjects' reports that delayed recall of the name was obtained from a visual code of the item.

It might be expected that the probability of recall would be related to the accuracy of this visual code. However, this was not the case. Instead, it was found that the ability to remember the object name ("teacup") was completely uncorrelated with the ability to pick out the particular teacup which had been seen. This suggests that the subjects could obtain the name of what they had seen from a visual representation, but not necessarily *the* visual representation of the particular teacup they had been shown.

One way to view these results makes them consistent with the abstractive quality of visual memory which has been emphasized in this discussion. The visual information presented to the subjects can become a part of the trace system which summarizes past visual experience with teacups. Thus the particular teacup which the subjects bring to mind at the time of recall is influenced not solely by the teacup which they saw, but also by information concerning the trace system representing their concept of teacups. Just as the unfamiliar object which Bartlett showed his subjects was reproduced more like a conventional cat, so the teacup brought to mind by Bahrick's subjects comes to take on the properties common to the category "teacup." This explanation fits with the lack of difference due to verbalization, since both groups would be using stored visual information. Moreover, it also agrees with the finding of no relation between accuracy of visual recall and likelihood of obtaining the correct category name. The failure to recognize the particular teacup which the subjects had seen would be due to the fact that this item had been assimilated into the subjects' overall concept.

How are visual memories of different objects arranged? So far we have discussed organization of visual memories of single objects (triangles or teacups) in terms of a trace system characterized by a central tendency and boundary. In Chapter 2 we discussed the importance of organizations which allow the thinker to go from one word to another. One experiment (Frost, 1971) has attempted to explore similar types of organization for visual memories. Subjects were shown pictures of familiar objects (e.g., dogs). They expected to have to recognize each picture from a set of pictures of the same objects (e.g., other dogs). The objects were drawn so that their orientation was either vertical, horizontal, or sloped at a 45-degree angle left or right. After seeing a number of pictures, subjects were required to recall the picture names. It was found that the names were clustered into categories based on the orientation of the picture. Like the subjects in the Bahrick and Boucher experiment, the subjects uniformly reported that their recall of the names was accomplished by first

imagining the picture and then naming it. They were usually unaware that orientation was a cue or that the names were organized in any particular way. Once having thought of a picture in a given orientation, subjects simply tended to think next of a picture which shared the same visual property. Thus orientation was the basis of association for these pictures. This experiment involved recall after brief (fifteen minute) delays. It is doubtful that orientation is a very important organizing property in long-term visual memory. However, this experiment does illustrate that visual memories have principles of organizaton which are independent of the verbal codes of the same items.

The assimilation of the particular into the general has important consequences for human memory and thought. It reduces the probability that we will be able to remember the exact details of what we have seen before, but it provides an economical storage system which can deal with a multitude of individual experiences without overloading the memory. Moreover, it gives us an internal reference system and code with which to think. When we think about teacups and attempt to find their characteristics, we may work from an abstracted visual code which represents our past experience with teacups. There is no need to bring to mind every individual teacup we have seen. Yet we are able to make judgments comparing a new teacup with our previous experience. For example, we may judge that the new cup is rather small or that its handle is bigger than usual. The internal reference for such judgments is the visual category formed from our past experience.

An experiment by Shepard and Chipman (1970) shows how we may study the relationships among our internal representations. Shepard chose fifteen states of the union of roughly the same size. He then made two decks of cards. In one deck each card consisted of the names of a pair of states, while the other deck had outline drawings of the same pairs. Subjects rated the similarity in shape of each pair of states. They first made ratings using only the name deck, so that the comparison rested entirely upon stored information. Then they made the same ratings from the picture deck. The results showed a very high correlation between the two sets of ratings.

Shepard and Chipman argued that the relationship among internal representations of information concerning the shape of the states was much the same as that which held among the corresponding external objects (principle of second-order isomorphism). This principle does not contend that internal iconic representations resemble the external events in any direct way, for that view would conflict with many findings that the nervous system stores not literal copies of experience, but highly abstracted representations of it. Rather, this principle merely suggests that iconic memories preserve the spatial relationships of the individual percepts which produced them. In this sense, iconic concepts resemble the external world in only a derivative or second-order way. Undoubted-

ly, it is this spatial character which makes such iconic representations important vehicles in many judgmental and problem-solving tasks.

ICONIC CONCEPTS AND AESTHETICS

Many aspects of our perception of patterns are governed less by the single event which is currently before us than by the set of patterns to which the present stimulus is related. The way in which an ambiguous figure is seen depends upon the situation. For example, the pattern |3 may be seen as a letter (B) if the subject is involved in a reading task, and as a number (13) if he is involved with arithmetic. The judgment of any particular pattern is affected by the entire set of related things which the pattern activates.

Galton (1907) found that composite photographs of faces produced a more aesthetically pleasurable response than the individual faces from which they were composed. In this special sense, an average face may be beautiful. Of course, a face which is average in each feature may be quite rare and unique. However, the idea of an average depends upon a set of inferred objects, not upon the present stimulus alone.

Some experiments have also suggested that our judgments of aesthetic preference depend upon the relationship of an individual pattern to an inferred set. In one experiment (Garner, 1970), ninety dot patterns were constructed, each consisting of five dots located on a three-inch-by-three-inch grid. Some of the patterns are shown in Figure 8. The top two patterns are unique in that they remain the same if they are rotated to successive 90-degree positions or if they are reflected. On the other hand, the bottom four patterns produce four different patterns when rotated or

FIGURE 8   DOT PATTERNS USED BY GARNER TO STUDY PREFERENCE FOR FIGURES

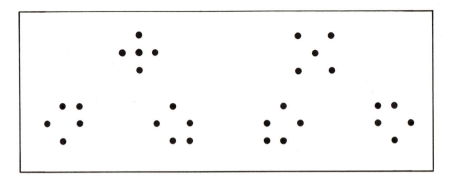

The two upper patterns are unique, while the two lower patterns can be rotated into one another. Reprinted from Garner, W. R. Good patterns have few alternatives. *American Scientist*, 1970, *58*, 34–42. Reprinted by permission.

reflected. One group of subjects sorted such patterns into piles which seemed to them to "belong" together, while another group rated each of the patterns for "goodness" (aesthetic preference) on a seven-point scale. It was shown that patterns which had few alternatives and were sorted into small categories also tended to be rated as "good" figures. This high correlation tended to support Garner's view that a pattern which is seen as being unique or one of a small set will tend to be seen as a good figure.

Another study (Alexander & Carey, 1968) used linear arrays of seven squares, each of which was either black or white. They found a very high relationship between patterns which were (1) easily described to others, (2) found rapidly when searching, (3) memorized easily, and (4) rated as "simple" in form. Patterns unique in the sense of being easily described and memorized were also seen as "simple." No "goodness" rating was taken. However, other studies (Munsinger & Kessen, 1966) suggest that there is a relationship between the simplicity of a form and its "goodness." If forms are arranged on a scale of complexity, different subjects place their ideal point at different positions on the scale. The preferences of an individual subject may be obtained by finding the distance on the simplicity scale from any pattern to the subject's ideal point. For many adult subjects, the ideal point is neither the simplest nor the most complex, but some place intermediate on the scale. There is some evidence that older subjects prefer more complex figures than younger ones do, and that increased exposure or artistic training also increases the optimal level of complexity. These results support Garner's general point that our judgment of a pattern depends heavily upon the set of related patterns which are stored in memory.

SUMMARY

This chapter has reviewed evidence on the construction of iconic concepts, which are trace systems constructed from many individual instances. Iconic concepts provide one kind of answer to the old philosophical dispute about how universals are represented in memory. The iconic concept allows us both to consider a representative case *(schema)* which approximates the central tendency of a set of instances and also to know something about the variability of instances within the concept.

The ability to form iconic concepts follows from the abstractive and grouping properties of the human memory system discussed in Chapter 2. It is not necessary that we be able to verbalize the rules which underlie such concepts in order to form them. Nonverbal concept formation connects human memory with that of nonhuman animals.

Iconic concepts give us a basis for the recognition and classification of new instances which we have never before experienced. They provide a basis for internal imagination and reasoning from past visual experience. They also serve as a reference for many kinds of judgments, including those underlying aesthetic preference.

4

Symbolic Concepts and Mental Structures

The lowest form of thinking is the bare recognition of the object. The highest, the comprehensive intuition of the man who sees all things as part of a system.

Plato

Plato emphasizes the hierarchical nature of the many processes by which humans impose order upon their world. The last chapter reviewed iconic concepts, which involve the combining of different perceptual experiences into an overall trace system that allows us to recognize a stimulus or, in its absence, to represent it to ourselves. This chapter will show how we use the power of symbolism to impose new conceptual organizations upon stored information which differs from the actual objects experienced.

In dealing with iconic concepts, the unit of analysis was the object as perceived. However, it is possible to disassemble objects into the component attributes[1] which constitute them. For example, we might view a face in terms of its shape, color, or size. This dimensionalization of input plays an important role in many aspects of human cognition. Disassembling objects allows us to make comparisons among things which are physically quite different. Thus the ability to separate the dimensions of perceptual objects underlies the human capacity for complicated analogies and judgments.

---

[1] In what follows, the terms *attribute* and *dimension* will be used interchangeably. For example, color, shape, and size will be called both attributes and dimensions. In other areas of psychology, the term *dimension* may have a somewhat more technical use, implying variation of a single physical quantity.

If you were asked to judge which of two houses was better, you might begin the judgment process by looking at the ways in which the houses differed. These might include such things as size, shape, and number of floors. Only by isolating these attributes and comparing the houses with respect to them would it be possible to arrive at a reasonable judgment about which of the two houses was superior.

Dimensionalization may apply not only to input, but also to material stored within long-term memory. For example, suppose you were asked what there was in common among the states of Alabama, Oregon, New Hampshire, and Texas. Bringing to mind stored information about the states, you might then attempt to derive an attribute which all the states had in common. One possibility would be that they all have a coastline. The process of grouping states in this way is one of effortful retrieval. You might scan an internal representation of a map or a verbal description of the states and bring together into active memory those which have coasts. The states could then be stored not only in their original locations, but also as part of a separate memory cell of states which have seacoasts. This structure would serve as a unit for future effortless retrieval of some or all states which have seacoasts. Thus the ability to derive attributes of objects provides new ways of organizing semantic memory.

This chapter will first examine learning to isolate attributes. Then it will examine the recombination of attributes in the process of classification and judgment. Finally, there will be a consideration of some types of semantic structures which may be used to store concepts abstracted from experience.

OBJECTS AND ATTRIBUTES

Kasanin and Hanfmann (1942) have described tests used by Vygotsky (1962) which seek to measure the stages through which children pass in learning to form dimensional concepts as follows:

> The material used in the concept formation tests consists of 22 wooden blocks varying in color, shape, height, and size. There are 5 different colors, 6 different shapes, 2 heights (the tall blocks and the flat blocks), and 2 sizes of the horizontal surface (large and small). On the underside of each figure, which is not seen by the subject, is written one of the four nonsense words: *lag, bik, mur, cev.* Regardless of color or shape, *lag* is written on all tall large figures, *bik* on all flat large figures, *mur* on the tall small ones, and *cev* on the flat small ones. At the beginning of the experiment all blocks, well mixed as to color, size and shape, are scattered on a table in front of the subject. . . . The examiner turns up one of the blocks (the "sample"), shows and reads its name to the subject, and asks him to pick out all the blocks which he thinks might belong to the

same kind. After the subject has done so . . . the examiner turns up one of the "wrongly" selected blocks, shows that this is a block of a different kind, and encourages the subject to continue trying. After each new attempt another of the wrongly placed blocks is turned up. As the number of the turned blocks increases, the subject by degrees obtains a basis for discovering to which characteristics of the blocks the nonsense words refer. As soon as he makes this discovery the . . . words . . . come to stand for definite kinds of objects (e.g., *lag* for large tall blocks, *bik* for large flat ones), and new concepts for which the language provides no names are thus built up. The subject is then able to complete the task of separating the four kinds of blocks indicated by the nonsense words. Thus the use of concepts has a definite functional value for the performance required by this test. Whether the subject actually uses conceptual thinking in trying to solve the problem . . . can be inferred from the nature of the groups he builds and from his procedure in building them: Nearly every step in his reasoning is reflected in his manipulations of the blocks. The first attack on the problem; the handling of the sample; the response to correction; the finding of the solution—all these stages of the experiment provide data that can serve as indicators of the subject's level of thinking [pp. 9–10].

Vygotsky (1962) distinguishes three phases through which children pass in learning to form true concepts. In the first phase they produce what he calls *heaps*. These heaps consist of a number of different blocks which have no similarity other than spatial position. They are like the list of letters of the alphabet in having no internal structure. The main cue used to form the heaps is the spatial position of the block within the field of view. The child tends to take one group of contiguous blocks and push them together as one concept without regard to their dimensions.

At a later age children form what Vygotsky calls *complexes.* Complexes are based, to some degree, upon the perceptual similarity among groups of blocks. One example of building a complex is to take one particular block as the focus for one pile, and add to it blocks which resemble it along first one dimension and then another. In using the block as a focus, the child selects no special attribute of the block, but perhaps adds one which has the same color, another which has the same size, and yet another which has the same width. More systematic complexes may be formed if the child picks one particular attribute, such as color, and sorts on the basis of that attribute alone. These discriminations are akin to the iconic concepts discussed previously.

Finally, Vygotsky argues, at about the age of puberty children begin to develop true concepts. That is, they learn the relevant attributes, in this case form, color, size, and height, and the values of these dimensions are associated with each label. For example, tall and large blocks are

systematically classified together. Thus children learn first to form classes based on perceptual similarity, and only later to use the attributes as a systematic basis for classifications which are no longer limited to the specific set of objects with which they have had experience.

Another experimental situation stresses the kinds of problems which can be solved once attributes are learned (Kendler & Kendler, 1962). The stimuli in this situation consist of two attributes, color and form. The color dimension has two values, black and white, and the form attribute has triangle and square as values. In this experimental paradigm, the subject is first taught to select black objects. Since the form of the object is irrelevant to the choice, black triangles and black squares are both positive, whereas white triangles and white squares are negative. At this point two new problem situations are compared. In one condition the subject changes to a problem in which white becomes the positive value and black the negative one. This is called a *reversal shift* because all previously positive objects have become negative. In the second situation the relevant attribute changes. In this situation squares become positive and triangles negative, regardless of color. This is called an *extradimensional shift* because the previously irrelevant attribute has become relevant. Most studies have indicated that animals and very young children find the reversal shift more difficult than the extradimensional shift. This suggests that what they have learned is to select particular objects. When a previously negative object becomes positive, the learning must be reversed.

Adults, however, do not follow this rule. Instead, they find extradimensional shifts generally more difficult than reversal shifts. An explanation for this is that adults learn not only to select the black and avoid the white, but to attend to a particular attribute (e.g., color) and to ignore the other attribute (e.g., form). Thus changes which involve attention to the same attribute are less disrupting than those which require a shift to a previously irrelevant attribute.

Kendler and Kendler (1962) have suggested that the use of verbal labels is a crucial aspect of learning to attend to an attribute. They argue that when children begin to use verbal labels, they are then able to instruct themselves, "I am attending now to the color dimension," and maintain their attention on that dimension. It is unclear whether words are really necessary for this ability (Tighe & Tighe, 1968), but whether they are or not, the ability to label the dimension does help free it from the particular perceptual context in which it occurs.

A third example which illustrates learning to deal with attributes is called *transposition* (Reese, 1968). Transposition problems involve a comparison of the learning of relations (such as "greater than") with the learning of objects. Obviously, relationships are difficult to learn on a purely iconic basis. In one form of the transposition task, the subject is rewarded every time he selects a 100-cm. rectangle, and not rewarded when he selects a 25-cm. rectangle. After learning, he is switched to a

choice between a 100-cm. and a 200-cm. rectangle. If the subject has learned that the 100-cm. rectangle is correct, then following the shift he ought to accept the 100-cm. rather than the 200-cm. rectangle. If, however, he is responding to the relationship "larger than," he will choose the 200-cm. rectangle. It has been shown in a variety of studies (Reese, 1968) that most animals make choices in accord with the relational rule, provided that two things apply: one, that there is only a single dimension present, and two, that the shift between the first problem and the second problem is relatively small. Nonhuman organisms tend not to make the relational shift when either irrelevant dimensions are present or the shift is too large, indicating their difficulty in freeing the relation from the individual objects which exhibit it.

The adult human can learn and use relationships of this kind. Once having verbalized the relationship "larger than," he can apply it freely in a variety of situations with different stimuli and even different relevant dimensions. Through the use of language, the relationship "larger than" becomes an abstraction which the subject can free from the specific visual stimuli presented. He can use this abstraction in a new situation without depending upon the perceptual characteristics of the input.

These three examples show that human subjects develop the ability to deal with the individual attributes of stimulus objects. Since this ability matures more slowly than the ability to recognize visual objects, it seems unreasonable to base iconic recognition upon it. Rather, dimensionalization reduces the reliance of the human cognitive system upon the specific objects which are presented and aids judgments based upon certain systematic aspects of the stimuli.

An important practical example of the difficulty which people have in disassembling a unified experience into its attributes is learning to read. An alphabetic language, like English, requires that words which are perceived and used as units be broken down into constituent sounds (phonemes) which are represented in the written language as letters. This seems like a trivial operation since the child already is familiar with the spoken word and its meaning. All he need do is learn the sounds of each letter and recognize that they make up the familiar words which he is using in his spoken language. Yet this appears to be an extremely difficult step. The auditory word is a unit which is not easily decomposed into the artificial segments necessary for the written language (Savin, 1972). The mental achievement in analyzing unitary experiences into their attributes is rarely appreciated.

The contrast between the perception of objects and the storage of iconic concepts on the one hand and the abstraction of attributes and their combination into semantic concepts on the other affects adult thinking. Of particular interest in this regard are the studies by Heidbreder (1946ab). Her basic method was to teach subjects to associate nonsense syllables with pictures of simple objects. The objects varied in type, color, and number. She found that classifications based upon the type of object (e.g.,

automobiles, books) were easier to make than concepts based upon the color of the object (e.g., red objects), which in turn were easier than concepts based upon the number of objects present. Heidbreder supposed that this ordering represented a tendency of subjects to perceive the stimulus patterns as whole objects and to use the names of the objects as the basic descriptors upon which to form the concepts. Only if the development of concepts based upon the name of the object failed did subjects turn to physical attributes like color, and then finally to more abstract aspects of the situation like the number of objects which might appear on a card. She concluded from these studies that human cognition may be ordered with respect to two kinds of performances, the first being the perception of concrete objects, and the second being the attainment of concepts. Her distinction is similar to the one being made here between iconic and symbolic concepts.

Heidbreder's conclusion has been criticized on the grounds that objects simply look more alike than do colors or numbers. That is, the set of all birds is more similar than the set of all yellow things or the set of things with two elements (Baum, 1954; Osgood, 1953). This is certainly true and is what allows concepts based upon objects to take advantage of the iconic abstraction discussed in the last chapter. Moreover, an object is usually coded verbally in terms of its name and not in terms of individual attributes such as size or color. Of course, the advantage of object coding is not universal. An obscure object in a striking color might well be coded in terms of being a "red-and-white-striped something," but this is a less frequent method of coding. Both the perceptual similarity and the familiarity of object codes help explain why Heidbreder found that object concepts were simple. In cases in which the object type does not succeed in producing the concept, the subjects are able to discover other commonalities among instances. How are these attributes used to define new concepts? A large number of psychological experiments (Bourne, 1966) have been directed at finding out some of the factors which affect the identification of concepts.

CONCEPT IDENTIFICATION

For the purposes of description, objects may be divided into attributes. In studying acquisition and identification of concepts, psychologists usually present materials which can be divided easily into attributes. Figure 9 shows the location of a variety of objects which vary in the attributes of form and size. This simple description space allows the location of twelve discriminably different stimuli.

Obviously, as the number of attributes and values increase, so do the number of possible stimulus objects which can be defined by that description space. In general, for N attributes, each with R values, the number of stimulus objects which can be defined is RN. Thus a relatively few attributes can produce vast numbers of discriminably different

FIGURE 9   ILLUSTRATION OF ALL PATTERNS MADE FROM FOUR LEVELS OF THE
DIMENSIONS SIZE AND SHAPE

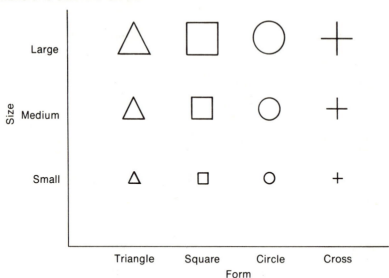

objects. A description of objects in terms of their attributes makes the task of classification logically simpler. In many laboratory experiments such a description is provided by the experimenter. In most real problems the subject must discover the attributes of variation which are important to problem solution.

In many laboratory concept-identification problems, only some of the attributes are related to the required categorization. The problem may be solved by selection of one or more attributes and a rule for combining them. The concept consists of the values of the relevant attributes which must be present for the instance to be positive (e.g., large triangle). In experiments of this type, subjects are shown some positive and some negative instances (see Figure 10). Their task is to learn to classify the patterns into those which are or are not instances of the concept.

The difficulty in solving such a problem depends upon the number of attributes which are allowed to vary. The more attributes, the more difficult it is to find the ones which are relevant to problem solution. The irrelevant attributes may be thought of as noise or static. The more noise, the harder it is to detect the important features of the patterns. On the other hand, if more than one combination of attributes can serve as a basis for solving the problem (redundant attributes), the rate at which the concept is learned is increased.

Heidbreder observed two rather different methods by which subjects might arrive at the concept. One corresponds to the development of iconic

FIGURE 10   EXAMPLES OF THREE CLASSIFICATION SCHEMES FOR EIGHT PAT-
TERNS

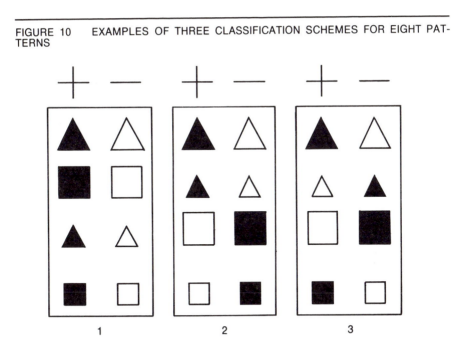

The left panel uses one dimension (color), the middle two dimensions (color and form),
and the right panel all three dimensions (color, form, and size).

concepts and involves passive observation of the positive instances.
Heidbreder called this method *spectator behavior.* The other method,
involving deliberate selection and active hypotheses on the part of the
subject, she called *participant behavior.*

Spectator Behavior

If one examines the positive instances in the left panel of Figure 10, it
should be clear that they tend to look alike since they have the same color.
Even without knowing at the verbal level that they all contain black
figures, it would be possible to accept a new pattern as an instance of the
concept because it looked like the positive instances. This is the kind of
pattern recognition discussed in Chapter 3. In this mode of processing, the
subject does not attempt to deal with individual attributes or to propose
verbal rules which allow classification. Rather, he tries to develop an
impression of what the positive instances look like. In this case he relies
upon the type of memorial structures we discussed earlier. He may not be
able to say why he has made a choice, but, like the subjects in Hull's
experiments, he chooses it because it looks right to him.

The solution of problems based upon spectator behavior is sometimes called *intuitive*. The idea is that the subject is able to classify instances without being able to state a rule for such classifications. We do not know the limits of the complexity of problems which may be solved by spectator behavior. However, one example which is frequently cited is a study by Bouthilet (1948). In this experiment the subject was given twenty trials, each consisting of a list of forty paired words. The second member of each pair was formed from the letters of the first member (e.g., "leopard" . . . "pole"), but this simple rule was not known to the subject. After viewing each list he was given a test list, each member of which consisted of a single word followed by five choices (e.g., "elephant" . . . "zero," "path," "this," "wood," "hole"). Some of the words were new to the subject, while others had been included in the previous training trial. In all cases, one of the choices was constructed from the letters of the single word. Some of the subjects showed near-chance performance and then very sudden increases to perfect performance, as if they had suddenly realized the rule. Others showed gradual improvements which appeared to be above chance, but which were too low for them to have derived the actual rule. It is possible, of course, that these subjects operated upon some rule which was correlated with the correct one, but it is also possible that they were operating on the basis of perceived similarities between the single word and the correct choice which were developed on an iconic basis. We are all familiar with our ability to "recognize" the improper spelling of a word which does not look like a correct English construction (e.g., "ngith"), even though we could not verbalize the rule which it violates. Human ability to combine and to abstract at an iconic level is not completely eliminated when subjects are placed in a complex concept-learning situation.

Hypothesis Testing

The more active strategy which Heidbreder observed she called *participant behavior.* In this mode of processing, the subject guesses which are the correct attributes and then tests these guesses against the information provided by the experimenter. This kind of active testing has a natural relationship to the scientific method and the strategies which philosophers have formulated under the laws of induction (see Chapter 1). Heidbreder found that participant behavior dominated the reports of most of her college-student subjects.

The tendency to believe that there is a pattern or rule underlying a sequence of events is extremely strong. Just how strong can be seen in situations in which input is random and there is no objective rule for the subject to discover. A favorite technique in experimental psychology is to present a sequence of events and require a prediction of which one will come next. If the experimenter randomizes the events, there is no way for

subjects to learn an objective pattern because none exists. Yet subjects in these experiments persist, over many trials, in attempting to extract some sort of rule governing the sequence. In one such study (Feldman, 1963), subjects predicted which of two events would occur next. The subjects were encouraged to speak aloud while trying to predict what was actually a random series of two hundred events. During the course of one sequence, a subject produced nine different hypotheses about the course of events. Many philosophers have commented upon our desire to discover some regularity in the world about us. It should be no surprise that even in the absence of a concept, people try to develop a rule to predict what will occur. When sequences are built to reflect rules, subjects are very fast in learning the sequences (Restle & Brown, 1970), indicating that they are sensitive to regularities in the order in which events occur.

Most experiments which have tried to study hypothesis behavior in humans have required subjects to verbalize their hypotheses. This might well induce behavior which would not be typical in the absence of forced verbalization. However, if the experimenter has arranged the situation properly, he can check to see if the subject is behaving in accordance with a particular hypothesis, even in the absence of verbal reports.

Levine (1969) constructed pairs of stimuli which were formed by four two-valued attributes. These were "black" or "white," "X" or "T," "large" or "small," and "left" or "right." He informed his subjects that the correct concept was one of these eight values (e.g., "X," "right," etc.). If the subjects were behaving in accordance with a hypothesis, three successive trials would be just sufficient for the experimenter to tell which hypothesis it was. There were eight patterns of choice which could have been made in three trials and each one was associated with one of the eight possible hypotheses (see Figure 11). In his experiments, Levine gave his subjects a series of four trials without information as to the correctness of their choice (feedback). Thus half of the sixteen possible patterns of choice were in accord with one of the hypotheses and the other half agreed with no hypothesis. He found that in about 92 percent of the responses, the college students used choice patterns consistent with one of the hypotheses. When subjects were then given feedback concerning their choices, it was possible to see how these hypotheses were modified by new information. If a hypothesis was confirmed on a trial, a choice consistent with that hypothesis occurred on the next trial 95 percent of the time. If a subject was informed that his choice was wrong, there was a strong tendency to change hypotheses. This happened on 98 percent of the incorrect trials. Thus hypothesis behavior, as defined by Levine, seems to fit with expectations.

Of greater interest was whether a subject tested more than the single hypothesis which he was using to make his choices. Suppose one thought that the most likely answer was "X." On each trial the response alternative "X" would be chosen. However, on each feedback trial, information

FIGURE 11   EIGHT PATTERNS OF CHOICE (REPRESENTED BY THE COLUMNS OF
DOTS), EACH OF WHICH CORRESPONDS TO ONE HYPOTHESIS WHEN THE FOUR
STIMULUS PAIRS ARE PRESENTED ON CONSECUTIVE BLANK TRIALS

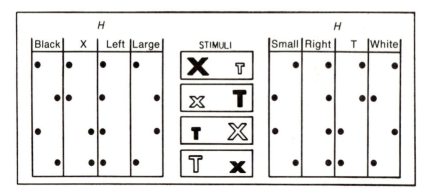

Reprinted from Levine, M. Hypothesis behavior by humans during discrimination learning.
Journal of Experimental Psychology, 1966, *71*(3), 331–338. Copyright © 1966 by the
American Psychological Association. Reprinted by permission.

would also be available about other hypotheses. For example, suppose an
X on the right side was chosen and was correct. This should eliminate the
possibility that the correct answer was "left."

Is this strategy learned? To answer this question, suppose a subject
considered only one hypothesis at a time. In that case, each time he
received feedback he would eliminate, at most, one hypothesis from the
total. For example, if on the first trial he chose "X" and was told he was
correct, he would eliminate no hypothesis; if he was told that he was
wrong, he would eliminate "X." On the other hand, suppose the subject
extracted all the information possible from the feedback trial. If he chose a
large black X on the left and was told that he was correct, this information
would eliminate "right," "T," "small," and "white." In general, each
feedback trial would eliminate half of the remaining hypotheses. After
three feedback trials, the subject would have only one hypothesis remaining. This strategy, an example of Mill's inductive method of elimination
(see Chapter 1), eliminates all hypotheses which are inconsistent with the
outcome on any single trial.

Levine was able to evaluate his subjects by taking the proportion of
correct hypotheses on any series of nonfeedback trials as a measure of the
number of hypotheses being used. These data are plotted in the dotted
line in Figure 12. It can be seen that the subjects in Levine's experiment
were eliminating more than the hypothesis with which they were
operating, but not quite all of the hypotheses possible if they were to
follow Mill's method. Presumably one of the reasons for their failure to

FIGURE 12   NUMBER OF HYPOTHESES (SIZE OF SET) FROM WHICH S SAMPLES ON EACH OUTCOME TRIAL

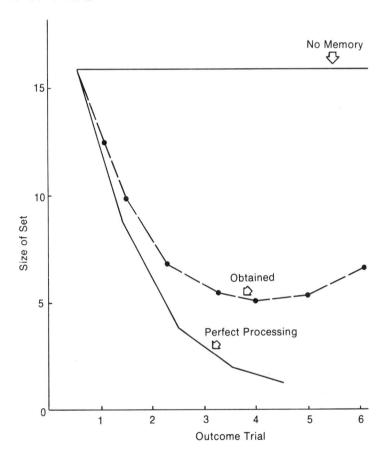

The upper line is based upon a zero-memory assumption, the bottom line upon an optimal strategy, and the middle line is the obtained results. Redrawn from Levine, M. Neo-noncontinuity theory. In G. H. Bower and J. T. Spence (Eds.), *The psychology of learning and motivation.* Vol. 3. New York: Academic Press, Inc., 1969. Pp. 101–134.

follow Mill's method was the difficulty in keeping track of the hypotheses still viable at any given time.

Levine investigated this possibility by creating two situations which differed in the extent of the corrections the subject had to make when feedback information was given. Suppose the subject is considering four hypotheses. His active memory might contain, for example, "black," "large," "X," and "left." Suppose he uses "X" as his overt choice. If he is told "correct," he can maintain his behavior of checking "X." The feedback also allows the elimination of other hypotheses (e.g., "left" and

"black"), which he can drop from active memory. Suppose, instead, the subject is told "incorrect." Then he must drop "X" as his choice and select a new one. He should also eliminate "left" and "black" on the basis of the feedback information.

In Chapter 2 it was shown that it is difficult to retain information in active memory and to perform reorganizations upon it at the same time. Mental operations interfere with the likelihood of maintaining the correct information in active memory. From this point of view, one might expect that being told "incorrect" would allow less elimination of wrong hypotheses than being told "correct." This is exactly the result Levine found. This finding is of particular interest because it is opposite what one might expect on intuitive grounds. When one is told he is incorrect, he ought to be motivated to reject hypotheses, while information that he is correct would not provide such motivation.

In addition to providing an overall measure of the number of hypotheses which the subject is using at any given time, Levine's technique also sheds some light on the dynamics of retention in active memory during the performance of the mental operations of comparison and elimination. In the next chapter we will consider in more detail these kinds of mental processes. For the time being, the main point of the Levine experiment is that subjects consider a number of different hypotheses on each trial and can reject some, but not all, of those which are not consistent with the feedback. The larger the memory load involved and the more difficult the mental operations required, the more we should expect the subjects to depart from optimal performance. The slower the pace of the task and the more use that can be made of artificial devices like paper and pencil, the more efficient their behavior is.

These general points are backed up by a variety of studies of concept learning. For example, Bower and Trabasso (1963) have found conditions under which subjects showed no evidence of elimination of hypotheses other than the specific one with which they were working. In these experiments the subjects' behavior was consistent with the upper line in Figure 12. That is, they seemed to formulate a hypothesis, test that hypothesis until it was proven wrong, and then discard it. Information related to hypotheses other than the one currently being tested was ignored completely. In another extensive series of concept-learning studies, Bruner and his associates (Bruner, Goodnow, & Austin, 1956) found conditions under which the subjects would closely approximate the ideal elimination of hypotheses allowed by Mill's method. This occurred under conditions in which the memory load was relatively low, particularly when subjects were allowed to determine which stimuli they saw. When the memory load was high and the problem difficulty great, the results approached those of Bower and Trabasso. While humans are capable of operating over a whole range of strategies, their choices are constrained by overall limitations on their memory and performance

capacities. It is these capacities and their influence upon the choice of strategies which will be the focus of Section II of this book.

Interaction of Spectator and Participant Behavior

One reason for separating iconic abstraction and hypothesis testing as modes of processing is that it becomes possible to ask how they affect one another. Hypotheses shape the information we remember about the world. They allow us to select which information should be considered, thus reducing the strain upon our memory capacities. Such selections limit what we retain about aspects of the situation not relevant to our current hypothesis. The consequence of such selection is that we may not have information available to develop new hypotheses should our current view prove inadequate. Bartlett (1958) has summarized this dilemma by suggesting that thought shows a "point of no return"—that is, a point at which the thought process continues to completion regardless of negative evidence. These ideas suggest that too early or too strong a reliance upon hypothesis testing may reduce performance by interfering with spectator behavior. This possibility has been explored in several experiments.

One study (Bruner & Potter, 1964) showed subjects pictures of complicated objects or scenes out of focus. The pictures were slowly focused until they reached a predetermined position which was clear enough for subjects to respond correctly on a reasonable percentage of trials. Three separate groups of subjects were used. One was introduced to the pictures when they were far out of focus, one when they were moderately blurred, and one when they were slightly blurred. For each group the pictures were focused until they reached the predetermined point. The experimenters measured the probability of a correct identification of the picture as a function of the degree of focus when they were originally introduced. It was found that subjects who were introduced to the pictures when they were very blurred did significantly worse than those who were introduced to the pictures when they were slightly blurred. The authors summarized their findings as follows:

> Exposure to a substandard visual display has the effect of interfering with its subsequent recognition. The longer the exposure and the worse the display, the greater the effect. Examination of the responses of the standardizing subjects, who reported aloud from the start of each picture, provides a clue as to the nature of the interference effect. Hypotheses about the identity of the picture are made despite the blur. The ambiguity of the stimulus is such that no obvious contradiction appears for a time, and the initial interpretation is maintained, even when the subject is doubtful of its correctness [p. 425].

A striking confirmation of this interpretation comes from a concept-formation experiment which has been reported only briefly in English (Kozielecki, 1961, cited by Du Charme & Peterson, 1969). In this experiment subjects were informed that on a specified proportion of the trials they would receive purposely false answers to questions about whether an event was a positive or negative instance of the concept they were to form. After the subjects chose a tenable hypothesis, they had a strong tendency to regard data confirming their hypothesis as true and data weakening their hypothesis as false. Consequently, subjects had increasing confidence in the stated hypothesis as a result of any confirming data they received, but did not decrease in confidence as a result of negative data. They simply chose to interpret information against that hypothesis as false.

Levine (1971) showed subjects a sequence of cards containing a large and a small circle. After each card, subjects were told "correct" if they indicated the large circle and "incorrect" if they indicated the small circle. This kind of problem can be solved in a few trials. If the subjects were first given problems which involved a complex position hypothesis (e.g., "3-left," "2-right," "3-left," "2-right," etc.), few were able to solve the simple size discrimination even after a hundred or more trials. Having been prepared to hypothesize about the position of the circle on the card, the subjects did not seem to notice the systematic relation between size and "correct."

In another study which illustrates the negative effects of hypotheses (Hislop & Brooks, 1968), subjects were shown cards which they had to categorize. The cards depicted cartoon animals which varied in color, size, type of animal, number of figures, and the presence or absence of letters and numerals. The correct rule was to classify as positive all instances containing two or more animals of the same species. Subjects were asked to make their categorizations as rapidly as possible. In one condition, subjects were required to verbalize the rule under which they were operating before their classification, while another group made the classification before verbalizing. It was found that the group classifying first made significantly more correct classifications than the group verbalizing first. The authors concluded that the subjects who had to verbalize first tended to let their behavior be governed by their verbal hypotheses. Those who did not have to verbalize first responded on the basis of nonverbal information which they had coded from the cards. The experimenters also found that the subjects' verbal rules did not always correspond completely with their classifications. This suggests that the verbal hypotheses and other types of stored information operated together to determine the classification.

Hypotheses bias the direction of attention and consequently which information is retained. They free us from the concrete and allow us to deal with abstract dimensions of stimulation. However, as a consequence,

they tend to suppress the operation of spectator behavior. If current hypotheses are incorrect, the ability to make modifications may be reduced by the way data have been selected and organized. Perhaps this explains why it is often difficult to relinquish hypotheses. The difficulty of changing hypotheses has also been noted on a larger scale in the development of scientific laws (Kuhn, 1962). While information on the detailed interaction of spectator and participant behavior is still sketchy, it does help us understand some of the problems people have in viewing information from several standpoints and freeing themselves from past organizations (see Chapter 7). The organization imposed upon information by hypotheses has both positive and negative consequences for the thought processes.

Combinatorial Rules

Knowledge of the relevant attributes is not a sufficient basis for making a classification in concept-identification experiments (Bourne, 1966). Even if the subject knows that the concept consists of the attributes "red" and "triangle," there are still ways of combining these attributes which will change the positive instances. Red triangles may be the positive set, or all red things and all triangular things, or red things and triangular things but not both. These represent three methods of combining relevant attributes to determine the classification.

Haygood and Bourne (1965) considered the ways in which a subject could combine two relevant attributes to arrive at a classification. The five basic types of rules are shown in Figure 13. Each of the five ways of combining the two relevant attributes may be called a rule in that it

FIGURE 13 FOUR LEVELS USED TO COMBINE ATTRIBUTES

Level	*Name*	*Symbol Description*	*Verbal Description*	*Real-Life Example*
1	Affirmation	R	Red patterns	Any attribute will do
2	Conjunction	R and S	Small red patterns	Bachelors degree: X credits and Y grade-point average
2	Inclusive Disjunction	R or S	Either small or red patterns	Doctor title: MD or PhD
3	Conditional	R implies S Not R or S	If the pattern is red, it must be small	Voter: If over X years, then register
4	Exclusive Disjunction	R or S Not R and S	Red and small but not both	Safety: Drink or drive

Adapted from Bourne, L. E., Jr., Ekstrand, B. R., and Dominowski, R. L. *The psychology of thinking.* Englewood Cliffs, N.J.: Prentice-Hall, Inc., 1971.

provides a unique classification of all patterns containing those attributes. The rules are *affirmation, conjunction, inclusive disjunction, conditional* and *exclusive disjunction.* These may be divided into three levels. Level 1 consists of rules with one relevant attribute. All instances of the rules have in common either the possession of the single attribute or its absence. In Level-2 concepts, two attributes are necessary for pattern classification. All of the dimensions are combined either by a single conjunctive ("and") operation or a single disjunctive ("or") operation. Level 3 requires either more than one conjunction/disjunction or a combination of conjunction and disjunction. The levels form a hierarchical structure, with the elements of Level-2 expressions being the Level-1 statements and the elements of Level-3 being Level-2 statements.

Experiments (Neisser & Weene, 1962; Haygood & Bourne, 1965) have shown that Level-1 concepts are easiest to learn, while Level-3 are hardest. There are several possible reasons for this. For one thing, affirmations and conjunctions produce positive instances which are perceptually similar. This allows spectator behavior to play a role in the classification process. Second, the conjunctive and affirmative rules may be more familiar than the higher-level concepts. There is, however, some reason to think that familiarity is not the complete explanation, since even subjects who have practiced on Level-3 rules still find them more difficult. Finally, the learning of high-level classification rules may be difficult because they require more complex suboperations.

All of the rules in Figure 13 involve three types of logical operations: conjunction, disjunction, and negation. Because these operations are important in the study of many learning and problem-solving tasks (Bourne, 1966; Piaget, 1957), psychologists have attempted to isolate them as parts of more complex performance. This work will be outlined in greater detail in the next chapter, on mental operations.

JUDGMENT

The concept literature which we have been considering is a rather restricted one. In the problems, a set of relatively obvious attributes are provided to the subject and his job is to learn which ones are relevant and how they are combined. At each step he receives information about the correctness of his response from the experimenter. Experiments which deal with choice and judgment appear to be very different. It will be instructive to see if some of the same analysis is appropriate.

Attributes

A favorite situation for psychologists interested in studying choice is gambling. Suppose you were offered a choice between the two gambles outlined in Figure 14. How could you make your choice? It is obvious

FIGURE 14   TWO BETS BETWEEN WHICH *S* IS REQUIRED TO MAKE A CHOICE

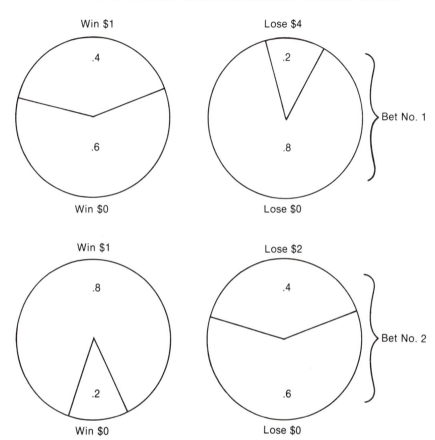

The diagram illustrates the four relevant attributes. Adapted from Slovic., P., and Lichtenstein, S. Relative importance of probabilities and payoffs in risk taking. *Journal of Experimental Psychology, Monograph Supplement*, 1968, *78*(3, pt. 2), 1–18. Copyright © 1968 by the American Psychological Association. Adapted by permission.

from the structure of Figure 14 that there are four relevant attributes: the probability of winning, the amount to win, the probability of losing, and the amount to lose. Moreover, it is possible to define a mathematical function called *expected value,* which consists of the probability of winning times the amount to win minus the probability of losing times the amount to lose. The expected value is an estimate of the amount of money you win or lose if the gamble is repeated many times. A rational rule might be to adopt the bet with the larger expected value, but it is well known that human behavior is not always "rational" in this sense. For example, we buy insurance which has a negative expected value because

the catastrophe of losing (dying early) is so great. We may select a long shot which has a negative expected value because the small likelihood of winning a large amount of money outweighs the much larger probability of losing a small amount.

One reason why the behavior of subjects in this situation is not fully in accord with expected value is that people do not use all the relevant attributes. Rather, they seem to focus on a subset of the four attributes to make their judgment. In one study (Slovic & Lichtenstein, 1968), subjects were allowed to choose among gambles in which the four relevant attributes could be manipulated separately. The authors developed a statistical method of finding out the emphasis subjects placed upon the different attributes. They discovered great individual differences in the weighting of the attributes. For example, some subjects attended only to the probability of losing and paid no attention to the other aspects of the gamble. Other subjects placed heavy emphasis on two attributes, such as the probability of winning and the amount to lose. Only a minority gave equal or near-equal weightings to all four attributes. The picture which the authors drew of the decision-making process was far closer to what we would conclude from the concept literature than it was to what the mathematician might expect from his analysis of expected values. The subjects formed their decisions after considering only a small part of the total relevant information. Since judgment situations provided relatively little feedback about which were the correct attributes, subjects selected and maintained sets which appeared to them to be appropriate.

The experimenters found that they could manipulate the attributes used. In one task they asked the subjects to rate their preference for each gamble. In this situation, the majority of the subjects tended to use the probability of winning as the main attribute. That is, bets which had high probabilities of winning were rated as generally desirable. However, when subjects were asked to state an amount of money they would be willing to pay in order to play the gamble, they tended to focus primarily on the amount to lose. Most theories of rational decision making assume that people will attend to the same relevant attributes in each choice; that is, if they prefer Gamble A to B and B to C, it is assumed that they will choose A to C. However, the tendency to shift relevant attributes when faced with different alternatives leads to violations of this principle in actual experience (Tversky, 1969).

Why do subjects attempt to reduce the complexity of the overall situation by attending to only certain relevant aspects, even at the risk of losing more money than they would if they attended to all the information? It might be argued that subjects simply do not realize that all the attributes are relevant to their choice. However, the tendency to use new attributes as the problem changes suggests that, in some sense, subjects realize that more attributes are relevant than they actually use. They find it difficult, in a rapidly moving situation, to take into account different

attributes. Even in the concept-learning experiments in which dimensions are continually pointed out to the subjects and in which the experimenter provides information concerning the correctness of the choice, it is difficult for the subjects to deal with all information. In the gambling situation such limitations become more critical.

The problems of attribute selection which we have been discussing are relevant to the decisions people make in complex real-life situations. A number of experimental studies have involved judgments by radiologists (Hoffman, Slovic, & Rorer, 1968), clinical psychologists (Goldberg, 1965), and stockbrokers (Slovic, 1969). In all these studies, the information was provided in the form of a number or rating on each dimension. For example, the radiologists did not see actual X rays, but were given information on the size, shape, texture, etc., of the film. This eliminated iconic aspects of judgment and might account for the relatively simple model which fit the data. The judgments which these people made could often be described quite accurately by an additive combination of some of the relevant attributes (Goldberg, 1968). These descriptions, however, are not necessarily related to the actual operations people use in making their judgments. When many attributes are involved, it is unlikely that people could, or would, be able to weight each attribute and calculate a sum. Indeed, it is more likely that subjects actually go through a sequence of subdecisions to produce judgments which resemble an additive combination.

Slovic (1966) studied a task in which nine different attributes related to success in college were given to subjects who then had to rate overall intelligence. He found that most of the subjects relied on only two cues, high-school record and English effectiveness. When these two cues were inconsistent, they discarded one of them. This tendency to discard attributes which are inconsistent has been found in other studies of judgment (Anderson & Jacobson, 1965). It is typical for one or two attributes to be used as a focus and small corrections made by reference to other attributes. In a study of skilled radiologists (Hoffman et al., 1968) six attributes were present, each of which was considered an important factor in the judgment of ulcer malignancy. However, when the actual judgments were analyzed, few of the physicians used more than two of the attributes to any substantial degree. Even with only two cues, Slovic (1966) found a strong tendency to focus on one, with the second used to make small corrections. This illustrates the tendency to simplify judgment by selecting a narrow focus of relevant attributes.

Heuristics

Heuristics are simple rules of thumb which people use in making complex judgments of symbolic material. They are ways of simplifying reality. We have already reviewed the tendency of subjects to focus on

only a small number of relevant attributes. There is also a strong tendency to summarize past experience in terms of a "representative" or "average" case. This is similar to the schema-formation process discussed in Chapter 3.

Bransford and Franks (1971) demonstrated that this process occurs in the comprehension of sentences which describe scenes. In these studies the experimenter constructs a prototype sentence which contains all the ideas in a scene (see Figure 15). Subjects are then read simpler sentences which describe the separate ideas in the scene. When tested for recognition, the subjects are more likely to recognize the prototype sentence as one they had heard than the actual sentences which were presented to them. As in schema formation, the memory trace has lost information about the individual instances and stored a representation which captures the overall idea.

FIGURE 15   PROTOTYPE SENTENCE AND THREE IDEAS

Prototype   The ants in the kitchen ate the sweet jelly which was on the table.
              (On Recognition Only)

Three   The ants ate the sweet jelly which was on the table.
Ideas   (On Acquisition Only)
              The ants in the kitchen ate the jelly which was on the table.
              (On Acquisition Only)
              The ants in the kitchen ate the sweet jelly.
              (On Recognition Only)

Two   The ants in the kitchen ate the jelly.
Ideas   (On Acquisition Only)
              The ants ate the sweet jelly.
              (On Both Acquisition and Recognition)
              The sweet jelly was on the table.
              (On Recognition Only)
              The ants ate the jelly which was on the table.
              (On Recognition Only)

One   The ants were in the kitchen.
Idea   (On Acquisition Only)
              The jelly was on the table.
              (On Acquisition Only)
              The jelly was sweet.
              (On Recognition Only)
              The ants ate the jelly.
              (On Recognition Only)

The top sentence is the prototype sentence. The remaining sentences present one or more ideas from the prototype. Each sentence is presented either during learning or during recognition. Reprinted from Bransford, J. D., and Franks, J. J. Abstraction of linguistic ideas. *Cognitive Psychology*, 1971, *2*, 331–350.

Studies of how one person forms an impression of another person (Anderson, 1972) have a very similar character. In these studies, subjects rate their overall impression of a person after hearing a set of descriptive adjectives. It is most often possible to describe the overall impression as a weighted average of the values of the individual adjectives (Anderson, 1972). Adjectives early in the list tend to be weighted more strongly than those later in the list. Moreover, adjectives which are inconsistent with the overall impression tend to be discounted. Thus, the overall impression may not reflect all the items equally, but only a reduced set of them.

Studies by Kahneman and Tversky (1972, 1973) reveal some important principles concerning the type of focus people use. They outline several heuristics which their subjects used to simplify the judgment task. One heuristic they call *representativeness*. When asked to make a judgment, people often reason from a typical or representative case, treating that case as though it were truly descriptive of the full range of possible cases. For example, suppose you were asked which of the following sequences of boy (B) and girl (G) births is most likely:

(1)   BBBGGG
(2)   BGBGBG
(3)   BGGBBG

Most people reply that (3) is the most likely, even though all sequences are equally probable. What they appear to mean is that (3) is more representative since it has no features which distinguish it from most of the possible orders. People who are asked to describe the properties of a general class (e.g., animal) will sometimes include properties which are true of some specific animal (e.g., dog) and not of all animals. They seem to think first of a representative of the class and then enumerate its properties as though these were true of the class as a whole. This principle suggests that subjects in the studies by Anderson may have used some of the adjectives to suggest a typical person and then rated him. The principle of representativeness appears to be an example in the study of judgment of a kind of abstraction process similar to that discussed in the section on abstraction of the schema (pp. 49–52).

Tversky and Kahneman (1973) report another heuristic which they call *availability*. This principle says that judgments of the frequency of an event are often based on how quickly or easily we find that event in memory. When asked whether it is more probable that an English word starts with a K or has a K in the third position, subjects most frequently replied that the former was more likely. In fact, about three times as many words have K in the third position. However, since the first letter of a word is a better retrieval cue, people can find words starting with K more quickly and thus judge them more frequent.

The study of judgment is starting to emerge from a period in which the primary interest was in testing mathematical models into one in which the focus is upon the cognitive operations people actually perform while

trying to arrive at a judgment. More experimental work must be focused upon how people select attributes for use in their judgments and the rules they use to combine them.

The studies discussed so far give rise to the view that human judgments involve a greatly simplified view of reality. There may be important limitations to this conclusion. In Chapter 3 we reviewed iconic judgments which take advantage of complex structures stored in long-term memory to recognize patterns. Human pattern recognition is a complex process which cannot be simulated by additive models such as those used in studying judgment. Yet such pattern recognition occurs effortlessly and with much less conscious involvement than the simple judgments discussed above. This suggests that more complex judgments may be made when appropriate memory structures evolved from past experience allow the judgment to bypass highly conscious processing. Memory structures which can be accessed effortlessly may be involved, for example, in the development of skills achieved by chess masters, or experts within any field. Such experts can use the richness of their past experience to improve their performance. Before considering these performances in greater detail, let us look at efforts to study the types of structures which might be present in long-term memory to aid in processing symbolic information.

MENTAL STRUCTURES

Lists

The simplest kind of mental structure is an ordered list. We have encountered this structure previously in discussing the internal representation of the digits and the alphabet. You may recall that both free-association studies and reaction-time studies indicate that the strongest association to any letter or digit is the next one in the sequence.

You might expect that such list structures are rather rare and that most human thinking depends upon more complex structures. However, many of our personal experiences appear to be stored in memory cells which have the character of lists (see Chapter 2).

One reason that the judgment studies cited in the last section may seem somewhat artificial is because they presume that people have impressions of others which range along a single dimension or list. Yet a one-dimensional view is surprisingly close to the truth in characterizing many aspects of human judgment. This was pointed out by DeSoto (1961) in a paper called "The Predilection for Single Orderings." DeSoto noted that when subjects are asked to rate others in such diverse things as voice quality and intelligence, they tend to see those high in one quality as also high in others. In social psychology this has been called the *halo effect.* It suggests an inclination to view someone who is high in one trait as high in

every trait. DeSoto argued that even in everyday language, one can detect a tendency to act as though there were only one ordering for a group of people. Use of expressions like "Joe's tops" or "Joe's the greatest" avoids any hint that there may be any orderings on which Joe does not stand uppermost.

DeSoto's experiments indicate that we have difficulty learning and remembering lists which involve different orderings of the same people. It is as though we stored a master list of people, just as we do of the alphabet. New orderings might be tried out on a provisional basis, but it is easier not to store separate orderings on different dimensions. In this sense the overall list structure tends to distort our thinking.

Spaces

It should not be thought, however, that lists are the only way in which attributes abstracted from the world are represented. Some studies of meaning (Deese, 1966; Osgood, Suci, & Tannenbaum, 1957) have attempted to uncover more complex multiattribute spaces which represent information. Some efforts to do this (Wallace & Atkins, 1960; Romney & D'Andrade, 1964) involved the study of the psychological meaning of kinship terms such as "mother," "father," "brother," "sister," "son," "daughter," "uncle," "aunt," "cousin," "nephew," and "niece." These terms may be seen as varying along three separate attributes: sex (S), generation (G), and lineality (L). The values on the sex dimension may be either male or female. Certain terms, such as "cousin," receive no values on the sex dimension since they do not distinguish between the sexes. The generation dimension can be seen as the older generation, the adult generation, or the younger generation. Lineality varies in two steps, members of the direct or nuclear family and those of more distant relationship. Each term in the kinship system may be seen as a unique point along these three dimensions, as shown in Figure 16.

It is clear that most subjects do not consciously think of kinship in terms of sex, generation, and lineality. How can we determine if in fact the terms are structured as Figure 16 suggests? One means of doing this uses ratings of similarity. It might be predicted that terms which differ along only the generation dimension (e.g., "father"-"son") would be psychologically closer than those which differ in both generation and sex (e.g., "father"-"daughter"). In fact, efforts have been made to use such similarity ratings to infer the cognitive structure which underlies kinship terms (Slobin, 1971). The results suggest that multiattribute spaces (although not necessarily the one shown in Figure 16) may be found which represent the internal organization of these terms in memory.

The same notion used to study kinship terms has been applied more widely to aspects of word meaning (Fillenbaum & Rappoport, 1971). Studies of the emotional connotation of words (Osgood, Suci, & Tan-

FIGURE 16   DIAGRAM OF ONE POSSIBLE STRUCTURAL REPRESENTATION OF THE KINSHIP SYSTEM

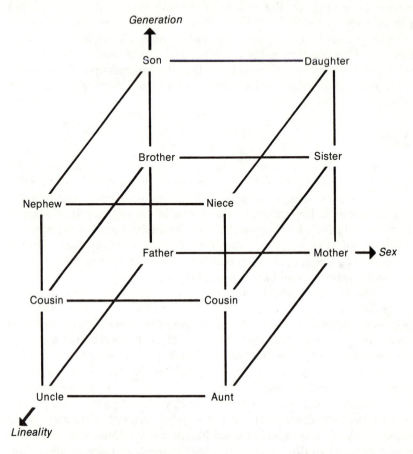

Redrawn from Miller, G. A. Psycholinguistic approaches to the study of communication. In D. L. Arm (Ed.), *Journeys in science*. Albuquerque: The University of New Mexico Press, 1967. Copyright © 1967 by the University of New Mexico Press. Redrawn by permission.

nenbaum, 1957) suggest that words may be stored in a three-dimensional space which summarizes the emotional impact of the word. The dimensions can be labeled as *evaluation* ("good" vs. "bad"), *strength* ("strong" vs. "weak"), and *potency* ("active" vs. "passive"). Important aspects of behavior seem to be related to such spatial structures. For example, if a neutral word is paired with words which are all "good" on the evaluation dimension, it will tend to be rated "good" and to elicit as associates words which are rated "good" (Staats & Staats, 1957). Moreover, if words which are all rated "good" are presented on successive trials of a memory

experiment, a shift to "bad" words will cause a release from proactive interference (Wickens, 1970). As was suggested in Chapter 2, such release is related to a shift in the ability of people to retrieve words from long-term memory.

This kind of evidence supports the notion of spatial structures which provide organization for memory. Such structures may well combine iconic, symbolic, and enactive codes within the same abstract framework. Unfortunately, we are far from having produced satisfactory methods for exploring such structures.

Hierarchies

One proposed structure is of special interest for our purposes because it relates to the hierarchical analysis of memory developed in Chapter 2. There are many reasons to believe that hierarchical structures are important in memory. For example, the presentation of a word appears to activate not only its own representation in memory, but also the name of the category of which it is a member. You may recall that subjects sometimes recognize associates to words they have experienced as if these associates themselves had been presented (see p. 28).

One study argues strongly for the automatic activation of superordinates. In this study (Warren, 1972), subjects were presented with lists of three words which they were to remember. The three words came from the same category (e.g., "maple," "oak," "elm"). The subjects were then shown one of the words in the list (e.g., "oak"), the name of the category (e.g., "tree"), or a neutral word unrelated to the list. These visually presented words were written in colored ink. The subjects were asked to name the color of the ink as rapidly as possible. Based on the Stroop effect (see p. 26), Warren reasoned that if the word shown to the subject was in activated memory, the subjects would have greater trouble inhibiting a tendency to vocalize the word name. Such a tendency would slow their response to naming the ink color. His data showed that words from the list ("maple," "oak," "elm") and the category name ("tree") produced greater interference with color naming than control words. This study suggests that the category name is activated when a list word is presented, even without any requirement to do so, and it thus supports the reality of hierarchical structures in memory.

Hierarchical structures such as the one shown in Figure 17 have a high degree of potential economy. By assigning certain properties to the level "animal," it is possible to avoid reassigning each of these to all the different subspecies of "animal." For example, knowing that an animal eats allows us to infer that birds, fish, mammals, and amphibians all eat, without having to specifically state that property for each lower position in the hierarchy. Moreover, such hierarchical organizations carry within them the relationships of conjunction and disjunction discussed in this

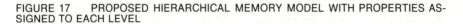

FIGURE 17   PROPOSED HIERARCHICAL MEMORY MODEL WITH PROPERTIES AS-
SIGNED TO EACH LEVEL

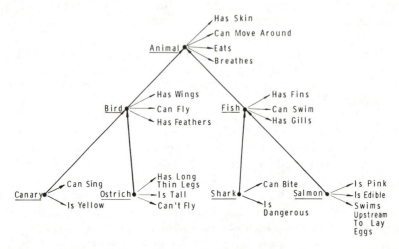

Reprinted from Collins, A. M., and Quillian, M. R. Retrieval time from semantic memory.
Journal of Verbal Learning and Verbal Behavior, 1969, *8,* 240–247.

chapter. The category "bird" is a disjunction of the various species of bird
("robin" or "jay," etc.). On the other hand, a bird is a conjunction of the
properties assigned at that level (flies and has feathers, etc.). Not all the
properties of a bird are necessarily critical to something's being a bird.
"Can fly" is a descriptor which applies to most birds, but something can
be a bird and have the special descriptor "cannot fly." A hierarchical
structure may occur as the result of abstracting from actual objects or
words attributes which may then be built into the structure under the
influence of conjunctive and disjunctive operations. The structure illustrated in Figure 17 is a part of a more complex model of human memory
(Quillian, 1968).

   In order to see if the structure of Figure 17 described human memory,
Collins and Quillian (1969) ran an experiment in which subjects were
given sentences which they had to classify as true or false. The sentences
referred either to names of objects (e.g., "canary," "bird," and "animal")
or to the properties of these objects. Their hypothesis was that responses
would be more rapid if the concepts named in the sentences were close
together in the memory hierarchy. Many different objects and properties
in addition to the ones shown in Figure 17 were used as examples.

   First consider the use of category names. A zero-order relationship
would be simply a repeat of the item, e.g., "A canary is a canary." A
first-order relationship would deal with a pair of concepts one position
apart in the hierarchy, e.g., "A canary is a bird," while a second-order

relationship would be "A canary is an animal." The speed with which such sentences can be classified is shown in Figure 18 (lower line). It seems clear from these data that the hierarchical relationships of Figure 17 are related to the way in which this information is used by the subject in classifying the sentences.

Several other studies have confirmed some aspects of the structural representation outlined in Figure 17. Schaeffer and Wallace (1969) showed that two words were classified faster if they fell within a subcategory than if they fell within a larger category. Subjects were instructed to press a "same" key if the two words were both living things; if not, they were to press a "different" key. The classification times were much faster if both words were mammals or both fabrics than, for example, if one was a mammal and the other a fabric. In terms of Figure 17, it was as though subjects were able to terminate their search on a lower level if both words had a lower-order category in common. Other studies (Dawes, 1966) have shown that statements which are not easily represented by hierarchical structures have a tendency to be altered in memory so that they can be. Dawes compared memory for statements of the form

FIGURE 18   RESULTS OF REACTION-TIME STUDIES IN WHICH SS WERE REQUIRED TO ANSWER QUESTION RELATING TO THE HIERARCHY PRESENTED IN FIGURE 17 AS QUICKLY AS THEY COULD

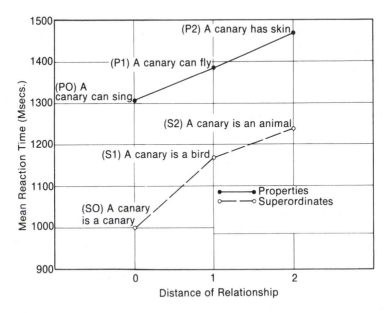

Reprinted from Collins, A. M., and Quillian, M. R. Retrieval time from semantic memory. *Journal of Verbal Learning and Verbal Behavior*, 1969, *8*, 240–247.

"Some X are Y" with those of the form "All or no X are Y." He found that subjects were more likely to recall "some" statements as "all or no" statements than the reverse. Statements of the form "All or no X are Y" can be represented easily in Figure 17 because X is included either under Y or under not Y. On the other hand, "Some X are Y" requires X to be entered both under Y and not Y.

A second aspect of the Collins and Quillian study refers to the question of whether properties are assigned only at the highest level to which they apply. This suggests, for example, that we know directly that "a canary is yellow," but only infer that "a canary flies" from knowing that a canary is a bird. The ability to assign a property at the highest level of the hierarchy makes it an efficient system. The experiment provided favorable evidence for this idea. As can be seen in Figure 18, it took longer to respond the further the property was located from the category name. For example, it was fastest to respond "yes" to "A canary is yellow" and slowest to say that it eats. These results have not been confirmed by other studies (Conrad, 1972). There is also an inherent difficulty in drawing firm conclusions from them. The properties used at higher levels may have been less familiar or less firmly agreed upon than those at the lower levels. More evidence will be required before it is clear whether there is any tendency to assign properties to only one level.

Some consequences of a hierarchical organization of information are especially interesting. We have already noted that this type of organization is efficient because it saves room in long-term memory and allows flexible use of the limited-capacity active-memory system (p. 35). Another consequence of the organization is that properties assigned at one level become automatically incorporated into the description at lower levels. For concepts such as "bird" this is probably reasonable, although subjects have some beliefs about birds which are not generally true. For example, they believe that all birds fly, although some species of birds, as defined by zoologists, do not fly and many young birds cannot fly. This kind of assignment becomes more serious in cases in which it may result in what social psychologists have called *stereotyping.* If a general property is assigned to a class (e.g., "Turks are cruel," "Jews are shrewd"), there exists an implicit tendency to treat each member of the class in accord with those general assignments, without thinking through their applicability to each case. Stereotyping is a known characteristic of human thinking. It may be an inevitable consequence of the efficiency of hierarchical memory structures.

There is little reason to suppose that the human mind is limited to any particular type of mental structure. Indeed, there is much reason to believe that structures vary with different individuals and cultures and within an individual from time to time. However, experiments do suggest that the particular format or structure which we use to store information in the memory system guides the nature of our effortless-retrieval processes and thus has important consequences for our thinking.

The Testing of Structures

This section has attempted to outline some efforts to develop models of the kinds of cognitive structures which guide our thinking. These structures represent our current knowledge about the internal character of symbolic concepts. There is a problem in evaluating the reality of such structures. People can activate and organize their memories on the basis of nearly any feature. If you are told to list the alphabet backwards or to list words whose third letter is K, you can do this. The ability to perform such a task does not indicate that you had already sorted the words in memory on this basis. Rather, you used the cue as a basis for effortful retrieval of memories whose organization was on another basis. How can we insure that a given performance is based upon effortless retrieval from preexisting structure and not upon an effortful sorting of memory? Some of the experiments cited above are efforts to do this. For example, Warren (p. 86) tried to insure that subjects had no reason to activate the category name; thus, evidence of its activation supported a preexisting structure. The studies of Collins and Quillian instructed subjects to respond as rapidly as possible in order to tap preexisting structures. All analyses of structure face the difficulty of separating effortful and effortless retrieval. In the next two chapters we shall try to develop some ideas about the study of mental operations which may help us in the study of mental structures.

SUMMARY

This chapter has dealt with the ways in which the human mind frees itself from individual objects to produce a more general system for the classification of information. We began by examining the process of concept identification. This process may be divided into two parts: learning the attributes relevant to classification and learning the classification rules which allow instances to be assigned to a category. Two different processes for obtaining concepts were discussed. Many of our concepts come from a rather passive spectator behavior akin to the abstraction and iconic information processing described in Chapter 3. At the same time, we form hypotheses which allow us to test categorization rules against the examples provided by experience.

This same analysis has relevance for the study of judgment. Here the attributes are suggested by the structure of the problem and the variability of the instances with which the subject is provided. Attention is drawn to certain attributes and these are used in making the judgment. The study of the rules governing such combinations is one of active interest.

The tendency of subjects to use only a few attributes leads to simplifications. One such simplification is the use of a single ordered list. More complex structures in human memory are also possible, some of which are outlined in the final section. Of particular interest is a hierarchical

structure which produces an economical use of long-term memory and efficient matching of concepts to the limitations of active memory.

It should be apparent that the memory structures which underlie human cognition are not simple. The goal of this chapter has been to review some possible types of structures among many which might be used. It is unlikely that any single cognitive structure exists for all kinds of material. Rather, it is the task of psychologists to understand different types of structures and their consequences for thought.

Section II
DYNAMICS OF COGNITION

5

Mental Operations

In short, the essential element of logical thought is that it is operational, i.e., it extends the scope of action by internalizing it.

J. Piaget

Representation in memory is not a sufficient basis for thought. We must be able to reorganize information in order to solve problems, develop new structures, and interpret the world around us. To accomplish this we must operate upon the structures stored in our memories in a way analogous to the carpenter's shaping of wood. A mental operation is an internal transformation of information from one form to another. Such operations do not obliterate the structures which existed before, but create new structures which themselves can be coded into long-term memory (p. 35). Since mental operations often allow the retention of the original information, they can frequently be reversed. For example, if you add fifty-four and twenty-one, you may store the sum in long-term memory. With the sum and either of the original numbers, you may subtract and recover the other number. On the other hand, if attention is directed to the sum, you may not retain either original number and will thus be unable to recover the separate numbers from the sum. Mental operations are reversible in principle (Piaget & Inhelder, 1969), but forgetting may make it impossible in practice.

Is it possible to observe mental operations? It may seem that these internal operations are hidden from observation. Certainly they are not observable in behavior and often not even in introspection. Try multiplying seven and eight. It is easy to obtain the answer, but what can be said about the operations which produced it? The failure of introspection to

suggest anything interesting about such mental operations led the Wurz-burg School (p. 7) to attribute them to vague "determining tendencies" laid down by the instruction "multiply."

Current psychological methods allow us to measure and trace the sequence of mental operations which intervene between the numbers and their product. Such measurements do not provide us with direct observa-tion of mental operations, but they can lead to detailed inferences about them. Mental operations can be measured because they have characteris-tics which are observable by appropriate experiments. First, they require *time;* and second, they may also require some of the limited capacity available for conscious processing of information *(space).*

The measurement of mental operations by their requirements for time and space may seem obvious. But in another sense, such measurements are revolutionary. Descartes excluded mental activity from the domain of natural law partly because he felt that mental events were fundamentally nonmeasurable and thus not subject to the mathematical laws which, at the time he wrote, were beginning to impose order on the study of matter. Descartes' exclusion of mental phenomenon from natural law was one factor instrumental in producing the long separation of the study of the mind from science and the notion that there was an impassable barrier between mind and body. Moreover, some philosophical theories have held that mental events are not extended and that, unlike material objects, they do not require space. Thus the idea that mental operations may compete for limited capacity within a central processing system has profound implications for the general view of mind.

Experimental studies of the structure of mental operations via these two observable characteristics will be the subject of this and the next chapter. This chapter will concentrate upon the study of the time for mental operations, and the next chapter will deal with the requirements for space.

TYPES OF OPERATIONS

Mental operations represent important constituents of the process of thought. However, it is not easy to decide which mental operations to consider. Several writers have attempted to state a minimal set of such operations which would be sufficient to deal with human thinking. Chapter 1 mentioned John Locke's proposed five operations of the human mind: perception, retention, discrimination, comparison, and composi-tion. Jean Piaget has developed a set of operations necessary for the description of operational thought in the child. These operations cor-respond closely to the binary rules (e.g., conjunction) of symbolic logic (see Figure 13). The importance of such operations in adult concept formation was discussed in Chapter 4. Another statement of elementary operations comes from the development of computer programs to simu-

late thought. One such program, complex enough to solve conjunctive concepts of the type discussed in Chapter 4 (Reitman, 1965), requires only a few mental operations, including detection, storage, comparison, elimination, searching, and binary choice.

There is overlap among these suggestions, but they are by no means identical. All of them bear some relationship to the ideas discussed in the last chapter. There we used the logical combining operations such as conjunction, disjunction, and negation, together with code-changing operations such as abstraction, to account for the types of concepts subjects could learn and the structures they constructed and stored in long-term memory.

It is not possible at present to state a set of mental operations which is either necessary or sufficient to serve as the basis of human thought. Perhaps no such set will ever be specified in a rigorous way. Although some steps have been taken to develop universal rules of grammar appropriate to all languages (Greenberg, 1966), such a task is more difficult for thinking, since the types of structures involved in thought are of even greater variety and complexity than those which underlie language. Even so, the study of a few important mental operations may give us increased insight into the dynamics of human thought. The operations discussed in this chapter represent at least some of the elements which might be involved in learning the concepts outlined in Chapter 4 and in solving the problems discussed in Chapter 7. At the same time, these operations have been studied with sufficient precision to help illuminate the structure of mental activity in general.

This chapter will be divided into four major sections. The first will cover operations which involve the abstraction of information from sensory form to semantic structure. These operations result in a code which represents the input information in a condensed form. The second section will discuss operations involved in generating or elaborating information. Generation is the logical inverse of abstraction. The third section will be concerned with combining information in both arithmetical and logical form. And the final section will deal with the organization of sequences of mental operations.

TIME AND MENTAL OPERATIONS

The origin of the view that mental operations can be measured by the time they require extends back into the middle of the nineteenth century. In 1850 the German physiologist Helmholtz showed that the time for the nervous system to conduct impulses was measurable. Before his studies, the usual conception was that the speed of nervous conduction was infinite. He found that it required about 20 msec. for an impulse to travel from a man's foot to his brain. This was a rate of about 100 meters per second. Shortly before the work of Helmholtz, the astronomer Bessel had

observed characteristic delays in the observations which individual astronomers made of the time that a star was centered in their telescopes. These delays were due to differences in reaction time which are characteristic of individuals.

Putting together these two observations, the Dutch physiologist Donders (1868) proposed that mental processes might be measured by the time they require. He studied three tasks. In the first, a subject responded as rapidly as possible whenever a single event occurred *(detection)*. In the second situation there was more than one event, but the subject was to respond to only one of them and not to respond if any of the others occurred *(discrimination)*. This task required him to discriminate among the stimuli which were presented. The third task involved a separate response to each event *(choice)*. Donders reasoned that having to respond differently to each event would add a choice among responses to the mental operation of discrimination among stimuli required by Task 2. He proposed a subtractive method to obtain the time which was required by the mental operations of discrimination (Task 2 − Task 1) and choice (Task 3 − Task 2). Although the times for each individual task varied from trial to trial and from person to person, it was possible for Donders to obtain, and for others to replicate, stable differences between tasks. Donders concluded that he had succeeded in measuring the time for the mental operations of discrimination and choice.

The Donders measurement raised a good deal of controversy. First, it was argued that the times obtained by Donders for the two mental operations were not general. For example, these times would be different if the stimulus was visual rather than auditory. While this criticism is true, it does not disprove the notion that mental operations can be measured, but merely suggests that the values obtained are not constant over all tasks. Even so, these values may provide important insight into the sequencing and structure of such operations.

Others criticized Donders on the grounds that his method required the experimenter to invent a new task for each new mental operation. It is difficult to argue that a new task demands exactly what the old task required, plus one new operation. Indeed, psychologists of the Wurzburg School suggested that the instructions themselves were the most crucial aspect. It is possible, however, to use the subtractive method within a given task instruction and thus meet this criticism (Posner & Mitchell, 1967; Sternberg, 1969).

A third criticism was that introspection usually revealed little about the period between receiving the stimuli and making the response. This criticism assumes that all mental operations are conscious and thus available to introspection. However, introspection is relatively poor when tasks are rapid. Perhaps the subtractive method can go beyond what is available to introspection.

For many years these criticisms, together with a general bias against the

study of internal mental phenomena, tended to suppress the examination of the time required by mental operations. However, in recent years new experiments have repeated Donders' basic finding (Taylor, 1966) and have greatly extended both the logic of the method and the empirical results obtained through its use (Neisser, 1967; Sternberg, 1969).

ABSTRACTION

Information available to the sense organs can be abstracted in at least two ways. One way involves selection of one part of the input rather than another. The other involves classification of the input into more general categories. Both types of mental operations are abstractive in the sense that they result in representations which code the input in a reduced or condensed form. This section will concentrate upon classification of input because this classification illustrates the relationship between what is stored in memory and the processing of new information.

The words you are reading are, first of all, unique configurations of print. The names these words represent are abstractions in the sense that they stand for a variety of perceptually different visual forms (e.g., PLANT, plant) and auditory patterns (e.g., the word "plant" spoken by a man or a woman). The name of a word gains its meaning from the semantic structures to which it is related. The word "plant" may be related to a structure dealing with living things or to one dealing with labor unions and assembly lines (Quillian, 1968). At one level the word is a visual code, at another a name, and at still another an aspect of the overall semantic structure. Figure 19 illustrates this general scheme.

The mental operations to code input items for each level of Figure 19 can be observed in the time required for making classifications. Suppose a subject is shown a pair of items and asked to press one key as quickly as possible if they are the "same" and another key if they are "different." Figure 20a illustrates the results of an experiment in which the items were letters and the definition of "same" was "both vowels" or "both consonants" (Posner & Mitchell, 1967). If the letters were identical in physical form (AA), the reaction time was faster than if they had a name in common (e.g., Aa), which in turn was faster than items which shared only the same class (e.g., Ae). A similar result (Schaeffer & Beller, 1970) is shown in Figure 20b for an experiment in which words were shown and subjects were required to press the "same" key when the words were either both "living things" or both "nonliving things."

These figures illustrate the use of Donders' method of measuring the time for classifications in order to observe the mental operations involved in what appeared to be simple tasks. In these tasks the subjects were instructed to make their comparisons on the basis of semantic similarity. If the level of the instruction was varied, it became possible to separate the mental operations occurring at the different levels.

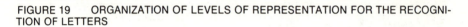

FIGURE 19   ORGANIZATION OF LEVELS OF REPRESENTATION FOR THE RECOGNITION OF LETTERS

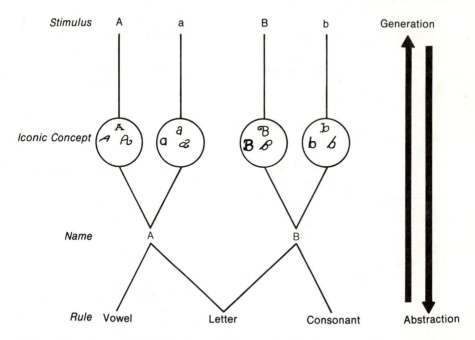

Redrawn from Posner, M. I. Abstraction and the process of recognition. In G. H. Bower and J. T. Spence (Eds.), *The psychology of learning and motivation.* Vol. 3. New York: Academic Press, Inc., 1969. Pp. 44–96.

Visual Processes

Can we isolate operations which are performed upon visual information? The problem is how to determine which operations performed on letters or words are using the visual representations rather than names. Suppose that a pair of items are presented simultaneously. The subject is required to press one key if they have the same name and another if their names are different. If the pair are physically identical (e.g., AA), it is logically possible to make the match based upon the visual form. On the other hand, for letters not similar in physical form (e.g., Aa), the match must be based upon a previously learned correspondence. Experimental results have suggested that these logical distinctions apply to the actual performance of subjects. Not only is the time to match physically identical letters about 80 msec. faster than letters having only names in common (see Figure 20), but the physical matches are affected by the visual similarity of the letters (Chase & Posner, 1965), while the name matches are affected by factors related to the letter names (Cohen, 1969b;

FIGURE 20   RESULTS OF REACTION-TIME STUDIES ASKING SUBJECTS TO CLAS-
SIFY WHETHER PAIRS OF ITEMS ARE EITHER BOTH VOWELS OR CONSONANTS OR
BOTH ANIMALS OR NONANIMALS

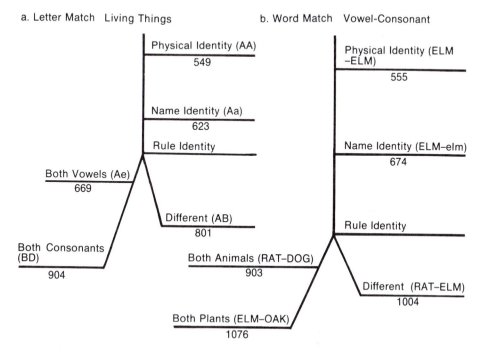

a. Letter Match   Living Things   b. Word Match   Vowel-Consonant

Physical Identity (AA)
549

Name Identity (Aa)
623

Rule Identity

Both Vowels (Ae)
669

Different (AB)
801

Both Consonants
(BD)
904

Both Animals (RAT–DOG)
903

Both Plants (ELM–OAK)
1076

Physical Identity (ELM
–ELM)
555

Name Identity (ELM–elm)
674

Rule Identity

Different (RAT–ELM)
1004

Reaction times are in milliseconds. a. Adapted from Posner, M. I., and Mitchell, R. F.
Chronometric analysis of classification. *Psychological Review,* 1967, *74,* 392–409. Copy-
right © 1967 by the American Psychological Association. Adapted by permission. b.
Adapted from Posner, M. I., Lewis, J. L., and Conrad, C. H. Component processes in
reading: A performance analysis. In J. Kavanaugh and I. Mattingly (Eds.), *Language by ear
and by eye: The relationship between speech and reading.* Cambridge: M.I.T. Press, 1972.
Pp. 159–192. Adapted by permission of The M.I.T. Press, Cambridge, Massachusetts.
Copyright © 1972 by The Massachusetts Institute of Technology.

Dainoff & Haber, 1970; Posner, 1969). Another reason for thinking that the
physical matches are independent of the letter names is that when
subjects are instructed to respond on the basis of physical similarity, they
show no delay in responding "different" to pairs like "Aa" which have
the same name. These findings suggest that subjects can match letters on
the basis of physical similarity prior to obtaining the letter names.

Can more complex mental operations be carried out upon the visual
code of letters? The answer appears to be yes. For example, consider the
letter pair "Cc." The time to respond that this pair has the same name is
only about 20 msec. longer than for its physical-identity controls (e.g., CC,
cc). Why should the pair "Cc" be faster than the pair "Aa"? If the match

were based upon the names, there would be little reason to suggest that the name "C" would be obtained faster than the name "A." It appears to require an additional visual process to equate two letters which differ in size. A similar result can be obtained (Buggie, 1970) if the two letters shown differ in orientation (e.g., A∀). The times to make physical and name matches are both markedly increased by this operation, but the former is more affected. When rotation is required to match at the physical level, subjects often show interference from the name level. That is, when instructed to respond on the basis of physical correspondence, there is a tendency to take longer to say "different" when the pair has the same name (e.g., ∀a). This does not occur when both pairs are upright.

This result suggests that the process of obtaining the name goes on at the same time that the subject attempts to match on the basis of the visual code. Because the rotation necessary for matching at the visual level takes time, on some occasions the name information is obtained first and interferes. The parallel execution of visual operations and naming is revealed more clearly when subjects are shown a single rotated letter (e.g., ∀) and required to indicate whether, when rotated to the upright, it is a correct letter or a mirror image. In this case the name is obtained faster than the visual rotation to the upright is performed.

In order to study the visual processes in isolation from names, it is often easier to use nonsense materials. One study (Shepard & Metzler, 1971) required subjects to respond "same" if the two complex patterns (see upper part of Figure 21) could be rotated into exact correspondence and "different" if they could not. The time to respond was a linear function of the amount of rotation required. These data are shown in the lower portion of Figure 21. They suggest that subjects had to rotate the figures mentally at a rate of about 50 degrees per second. This is striking evidence that subjects can perform very complex manipulations upon visual representations and that the time for such manipulations is an orderly function of the task requirements.

Iconic Concepts

Incoming visual information is brought into contact with previously learned iconic concepts, and it is by means of this contact that iconic concepts are formed and modified (see Chapter 3). This contact is experienced subjectively as *recognition.* It is clear that we can experience recognition of a visual form without knowing its name, as when a face seems familiar without our being able to recall the name or even the context in which it was previously experienced. Presumably in this situation the iconic representation is contacted, but the association to the name is not activated.

Experiments allow us to study the influence of past experience upon mental operations within the visual system. If a subject is required to

FIGURE 21   RESULTS OF A REACTION-TIME STUDY IN WHICH SUBJECTS WERE
REQUIRED TO INDICATE WHETHER TWO COMPLEX FORMS COULD BE MADE CON-
GRUENT BY ROTATION

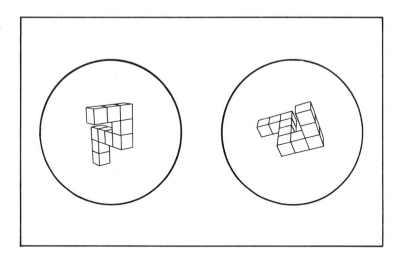

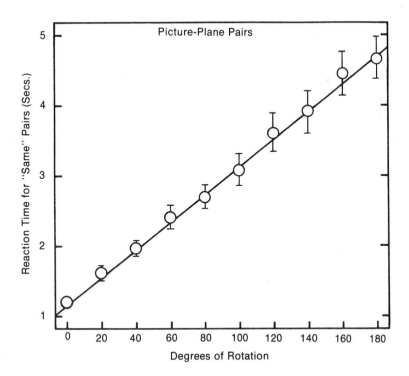

Reprinted from Shepard, R. N., and Metzler, J. Mental rotation of three-dimensional objects. *Science,* 1971, *171,* 701–703. Copyright © 1971 by the American Association for the Advancement of Science.

match two strings of letters to determine if they are physically identical, he can do so faster if they form a familiar word than if they are a nonsense string (Eichelman, 1970; Krueger, 1970a). Evidence indicates that this improvement is due not to naming the words, but rather to the efficiency of the visual matching operation when the letter sequence is familiar. If a subject has to recognize a given letter from a brief exposure of several letters, he can do so most efficiently if the letters form a word (Reicher, 1969). It thus appears that having had past experience with certain sequences of letters allows us to perform matching and other visual operations upon them with greater efficiency.

A visual word can be seen as a complex trace system which contains letters as elements. The trace system appears to be so flexible that it matters relatively little whether the visual pattern presented is "PLANT," "plant," or "PLAnt," either in the time to obtain the name or in the time to search for a particular word, provided the constituent letters are equated for visibility (Smith, Lott, & Cronnell, 1969). Exactly how such a trace system is characterized in terms of the details of its operation is a matter of dispute and active research (see, for example, Neisser, 1967; Gibson, 1969). The important point for our purposes is that experience affects mental operations at the visual level. Past experience of letter sequences (words) integrates the individual elements and makes their processing as visual units more efficient.

These principles apply even more strongly to perception of pictures and objects. Studies have shown (Fraisse, 1970; Wingfield, 1966) that the time differences found between matching pairs of pictures and matching a picture with its name are the same as those outlined for physical and name matches of letters. It appears that the recognition of an object involves excitation of the same kind of trace system of past visual experience that is involved in letter and word recognition.

Complex Visual Associations

Associations are often thought of as involving verbal descriptions of information. However, we have just seen that complex mental operations can be performed upon visual input. Moreover, it has been shown that visual memories may be clustered in recall by their distinctive spatial properties, independent of their names (Frost, 1971). These findings suggest the importance of associations between objects and actions which do not proceed by way of verbal links. It has long been known that word associations to objects and pictures are not identical with those obtained from the names of the pictures (Karwoski, Gramlich, & Arnott, 1944). Associations to pictures relate to active performance with the object (e.g., "shovel"-"dig") more often than is the case for associations to the picture's name (e.g., "shovel"-"tool"). The time to produce associations to pictures is greater than associations to words. This could be due to the time needed to name the pictures, but it might also indicate that the

pictures produce associated visual images which then must be translated into words. Indeed, it is this latter idea which corresponds to the introspective reports of subjects (Karwoski et al., 1944), and agrees with evidence that visual memories have their own principles of organization (Frost, 1971).

What complexity of classifications can be performed with purely visual information? This question is similar to one raised earlier with respect to spectator behavior (see Chapter 4). Many theories of speed reading suggest that visually presented words can be related directly to their semantic structures without locating their names. Indeed, some languages (e.g., Chinese) function by passing directly from the visual form to meaning. Others, like our own, make it possible to transform each visual form into a unique name. We know a little about the relative advantages of each. One advantage of visual symbols is communication across language groups. For example, the digit "8" has the same meaning in many languages, although its name is not the same (Kolers, 1969). On the other hand, languages like Chinese which use pictograms are probably harder to learn than those which use an alphabet.

There is reason to believe that visual-to-verbal encoding is particularly important when subjects are trying to learn or memorize material. For example, Conrad (1964) showed that visually presented strings of letters were recoded into the names of the letters before the subjects reproduced them in writing. The apparent reason for this was that the letters could be rehearsed and held in store more easily in terms of their names than in terms of visual representations.

It is possible to observe some of the consequences of different ways of learning classifications. In one experiment (Posner, 1970), subjects matched pairs of stimuli in two different conditions. In one they were required to respond "same" if both stimuli were vowels or both were consonants, while in the other they were required to respond "same" if both stimuli were letters or both were digits. A remarkably different structure of reaction times was obtained in the two experimental classifications. In the vowel-consonant classification, subjects were much faster for pairs having the same name (e.g., Aa) than for pairs having only the classification in common (e.g., AE). Moreover, it was shown that letter pairs which were hard to match at the name level were also hard to match when subjects used the vowel-consonant classification. However, when the classification scheme was letter-digit, subjects were almost equally fast in determining whether two stimuli were letters, regardless of whether they had the same name. Letters which were hard to match at the name level were not particularly difficult to match when the subjects were doing the letter-digit classification.

This evidence suggests that subjects use the name of the stimulus as a mediator when doing a vowel-consonant classification, but not when making a letter-digit classification. There is a vast difference in how these

two classifications are learned during childhood. Letters occur in reading tasks, whereas digits occur in arithmetic tasks. Experience with the two populations tends to be quite separate and visual associations may be developed between the visual forms and the class name "letter" or "digit." The vowel-consonant distinction, however, is learned rather differently. Children are generally told orally the list of vowels and are instructed that the other letters are consonants. Moreover, consonants and vowels always appear mixed together in reading. The results of learning are quite different methods of classification.

Separation of Physical and Name Codes

The separation between visual and verbal factors appears to play a basic role in the organization of the human brain. This is revealed in its clearest form in the study of patients whose brains have been bisected by cutting the fiber tracts which connect the left and right hemispheres (Gazzaniga, 1970). This operation is performed in cases of intractable epilepsy to prevent spread of the seizures. It has surprisingly little effect upon normal behavior. However, under special conditions in which information is confined to only one hemisphere, some interesting facts emerge. If visual information is presented to the right hemisphere (by use of a flash to the left side of the visual field), the subject is unable to make any verbal report of what he saw, since the centers controlling speech are located on the left side (at least in right-handed people). He denies knowing anything about what has been presented if asked about it. However, nonverbal behavior such as laughing does reflect the information presented to the right hemisphere. One woman, shown a nude photograph, was unable to say what she saw, but produced an embarrassed snicker. Subjects shown pictures of an apple could not report what they had seen, but were able to pick out an apple from among other items (provided they used the left hand, which is under control of the right hemisphere).

Studies of patients with brain damage to the left or right side also confirm the relative bias of the two hemispheres. Right-brain damage usually results in impaired spatial abilities, while left-brain damage is more related to loss of verbal skills. These same asymmetries between left and right hemispheres have been reported for normal people presented with special tests. For example, if normal subjects are required to make a physical match among letters, they are faster if information is presented to the right hemisphere, while if required to deal with names, they appear to do better with information presented to the left hemisphere. Somewhat the same thing has been found with auditory presentation. Processing of music tends to be better with stimulation of the left ear (predominantly right-hemisphere connections) (Kimura, 1967), while perception of words seems to be better with right-ear stimulation (Studdert-Kennedy & Shankweiler, 1970).

The specialization of the hemisphere for different kinds of processing may be important in tasks such as learning to read. It has been found that skills based upon manipulation of the visual code and those based upon auditory abilities, while both related to reading, are not closely related to each other (Calfee, Chapman, & Venezky, 1972). This suggests that visual perception and linguistic processing represent separate factors in learning reading tasks. There is also some evidence that problems in learning to read are related to the development of hemisphere dominance (Bryden, 1970; Gazzaniga, 1970).

The separation between physical and name codes is also important in normal adult information processing. In a real sense, we organize our world with the aid of two quite different languages. We have an internal visual language with its own concepts, complex rules, and associations. We may then map a part of that visual world into a verbal language which has concepts and rules of its own. Some philosophers and linguists have wondered if the particular language we speak shapes our perception, memories, and thoughts (Whorf, 1956). The answer for memory and thought certainly appears to be yes, as we have seen in Chapter 4. Visual perception, however, seems to have its own organization not entirely coincident with or dependent upon verbal concepts. As we shall see in Chapter 7, the solution of problems often depends upon the complex interactions of mental operations which occur in each domain.

Search of Active Memory

The rapidity with which words are read often masks the complexity of processing which may be done on the visual forms. A better idea of visual processing of letters may be obtained if subjects are required to look for a target in a list of items. If a subject scans a visual display looking for a particular set of target letters, his eyes move rapidly from one fixation to another. The time it takes him to locate the target is linearly related to the number of letters through which he must search (Neisser, 1967). In such a task, the subject reports that he does not know which letters he has been shown. He has no subjective impression of obtaining the letter names. Moreover, with sufficient practice the number of targets for which he is looking does not seem to affect the rate at which he scans (Neisser, 1967). The target letter or letters seem to pop effortlessly into mind. This process is prone to error, but it proceeds rapidly and is far better than chance performance. When engaged in this kind of task, the subject is strongly affected by visual factors such as the similarity of the letters through which he looks and whether or not they form words (Krueger, 1970b), but he is relatively unaffected by auditory factors, such as the experimenter's speaking irrelevant letter names (Gibson, 1969).

This search task is a good example of effortless retrieval. The visual forms of letters are rejected as targets with little or no relationship to the

number of target letters for which the subject is searching. It is as if the set of target letters formed a separate memory cell and the subject could tell that an item within that cell was active without identifying what letter it was. Indeed, this can be done without extensive practice if one takes advantage of distinctions learned in past experience. If a subject is required to scan a list of digits for a single target letter (e.g., A), he is no faster than if he scans the digits for any of twenty-six target letters (Brand, 1971). The visual form appears to activate the area of memory representing letters and this leads the subject to make the response without having to identify the letter presented.

In Chapter 2 it was suggested that when the information leading to retrieval was ambiguous, the stored items highly similar, or great accuracy demanded, effortless retrieval was followed by a scanning of the items which it activated. Can the time for this search be measured? A remarkable series of experiments (Sternberg, 1969) have developed the details of this process. In these experiments subjects were presented with a list of from one to four items (e.g., digits or faces). This was followed by a single probe item to which the subject had to respond "yes" as rapidly as possible when it was a member of the previous list and "no" when it was not. It was found that items in active memory were scanned at the rapid rate of 30 msec. per item. The rate was relatively constant, regardless of the type of item which the subject had to remember. Moreover, Sternberg was able to manipulate the start of the scan by presenting probes which were difficult to see because a visual-noise field (checkerboard) had been superimposed on them. When this was done, the time needed to begin the scan was increased, but the rate of scanning remained constant. This result suggests that visual-system operations (see p. 97) first free the probe from the effects of noise and then compare the abstracted probe against the items in active memory.

Apparently the rate of scanning in active memory depends in part upon the task the subject is required to perform. If the subject is to report the item following the probe, rather than whether or not the probe was in the list, the scanning time is increased tenfold, to about 300 msec. per item. However, the same increase in time is obtained for each new item in memory.

These experiments give us more confidence in the distinction between a rapid error-prone process of effortless retrieval (access to a memory cell) and a slower checking of the items activated by that process (effortful retrieval). In Chapter 2 we had to infer these two processes rather indirectly, but the experiments on search-with-speed measures suggest that they can be separated. As would be expected, most tasks involve a combination of the two processes. A rapid activation of information in some areas of long-term memory and a slower sifting of the activated items are both crucial aspects of thought.

In Sternberg's experiments it is difficult to know the representation of

the activated items which are being searched. In the case of face drawings the representation is probably visual, but for digits and letters the subject undoubtedly knows and uses the item names. How can we separate these two components and determine their relationship?

Suppose a subject is given two strings of letters (e.g., abCd, AbCd) and is then asked to determine if each pair has the same name (Beller, 1970). If all the pairs match physically (e.g., AA), it requires about 60 msec. per pair to do so. If all the pairs differ in case (e.g., Aa), the time per pair grows to about 140 msec., or about 80 msec. per pair longer than for physical matches. If only one pair is a name match and the others are physical matches, the overall time is 80 msec. longer than for physical matching. These results suggest that the physical- and name-matching processes go on together without interfering with each other. The time to make three physical matches is the same regardless of whether the fourth match is a physical or a name match.

The close relationship between the visual and verbal codes is best illustrated by an experiment (Cohen, 1969b) in which subjects received four lower-case letters. This was followed after 5 seconds by a single lower-case probe letter. On half the trials the single letter matched one of the stored items and on half it did not. It was expected that it would take longer to reject a probe letter if it was somehow made similar to the information which the subject had stored about the array letters. However, it was found that varying *either* the visual or the acoustic similarity of the probe to the stored items did not increase reaction time. However, when *both* visual and acoustic similarity were increased, reaction time did increase. The explanation which appears most likely is that matching on both bases proceeds simultaneously. In the presence of visual confusion, matches based upon the name are completed first, while in the presence of acoustic confusion, the match is made on the visual form. This experiment, taken with many others (Posner, 1969), argues that both the name and the visual form of the letters are activated. Subjects may match the new input against either representation.

If the names and the visual forms of letters can both be activated and examined, is there any rivalry between these codes? In Chapter 3 it was argued that iconic storage is sometimes suppressed when verbal hypotheses are made and tested (p. 74). On a miniature scale, the same processes can be found here (Posner, 1969). If the subject concentrates primarily upon the visual form, his reaction times for physical matching tend to maintain their superiority over the times for name matching. If he attends primarily to the name, the rate at which physical matching loses its superiority is increased. A still greater loss of physical-match efficiency occurs when the subject is asked to name the letter aloud.

These same results have been found with pictorial stimuli. For example, B. Tversky (1969) taught subjects to name a set of schematic faces. She found that subjects were fastest on matches involving a face if they

expected to see faces and on matches involving a name if they expected to see names. She argued that subjects could activate either faces or names depending upon what they expected.

Perhaps a more striking demonstration of the rivalry of visual and name codes is in a study by Frost (1972) on memory for simple outline pictures. All subjects were shown a series of sixteen pictures. Half of her subjects thought they were to recall the picture names and the other half thought they were to recognize the pictures. After fifteen minutes of a demanding activity the subjects were given a reaction-time test designed to determine what they had in memory about the pictures. The test presented subjects with either the identical picture they had seen during learning, the same picture rotated to another angle, or a different picture. The subjects were to respond "yes" if the picture was the same as the one shown during learning. The "recognition group" subjects were significantly faster and had fewer errors on pictures which were identical than on rotated pictures. The "recall" subjects were not faster on the identical pictures, but they had fewer errors on them. These results suggest that both groups had retained the physical form of the pictures which they had seen. Otherwise there would have been no reason for the two groups to do better on that picture than the same picture at another orientation. However, the recognition instruction appeared to have directed the attention of that group in a way which emphasized the physical form more than the recall instruction did for the recall group. The way the group directed its processing at the time of storage seemed to affect the relative efficiency of the codes fifteen minutes later.

The detailed study of abstraction has supported the distinction between effortless and effortful retrieval raised in Chapter 2. The time for each component is a separable aspect of overall performance. Some efforts have been made to work out more detailed models which are based on this separation (Atkinson & Joula, 1973). One basic principle of these models is that effortless retrieval is a relatively automatic process set in motion by the stimulus situation. Time is required to locate a particular memory cell, but the time does not reflect the size of that memory cell. Effortful search time increases uniformly with the number of target items. The rate of effortful search time can vary over a wide range, depending upon the task.

GENERATION

We have just considered the abstraction of more general classifications (e.g., letter) from specific input information (e.g., A). It is just as important to consider the location and activation of specific codes from more general instructions. For example, when asked to imagine a walrus with a cigar and top hat, subjects usually construct a particular representation which is only one of many possible formulations consistent with the instruction.

This section will be concerned with the time course of activating such representations. First we shall deal with simple representations which have already been stored in memory, and later we shall turn to some of the operations which allow the synthesis of new representations from stored components.

Alertness

One way to study generation is to tell subjects to get ready to process any event. At this simple level, there is a nonspecific common component in getting ready to perceive or to perform anything. To start a footrace the official says, "Get ready, get set, go." The sequence is designed to allow the runner to prepare his start to coincide with "go." Many reaction-time studies show that it takes from .2 to .5 seconds to reach a level of preparation which produces the fastest reaction time (Bertelson, 1967). What happens during such preparation? It is not easy to observe visible changes. However, there is a change in the pattern of brain activity (Walter et al., 1964) which is of the same type, although not as large, as changes which accompany the shift from sleep to waking. This change in performance and in brain activity appears to be related to a general increase in alertness which occurs not only during reaction-time tasks, but also when preparing to detect a weak signal, while receiving new information for storage and before the start of a voluntary movement (Karlin, 1970). The widespread character of the change suggests that it represents a very general effect which facilitates both sensory and motor systems.

Generating Visual Codes

We usually get ready to deal with some specific event or range of events. In fact, it is rather difficult to prepare without generating an expectancy about what will occur. In many reaction-time studies the data are consistent with the idea that subjects come to anticipate some particular signal or set of signals and do best when the expected event occurs (Fitts & Posner, 1967). Such expectancy often involves activation of an internal representation of the anticipated event.

Of particular interest is the generation of visual representation from a verbal instruction. In Chapter 3 we reviewed evidence that subjects can construct visual representations. Precise experimental techniques for studying the generation of such codes have been developed in work using letter-matching methods. When two successive visual letters are presented, subjects can perform matches at either the physical or the name level. Suppose a subject is given the name "A" orally, followed after a delay by a visual letter. The extent to which matching following auditory presentation is as efficient as visual matching provides an objective index

of the efficiency with which the subject can generate a visual code. Experiments suggest that when the first stimulus is presented orally, subjects are able to develop a representation which yields fast and efficient visual matching. These experiments indicate that the generation of the visual representation takes from about .5 to 1 second (Posner et al., 1969).

The results of the letter-matching experiment complement subjective data collected much earlier (Moore, 1915) in which subjects were asked to report when they first obtained an image of a familiar object (e.g., steamboat). Weber and Bach (1969) compared the time to generate successive letters of the alphabet verbally with the time to obtain a visual representation of each one. In this experiment subjects were instructed to go through the alphabet, either pronouncing each letter to themselves or getting a clear visual representation. Weber found that the former task took about 150 msec. per item, while visual imagery required nearly 500 msec. per item. There was no objective check on the criterion subjects used to determine if they were "pronouncing" or "seeing" the letters. Since subjective reporting methods do not provide any way of checking up on the completeness of the generation, it should not be too surprising that the reported times are somewhat faster than those found with objective methods. Indeed, when subjects were required to decide whether each generated lower-case letter was large (e.g., b, g) or small (e.g., a, c), times went up to about 1 second per letter, which is similar to those obtained with matching methods (Weber & Castleman, 1970).

The generation of a visual code has a complex relationship to our conscious perception. As we saw in Chapter 2, a generated representation is rarely confused with the actual stimuli. However, it does change the efficiency with which visual input can be matched. In some cases in which ambiguous information is presented, the information can affect what the subject experiences. This is illustrated in a recent study (Rommetveit, 1968) in which strings of typewritten letters were exposed for 120 msec. and subjects were told to report as accurately as possible what they saw. Two words were presented simultaneously, one to each eye. In most cases the words were identical, but in some cases they differed by a single letter. For example, one eye might see "mouth" and the other "south." In general, when two words were exposed simultaneously, the subjects reported seeing only one word. When a context word, such as the opposite of one of the words (e.g., "north"), was presented three seconds prior to the pair, subjects showed a definite bias to perceive the word more closely associated with the context word. These results suggest that, in this situation, the verbal context provides an expectancy as to what type of visual information will be presented to the subjects, and the subjects are conscious only of the input which is associated with the context. It is as if generation affected which word was seen.

A generated visual code has much in common with the residue of a just

previously presented visual item. In many ways it does not seem to matter if a visual item in active memory results from an actual visual experience or is generated by the subject. However, when expectancy and recent input are opposed, the latter may be more important. One study which bears on this issue used the perception of·an ambiguous figure as a test of generation (Epstein & Rock, 1960). The middle panel in Figure 22 may be seen as either an old lady or a young woman. If a subject is shown one of the side forms prior to seeing the ambiguous figure, his perception is more likely to be of the form just seen. However, if he is led to *expect* one form to occur by a systematic alternating of the left and right panels of Figure 22, he will tend to perceive the ambiguous figure as the one he last *saw* rather than the one he has been led to *expect.* The authors of this study felt that systematic alternation led to a visual expectancy of one form, but that this generated expectancy did not bias the perception as efficiently as an immediately past visual experience.

The details with which a generated code reproduces the experience it represents are still largely unexplored. The techniques outlined in this section may, however, make it possible to characterize in more detail the generated visual code.

Generation of Speech

The most common form of generation is the production of spoken and written language from the semantic structures which underlie them. Linguists have begun to develop some understanding of the rules by which such structures are turned into meaningful sentences. Their work

FIGURE 22   THE MIDDLE PANEL MAY BE SEEN EITHER AS AN OLD WOMAN (LEFT) OR AS A YOUNG LADY (RIGHT)

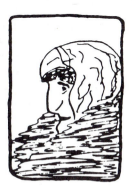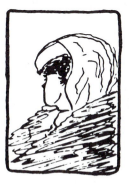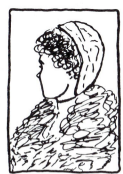

Reprinted from Leeper, R. W. A study of a neglected portion of the field of learning—The development of sensory organization. *Journal of Genetic Psychology*, 1935, *46,* 41–75.

is beyond the scope of this book (see Slobin, 1971). However, if such mental operations require time, it should be possible to use pauses in speech generation to investigate the type of semantic structures involved.

The generation of words has been used to analyze the underlying structures in which those words are embedded. If words are organized in a semantic space (see p. 85), long pauses should be associated with movement from one portion of the space to another. On the other hand, when responses are confined within an area of the space, the rate of production should be very high. Pollio (1964) required his subjects to produce associations to a single word for long periods of time (four minutes). He found that pauses were associated with shifts in the *connotative* meaning of the words (e.g., from words rated "good" to those rated "bad"), while rapid responses were associated with the production of words with similar connotations.

Another use of time measures in the study of speech involves pausing during the production of sentences. In one experimental condition (Goldman-Eisler, 1968), subjects were shown cartoons from the *New Yorker* magazine and were required to describe the story illustrated by the pictures. These results were compared with other conditions under which they read descriptions written by others or reproduced descriptions which they had composed previously. In all conditions subjects paused at many of the same places. However, there was both a dramatic reduction and a qualitative shift in pausing between the first production of a description and subsequent reproductions. It was found that in the initial production, hesitation was great at places where the next word was unpredictable. After the initial reproduction, hesitation was no longer greatest at places of low predictability, but appeared mainly at places where punctuation would be required in written language. It was as though the initial description was assembled from separate semantic structures, while the later representations were read from a single memory cell. The author argued that it was possible to isolate the pauses due to grammatical factors from those which were produced by the generation of the plan of the story. It does appear that the generation of linguistic strings from their underlying semantic structures requires time. As the rules of language become better understood, it may be possible to use generation time as a means of verifying their psychological reality.

COMBINATIONAL OPERATIONS

The operations reviewed so far have not involved combining information. However, as Piaget observed, "Operations such as the union of two classes (e.g., father united with mother constitutes the class parent) or the addition of two numbers . . . enter into all coordination of particular action [Piaget & Inhelder, 1969, p. 96]." In the remainder of this chapter we shall deal with experiments which are concerned with the combina-

tion of information and with the sequencing of operations in the solution of problems. Although the problems discussed have clearly specified goals, they begin to penetrate into the heart of thinking.

Implicit Counting and Addition

Perhaps the simplest way to study the combination of elements is to consider the operations of arithmetic. It was shown earlier that the digits are stored as a list in long-term memory and are organized in terms of their numerical magnitude (see pp. 16–17). It takes measurable time to move through this list. For example, it was shown that subjects required about 150 msec. per item to count silently from one to ten (Landauer, 1962). Moreover, the time to say which of two numbers was larger was reduced as the distance between the numbers was increased.

Time is needed to combine even the simplest numbers. Many investigators have measured the time to perform simple numerical calculations (Groen & Parkman, 1972; Restle, 1970; Schvaneveldt & Staudenmayer, 1970; Thomas, 1963). All of these studies have agreed in showing that the speed of response is related to the magnitude of the numbers being combined. It might seem surprising that the time to add three and two is less than the time to add three and four, because introspectively they both seem immediate. Nevertheless, it is true. These results do not depend upon the time to say the numbers aloud, since it is possible to eliminate that aspect by providing the subjects with, for example, two numbers and their sum, and requiring them to indicate whether or not the answer is correct.

Perhaps the simplest model of the internal operations involved in adding is the view that the subject takes the larger of the two numbers and increments it successively the number of times indicated by the smaller of the two numbers (Groen & Parkman, 1972). This model does fairly well in predicting the times obtained by young children using single-digit numbers. Applied to adults, this model would suggest that the time to add should be linearly related to the number of counts required, and that the slope of this function should be about 150 msec. per count, the time Landauer found for implicit counting. Neither of these predictions is confirmed for adult subjects. Instead the time per count is faster than this and often there appears a negatively accelerated rather than a linear increase with increment size (Schvaneveldt & Staudenmayer, 1970). There is some reason to suppose that adult subjects often retrieve the answer to such simple problems effortlessly without any counting.

Winkelman and Schmidt (1974) have provided some evidence for the idea of effortless retrieval in simple problems. They gave subjects a series of simple addition problems, together with answers (e.g., 3 + 2 = 5). The task was to indicate whether the answer was correct or not as quickly as possible. On some trials an answer was provided which, though incorrect

for addition, was correct for multiplication (e.g., $4 + 3 = 12$). The time to respond "no" to such problems was significantly longer than for similar problems in which the answers were incorrect for both addition and multiplication. This suggests that a number of familiar answers were activated by the problem statement, even though only one was accepted as correct for the particular operation in the problem.

Presumably, the likelihood of effortless retrieval increases with familiarity of the operation. When faced with the task of adding in an unfamiliar domain like the alphabet (e.g., $K + 3 = N$), the counting strategy reappears.

When more complex addition and multiplication problems are studied, it is possible to divide the overall problems into a number of substeps, such as add, carry, multiply, and to show that the time for solution is an orderly function of these substeps (Dansereau & Gregg, 1966; Thomas, 1963).

The results of these studies indicate that people use rather simple strategies while learning a skill such as addition or multiplication. These strategies involve a sequence of small steps, such as successive incrementing by one. As the skill develops, many of the individual results are stored in memory and can be retrieved effortlessly. Nevertheless, it is often possible to uncover a series of orderly steps by which complex problems are solved.

These same techniques have been used to study the mental processes of so-called lightning calculators. Lightning calculators are people who can perform complex numerical manipulations, such as multiplying multidigit numbers, in their heads. They are often gifted at using special shortcuts they have learned. However, by making up special problems, experimenters can reduce the use of such shortcuts. When this is done (Quastler, 1955), it is found that the time these people require to produce the answers indicates that the rates at which information is handled is well within the limits obtained for normal subjects. They differ primarily in their ability to hold in store the subproducts of operations so that they can complete and report the results.

Conjunction, Disjunction, and Negation

Numerical operations represent only a special set of combination rules. More general are the operations of conjunction ("and"), disjunction ("and/or"), and negation ("not"), which are involved in the study of concept identification and judgment (see Chapter 4). Can the time required for these mental operations be measured?

Previously we discussed the technique of asking subjects to match two simultaneous forms. If the forms are made up of easily specifiable attributes (e.g., color and shape), the task resembles a concept-

identification experiment. The subjects can be provided with a description of the rule and attributes for which they are to examine the two forms. When the forms are exposed, the time to determine whether they match the description can be measured.

One study (Trabasso, Rollins, & Shaughnessy, 1971) applied this method to different types of combining rules. In this study the attributes were form (triangle or circle), size (small or large), and color (orange or green). The description consisted of one value for each form (e.g., triangle, large, and green). The combining rules studied included conjunction, disjunction, and exclusive disjunction. These rules were illustrated in Figure 13. Since each attribute had only two values, it was possible to diagram the tests which would allow a subject to determine whether the description matched the pattern. Suppose he was told "red and green." He might then test to see if one figure was red; if it was not, he could answer "no," but if one figure was red, he would have to test the other figure to see if it was green. For each rule, a sequence of simple binary tests can be outlined which would allow the subject to arrive at the right answer. These tests are diagrammed in Figure 23a. It should be clear that the exclusive disjunctions would require more tests than conjunctions and disjunctions would. If the subject's internal behavior could be described in this task as a sequence of tests, and if each test required time, the rate at which the subject could determine if the description matched the pattern should be predictable.

In the experiment, subjects were first allowed to read the description, and when ready, they exposed the patterns. When the patterns appeared, they were to respond "yes" or "no" as fast as possible. The time required to read the description (storage time) and the time from the exposure of the pattern to their response (verification time) was measured. Figure 23b gives the storage time, match times, and error for conjunctive, disjunctive, and exclusive disjunctive rules. Several important facts emerge from this study. First, conjunctive and disjunctive rules were rather similar in overall efficiency, as predicted by Figure 23a. This result is different from that obtained in concept-identification studies, probably because in this study conjunctions describe attributes of separate objects rather than attributes of one object. Thus the perceptual factors which usually aid conjunctions were not involved. On the other hand, the exclusive disjunction, which involves a combination of conjunction and disjunction, took longer both in storage and in verification time.

These results suggest that the rules which are more difficult to specify in terms of binary operations also take longer to execute. Moreover, these differences are stable over many hours of practice. In Chapter 4 we saw that complex rules such as implication and exclusive disjunction were more difficult to learn. In the learning studies it was possible to attribute the difference to the degree of familiarity, but in the speeded classification tasks it is clear that the explanation must be more fundamental than that.

FIGURE 23   TREE DIAGRAMS OUTLINE POSSIBLE SEQUENCES OF TESTS FOR A
PARTICULAR RULE; TABLE CONTAINS DATA OBTAINED FROM A REACTION-TIME TEST
REQUIRING SUBJECTS TO VERIFY EACH OF THE THREE RULES

a.

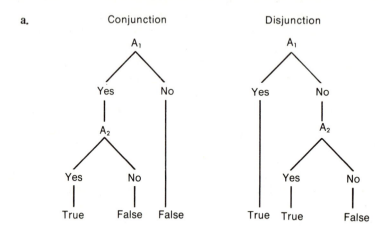

Exclusive Disjunction

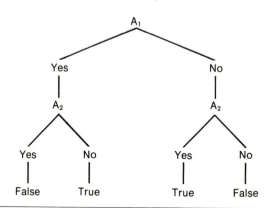

b.	Storage Time (Msec.)	Verify Time (Msec.)	% Errors
Conjunction	1082	895	14.3
Disjunction	1251	758	11.6
Exclusive Disjunction	1373	1330	23.6

Adapted from Trabasso, T., Rollins, H., and Shaughnessy, E. Storage and verification stages in processing concepts. *Cognitive Psychology,* 1971, *2,* 239–289.

Other aspects of the data also confirm that subjects were performing something equivalent to a set of binary tests, each of which took time. For example, if the description given to them was a conjunction, subjects were faster if the left object was false than if the right one was. This would be the case if they processed left to right and terminated their decision after seeing one negative instance, as indicated by Figure 23a.

The authors also found that the use of negatives in the descriptions led to a much longer storage time, but little difficulty during verification. The subjects appeared to convert each negative into its positive counterpart (e.g., "not orange" would mean "green"). This confirms many studies which suggest that subjects prefer to carry information in its positive form and that converting a negative requires time (Wason, 1959). In this study the use of binary attributes made it possible to transform each negative into a definite positive statement.

The results of this study provide evidence that concept tasks can be broken down into more basic mental operations, each of which takes a measurable time. However, it would be wrong to think that step-by-step testing of each attribute always characterizes the use of concepts. Chapters 3 and 4 drew a distinction between concept behavior based upon the use of separate attributes and behavior based upon a global iconic process. The same distinction can be observed in speeded classification tasks. Suppose subjects are given pairs of forms and are required to respond "same" when the two are identical. It matters little how many attributes are present. Subjects can match about as rapidly on several attributes as on any one (Hawkins, 1969; Nickerson, 1967). In this case attributes are not taken as separate attributes, but the object is treated as a whole.

SEQUENCES OF MENTAL OPERATIONS

How are mental operations controlled and organized in the process of solving a problem? A number of psychologists (Miller, Galanter, & Pribram, 1960; Newell, Shaw, & Simon, 1958) have proposed a unified framework for viewing the organization of mental operations. This framework consists of a goal to which the organism aspires and a hierarchy of tests and mental operations. The organism compares its present state with the goal and performs an operation which will move it in the direction of the goal. The resulting representation is then compared against the representation of the goal, and if there is a mismatch another operation is performed. This kind of unit is called a *TOTE* (Test-Operate-Test-Exit). It organizes mental operations in a sequence which results in a final match between the current state and the goal. An example of a TOTE-controlled process is hammering a nail. The goal state is a smooth junction between wood and nailhead. Each operation is a hammer blow, and it is followed by a test to see if the head is flush. When the test matches the desired state, the hammering stops. The TOTE concept

suggests that matching a present input against a goal state is a basic part of all mental processes. It suggests a framework within which the idea of direction toward a goal can be used to integrate and sequence mental operations. This idea is important if mental operations are to be organized in the process of solving problems.

Stages of Processing

Some mental acts may be broken down into stages which occur in sequence. Consider the task of responding whether a visually presented stimulus is a member of a just presented set (Sternberg, 1969). The task may be seen as consisting of four stages. The first involves abstracting the incoming stimulus item and forming a representation of it. As we have seen, this process is not simple and involves both visual and name components (p. 106). Abstraction must then be followed by a check against the items stored in active memory. When the checking process is finished, the subject can determine if his response is "yes" or "no." Finally the response must be initiated. These stages are outlined in Figure 24. Sternberg has shown that these stages have psychological reality. He has found a number of things which increase the time for a particular stage without varying the time for other stages.

To understand the nature of this evidence, consider once again the relationship between reaction time and the number of items in memory. This linear function is illustrated in Figure 24. The function has a *slope* and an *intercept*. The slope represents the time needed to check out the probe against the stored items (Stage 2). The intercept represents the time needed to encode the probe and respond to the results of Stage 2. Sternberg has shown, for example, that varying the clarity of the probe affects the intercept, but has little effect on Stage 2. This is reasonable since clarity ought to affect the encoding time. Varying the probability of a "yes" response or the difficulty of indicating the response also affects the intercept but not the slope. Increasing the number of items in active memory or requiring effortful search of long-term rather than active memory increases the time for Stage 2 without affecting the time for the remaining stages (Sternberg, 1969).

Comprehension

Can mental operations be observed as stages of more complex tasks? A study of the comprehension of simple logical relations shows how the experimenter may uncover these operations and tests as aspects of more complex thought. Meyer (1970) attempted to apply Sternberg's method to see how people understand simple logical propositions. In his task subjects were shown statements such as, "All dogs (S) are animals (P)" or, "Some typhoons (S) are wheat (P)." They were to answer as quickly as

FIGURE 24   UPPER PANEL INDICATES SOME STAGES IN THE TASK OF IDENTIFYING
WHETHER AN ITEM WAS A MEMBER OF A JUST-PRESENTED LIST; LOWER FIGURE
INDICATES HOW STAGE 2 MIGHT BE SEPARATED FROM THE OTHER STAGES

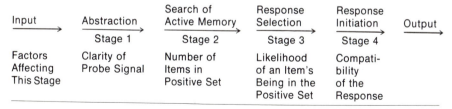

Input	Abstraction	Search of Active Memory	Response Selection	Response Initiation	Output
	Stage 1	Stage 2	Stage 3	Stage 4	
Factors Affecting This Stage	Clarity of Probe Signal	Number of Items in Positive Set	Likelihood of an Item's Being in the Positive Set	Compati-bility of the Response	

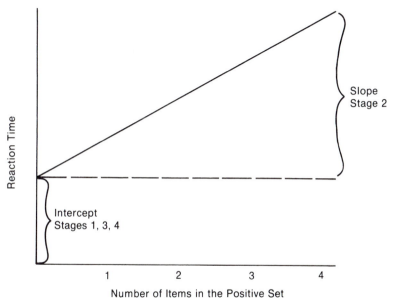

Adapted from Sternberg, S. Memory-scanning: Mental processes revealed by reaction-
time experiments. *American Scientist*, 1969, *57*, 421–457.

possible whether these statements were true or false. He varied the
relationship of the two elements (S & P). When people judged statements
with "some" (e.g., "Some S are P"), they were faster when the two
statements overlapped. On the other hand, when they were required to
judge "all" statements (e.g., "All S are P"), they were faster when S and P
did not overlap (e.g., "All typhoons are wheat") and slow when they did
(e.g., "All stones are rubies".) These findings are somewhat surprising
since it might be expected that subjects would find it easy both to say
"no" to statements involving two things far apart and to reject the idea
that a superordinate was contained in a subordinate.

Meyer's explanation illustrated in Figure 25. He suggests that subjects make two internal tests. The first essentially asks if there is overlap of the two statements. This is like deciding if there can be a conjunction of the two propositions. If the answer to this is "no," the subject can answer "false" to the statements at the bottom of the diagram. For this theory to be correct would require that false "all" and "some" statements show similar reaction times. This was found. If the answer is "yes," a further operation will be necessary when the statement involves "all." This new operation tests the order of the two statements. That is, it tells us if S or P is a superordinate. It is this operation which produces such long times for statements like, "All stones are rubies." Meyer then tries to develop details of the two operations and to determine the times they require.

Regardless of the eventual truth of the specific model, it illustrates several important trends in analysis of human thought. Note that a complex mental decision is seen as an orderly sequence of operations. The first operation is a global and effortless comparison of the similarity of the elements. The second operation is a slower and more effortful stage

FIGURE 25   SEQUENCE OF TESTS INVOLVED IN DETERMINING WHETHER A QUAN-
TIFIED STATEMENT IS TRUE OR FALSE

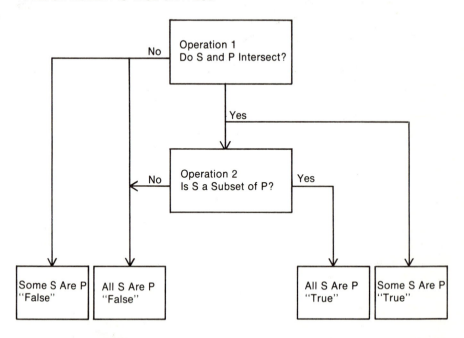

Adapted from Meyer, D. E. On the representation and retrieval of stored semantic information. *Cognitive Psychology*, 1970, *1*(3), 242–299.

which is inserted when some overlap is detected by the first operation. Each operation requires a certain time interval.

Perhaps the most extensive current effort to isolate mental operations within a simple problem is in work by Clark and Chase (1972). The study is of particular interest because it combines linguistic and pictorial relationships. In this study, subjects were given a simple sentence like, "The star is above the plus" or, "The plus is not above the star." They were to compare the sentence with one of two pictures (e.g,$\overset{*}{+}$,$\overset{+}{*}$) and respond "true" as rapidly as possible if the sentence described the picture and "false" if it did not. This could be a surprisingly difficult task which resulted in response times for unpracticed subjects in the range of 2 to 3 seconds.

The authors have conceived of the task as requiring five stages (see Figure 26). The stages follow one another in serial order. At each stage the subject has a tentative answer of either "true" or "false." This tentative answer is called the *index*. The index is always set at "true" to start.

The first stage involves abstracting the meaning of the sentence. The authors believe that this meaning is stored as an abstract proposition without any particular sensory quality.

The second stage involves abstracting the picture into an underlying proposition. The authors suggest that the picture is encoded to involve the same relationship (e.g., "above" or "below") as provided by the sentence. Thus if the sentence involved "below," the picture $\overset{*}{+}$ would be encoded "plus below star," while if the sentence involved "above," it would be encoded "star above plus."

In the third stage the subjects are thought to compare the first word of each proposition. If they match (e.g., both stars), the subjects continue to assume the answer is true (keep index value "true") and move to the fourth stage. If they do not match, the subjects assume the answer is false (set index value to "false") and move to the fourth stage.

The fourth stage involves checking the sentence for a negative. If the sentence has a negative (e.g., "Star is not above plus"), the subjects reverse their tentative answer and respond. If it does not have a negative, they keep their tentative answer and respond.

The authors present considerable evidence for their model. There are a number of factors which might reasonably be thought to affect only a single stage. For example, it is known that the word "above" is easier to encode than the word "below." Thus the presence of the term "below" ought to affect Stages 1 and 2, but not 3 and 4. On the other hand, the presence of a negative ("is not") in the sentence ought to affect Stage 4, but no other stage. The use of a picture which, when encoded, has the opposite order as the sentence ought to affect Stage 3, but no other. The reaction-time data support these ideas. Each variable seems to contribute an independent increase to the overall time without affecting the time of stages with which it is not thought to be involved. As an illustration,

FIGURE 26   SEQUENCE WITH FIVE STAGES INVOLVED IN MATCHING A SIMPLE SENTENCE WITH A PICTURE

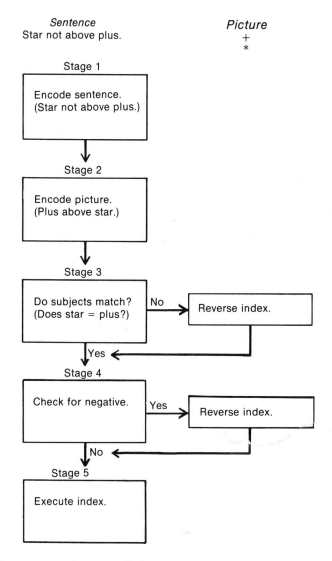

Adapted from Clark. H. H., and Chase, W. G. On the process of comparing sentences against pictures. Cognitive Psychology, *1972,* 3, *472–517.*

consider the sentence "Star is above plus," with the picture ⁎₊ . It takes an average of 1750 msec. to respond to this pair. If Stage 1 is increased by using the term "below," the time goes to about 1850 msec. If, instead, Stage 3 is increased by changing the picture to ₊⁎ , the time required is

about 1950 msec. If both changes are made so that the proposition is "Star is below plus" and the picture $\underset{*}{+}$, the time is increased to 2050 msec. The increases in Stages 1 and 3 combine to predict the total reaction time. This property of additivity among variables affecting different stages holds up for all comparisons in this study. Moreover, the authors suggest that their model corresponds quite well to the introspections of the subjects. This is especially interesting since introspections for speeded tasks tend to be rather poor. However, this task extends for nearly two seconds and, as we shall see, introspective methods tend to improve as problems lengthen so that conscious processes are more clearly involved.

There are a number of weaknesses to the approach represented by this study. The additivity principle implies that stages do not overlap in time, but follow each other in serial order. This may be unique either to low levels of practice or to problems in which the output of one stage is needed as input to the next. For example, it would be absurd to imagine that the matching stages (3 and 4) could come before the encoding stages (1 and 2). On the other hand, the automatic nature of the memory retrieval process suggests that at least some parts of picture and sentence encoding could overlap in time. The simultaneous exposure of sentence and picture may inhibit other possible strategies, such as reading the sentence and constructing the appropriate visual match. Despite these problems, the study illustrates important principles in human problem solving. The subjects tend to divide problems into a series of simple stages, each of which involves relatively elementary mental operations which approach the final goal. This tendency will be important in understanding the analysis of more complex problems discussed in Chapter 7.

SUMMARY

In this chapter we have examined mental operations in terms of the time they require. It has been shown that mental operations require measurable time. However, in the case of abstraction, many different operations may overlap. An object may simultaneously excite visual associations and associations to its verbal description. What is excited in such effortless retrieval is influenced by the structure of memory as discussed in previous chapters. Experiments indicate that visual and linguistic association are separable processes in the nervous system, even though they overlap in time.

Material may be activated either by external stimulation (abstraction) or by internal instruction (generation). Generation requires considerable time, particularly when it involves the construction of a visual representation from a verbal instruction. Material placed in active memory may be scanned by a deliberate, effortful process. The time for such scanning is an orderly function of the number of items to be examined.

Complex tasks such as those involved in comprehending relationships can be broken down into an orderly set of operations. In some tasks these operations occur in serial stages, the operations required at any stage being independent of those required at any other stage. Increases in the time for any stage contribute additively to overall processing time. As the task lengthens in time, subjects appear to be able to provide introspective accounts of their general processing stages.

6

Consciousness

We see that the mind is at every stage a theatre of possibilities. Selective consciousness consists in the comparison of these . . . the selection of some and the suppression of the rest.

W. James

No issue has been more central to the history of Western thought than the nature of consciousness. Centuries of speculation have attended the question of the relationship of our subjective experience to our external behavior. Philosophical theories have held that consciousness controls behavior, that it is a result of behavior, and that it is unrelated to behavior. In the terms of this book, the issue is the relationship between mental operations and consciousness. It is clear that we are not conscious of stimulus events themselves, but only of the results of abstractions performed by the nervous system.

As we saw in the last chapter, however, abstraction takes place at many levels. Are we aware of visual stimulation prior to its being related to past experience, or only after it has been related? Or perhaps consciousness may be directed to any level, but is unnecessary for certain mental operations. If our consciousness is not directed toward the visual form of a word, can we still perform the mental operations necessary to obtain the name? Can memory cells operate directly upon their stored representations, or does that require reliance upon mechanisms which mediate consciousness? These are questions which were implicit in the debates of philosophers of the past and which currently engage experimental psychologists.

The framework which we have constructed in our discussion so far might help clarify these issues if we had a notion of how to deal objectively with the question of consciousness. Introspective psychology

views questions of consciousness as subjective. Stimuli to which we attend give rise to an internal state of awareness quite familiar to all of us. Introspection tells us that the number of things of which we are aware at any given time is quite limited. In the analogy of William James, consciousness flows like a stream, relatively narrow at any given time. The difficulty is that verbal introspections are only a crude way of getting a detailed analysis of consciousness. This is especially true if we are dealing with short time periods or materials which are not verbal. Introspections about events which occur for very brief time periods are sparse in comparison with the information which experiments reveal. Does this mean that such operations are not conscious, or only that we do not have the language to describe them? Psychologists have been trying to develop objective methods which will reveal the role of conscious processing in the performance of mental operations.

LIMITED CAPACITY

Objective methods for studying mental operations began well before the formal birth of experimental psychology as an academic discipline. One of the earliest attempts was an effort to determine the span of attention. As described by Sir William Hamilton (1859, as cited by Woodworth & Schlosberg, 1954), "How many objects can the mind simultaneously survey?" His conclusion was that the number was about six or seven. Hamilton also realized that grouping objects into familiar units could increase the span. More recently this span has been measured by presenting a brief visual flash (less than the time for an eye movement) of varying numbers of dots. For numbers of dots below about seven, an increase in exposure duration of 10 msec. is sufficient to add an additional dot to the span. Above this number it takes 300 msec. to increase the span by another dot (Averbach, 1963). This difference supports Hamilton's idea of a limit to the attention span.

Another early effort to develop an objective analysis of conscious attention occurred at the end of the nineteenth century in the laboratory of Wilhelm Wundt. E. G. Boring, in his *History of Experimental Psychology* (1950), describes one of the earliest experiments of this type. The subject was instructed to listen for a bell and to watch a clock with a needle sweeping over its face. He was to indicate the number the needle was pointing at when the bell sounded. Note that the instruction directed the subject's attention to the bell. The surprising result of the study was that when the bell sounded with the needle at five, the average report was that the needle was at four. How could hearing the bell take place before it actually rang? This curious phenomenon led to the notion of temporal priority in dealing with events, sometimes called the *doctrine of prior entry*. This theory may be summarized as follows: A person is limited in his ability to attend to signals from more than one source. If signals arise

simultaneously from two sources, he will process them in order. In the experiment, the bell is processed first because of the instructions, and the visual information coming from the clockface is delayed. Thus the subject is still processing the needle at four when the bell is heard. If the instructions were changed to focus the subject's attention on the clock, then he would be expected to report the bell as occurring later, for example at six.

At about the same time, another demonstration of the effects of conscious attention was reported (Welch, 1898). In these experiments, muscular force was used to measure mental activity. Subjects were required to focus their attention upon mental calculations such as counting the beats of a metronome, adding, multiplying, or reading. At the same time, they were told to maintain maximal force on a hand dynamometer. The experimenter observed that the force exerted by the hand was reduced in relation to the extent of mental concentration on the task. Welch developed a coefficient of attention which was the reduction in maximum force caused by different mental activities.

There are many obvious similarities between these three objective techniques for measuring attention. They all suggest that there is a limitation to the total capacity available for attending to information. Moreover, this limitation seems to manifest itself very broadly, regardless of the sensory quality of the signals. These studies demonstrate the objective consequences of James' observations concerning the narrowness of consciousness.

The findings were not integrated into a general theory of attention until during and after World War II, when English and American psychologists began to resurrect them. These psychologists defined a system of limited capacity which was thought to be necessary, at some point, to select responses to stimuli. This theory rested in part upon important new observations made when subjects were required to listen to more than one event at a time. We have all had the experience of being at a party and trying to listen to one person while a buzz of other conversations goes on around us. Cherry (1953) and Broadbent (1958) attempted to investigate some of the characteristics of such behavior. Cherry instructed subjects to follow closely a message delivered to one ear by repeating back each word as soon after its presentation as possible (shadowing). He found that subjects were unable to report much of what was occurring in the opposite ear. They could report gross characteristics of the signal, such as whether it was speech or a musical tone, but they were unable to report shifts of content or language. Broadbent presented his subjects with simultaneous digits to each ear, in strings of three. He found that, at fast rates, subjects found it easiest to report all the digits in one ear followed by all those in the other. It was as if only after the information in one ear was perceived that the subjects switched and took in the information presented to the other ear.

These findings, together with the older ideas we have discussed, led Broadbent (1958) to postulate a limited-capacity system which corresponded to perception (p system). This system received information from the senses and could operate on only a restricted range of it. The exact properties of the system can be found in Broadbent's books (1958, 1971).

Broadbent's formulation stimulated research on the limitations of his p system. In Chapter 5 we reviewed the portion of that research which dealt with limitations in the rate at which information could be processed. Just as important, however, was the limited number of items which could enter and occupy the p system. Broadbent suggested that information from one channel excluded information from other sources. The excluded information was stored for a time, but unless attention was switched to it fairly quickly, it was lost.

Broadbent's suggestion that there was a limited capacity to the p system corresponded roughly to the introspective view of limited consciousness. Following a channel of input requires a certain amount of the mind's limited capacity and thus excludes or retards other operations. Even at the time of Cherry and Broadbent's earliest work, it was quite clear that the limitation did not function by excluding all other information entirely. Subjects shadowing material in one ear would pick up some signals from the other ear. For example, if a subject's name was repeated, or if a word which was related to one which occurred in the attended ear was used, then this information would be heard and reported later by the subject.

Despite these important exceptions, the basic idea that mental operations could be measured if they required a portion of the limited-capacity p system was established. The detailed relationship between the p system and consciousness as a subjective experience is still not clear. However, the basic idea of a limited processing capacity does provide an objective method for dealing with conscious operations. Experiments can tell us if a given type of mental operation places a load upon the central processor, and if so, how much. Moreover, this makes it possible to distinguish between mental processes which require access to such a processor and those which do not.

ALLOCATION OF CAPACITY

The work of Broadbent and Cherry involved an effort to focus the attention of the subject so completely on one course of sensory information that additional information would not rise to consciousness. We are all familiar with the difficulty of such intense concentration. Most of us find it extremely hard to concentrate attention on one subject for any length of time. The difficulty of mental concentration has a rough analogy in perception. When a visual stimulus remains fixed in a given position on the retina, by means of an optical system which compensates for

normal small fluctuations, it quickly disappears. In somewhat the same way, it is difficult to maintain in consciousness a single source of stimulation or a single subject matter for any length of time. The mind tends to wander. The difficulty of maintaining accurate attention is a prime problem in thinking.

Maintaining Alertness

In Chapter 5 we discussed the development of a general alertness to external signals. A major problem in thinking is maintaining alertness. One experimental analysis of this question involved the study of vigilance (see Broadbent, 1971, for a review). In many of these experiments, subjects were required to attend to a single source of sensory stimulation for a long period of time. For example, a subject was seated in front of a screen and asked to report whenever a dim light appeared. Because the light might appear infrequently and because it was very dim, this required close concentration. Alertness waned, and as time passed it became increasingly difficult to detect a signal.

Even when the rate of sensory information was high, as when signals appeared all the time, subjects still had difficulty maintaining attention. In one situation, for example, a subject was presented with rapid movements of a hand over a clockface. His job was to detect whenever the movement was slightly larger than usual. In this case the number of sensory events was high, but only a few of them were targets. The performance of the subject declined after a few minutes on this task. Even when a task was quite active, as in a reaction-time situation in which the subject pressed a new key each time a light came on, a decline in performance over time was detected (Mackworth, 1964).

These decrements with time often took the form of small blocks or gaps in the subject's performance. He appeared to switch off the task for brief periods of time. These switches showed up in increased reaction time to signals, or in signals which were missed completely. The rate of these switches tended to increase with the time spent taking in or responding to signals from some sensory source. If the task was designed to allow frequent shifts to new signals, the amount of this decline was systematically reduced.

Concentration

What happens when a person is instructed to commit as much processing as he can to one set of stimuli and to ignore all others? This was what Cherry and others sought to determine by means of the shadowing task. Insofar as possible, they attempted to rivet the subject's conscious processing on the task of repeating back the items coming in one ear. It was found (Moray, 1959) that subjects neither recalled nor

recognized a message repeated thirty-five times in the unattended ear. However, some things did break in on the shadowing and intruded upon attention sufficiently so that the subject either spontaneously reported them at the time or reported them after the shadowing task had finished (see p. 127).

These findings suggested that information in the unattended ear was processed, although it appeared to be blocked from entering the p system by the already heavy demands of the shadowing task. In the terms outlined in Chapter 5, unattended mental operations were sufficient to bring the input into contact with the semantic structures representing its meaning. Evidence for this was obtained in a study in which the speed at which subjects shadowed each word was measured (Lewis, 1970). It was shown that when a word in the unattended ear was a synonym of one in the attended ear, the reaction time to the shadowing task was delayed. This could not have occurred unless the unattended message had been processed sufficiently to have reached the semantic structures which related it to the attended message. Nevertheless, subjects were not able to report later any of the unattended words. A similar result (MacKay, 1973) was obtained when an ambiguous sentence such as "He is throwing stones at the bank" was presented to the attended ear while a single word, either "savings" or "river," was presented to the other ear. Subjects interpreted the sentence in accord with the word in the unattended ear, even though they did not remember its being presented.

Two ways of interpreting this kind of effect are possible. One suggests that the p system is unnecessary for obtaining the meaning of stimulus words. That is, effortless retrieval does not demand any p-system activity. Another theory is that the shadowing task is not sufficient to engage the p system fully and that a part of the system remains free to handle other signals. It is difficult to determine which of these two theories is correct because it is always possible that the subject switches his attention between words. Measuring the reaction time to the shadowed message, as Lewis did, helps reduce the possibility that this is the correct explanation, but a better method is to have detailed performance measures on both tasks, as in the studies discussed below.

Divided Attention

If you are instructed to process and respond to a certain signal as rapidly as possible, your response time to signals which arrive during this processing will be lengthened. Under some circumstances it will be lengthened less than the time spent processing the first signal, and under other circumstances the lengthening will be greater. In order to get an idea of how the difficulty of the two tasks relates to the delay in responding, it is useful to deal with two tasks which extend over a considerable time.

Fortunately, a study has been conducted showing the relationship of task difficulty to interference between two simultaneous tasks. In this experiment (Keele, 1967), the primary task was serial-reaction time. The subjects viewed a board containing eight lights in a vertical plane; for each light there was a corresponding key. Each time a key was touched, the next light came on immediately. The subjects proceeded through a series of sixty-four trials. Task difficulty was varied by manipulating the spatial correspondence between the lights and the keys. Figure 27 shows two arrangements, one with virtually exact correspondence and the other showing a very low degree of correspondence.

In the first phase of the experiment, subjects practiced until they knew the proper key to touch for each light. After reaching a high level of skill, they were required to time-share this serial-reaction task with a mental-arithmetic task that had three levels of difficulty. In the simplest condition, subjects had to count backward by ones, in the next most difficult, by threes, and in the most difficult, by sevens. In order to understand the effect of the difficulty of the two tasks on performance, the following data were collected: first, the time to count backward from a three-digit number by ones, threes, and sevens when this task was performed alone; second, the time to execute a series of sixty-four responses in the serial-reaction-time test; third, the time to execute the serial reaction and counts when both tasks were done together.

Figure 27 (lower panel) provides an overview of the findings. The surface represents the efficiency with which the two tasks could be performed simultaneously. Points lying on the zero plane indicate that performing the two tasks simultaneously required a time equal to performing each separately. That is, it required exactly the same length of time for the subjects to do the combined tasks as it would have if the times required for each individual task were added together. Points above the zero plane (+) indicate that simultaneous performance was superior to doing each task separately, while for points below the plane (−), mean performance on the combined tasks was worse than the sum of the two tasks taken apart.

When both tasks became relatively difficult, it was less efficient to perform them together than it was to perform them one at a time. Only in these cases could it be said that the subjects were truly acting as if they were unable to time-share at all and would be better off doing each task separately. In the majority of cases, the subjects were able to overlap the two tasks somewhat. Never, regardless of the ease of the two tasks, were the subjects able to perform the two tasks together with efficiency equal to performing either one alone. This evidence is the most complete description of the overall limitations in simultaneous performance that has yet been obtained. It suggests that humans are indeed limited in their ability to perform simultaneous tasks, but that the limitation is nothing like what it would be if, in fact, they could perform only one thing at a time.

FIGURE 27   UPPER PANEL ILLUSTRATES TWO LEVELS OF DIFFICULTY IN A REAC-
TION-TIME TASK; LOWER PANEL ILLUSTRATES THE DEGREE OF INTERFERENCE
BETWEEN THE SERIAL-REACTION-TIME TASK (TASK 1) AND A MENTAL-ARITHMETIC
TASK (TASK 2) AS A FUNCTION OF THEIR DIFFICULTY

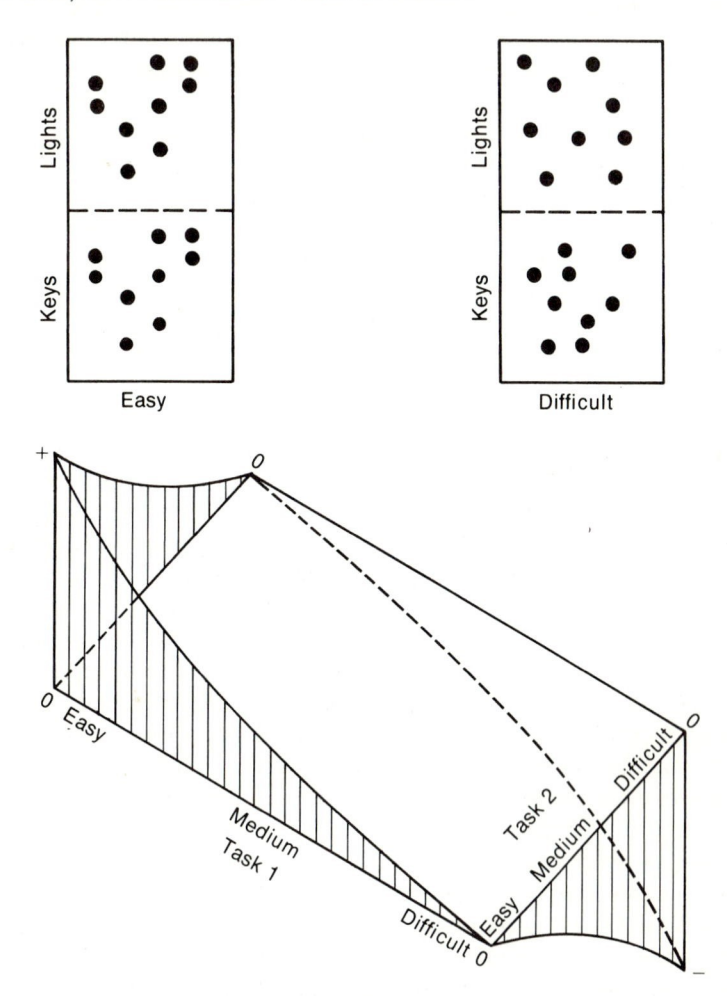

Adapted from Keele, S. W. Compatibility and time sharing in serial reaction time. *Journal
of Experimental Psychology*, 1967, *75*, 529–539.

Humans time-share quite well, with the extent of interference being a
function of task difficulty.

The difficulty of a task depends not only upon objective aspects of the
task itself, but also upon the training of the person performing it. People
with extremely high levels of skill in tasks like typing, playing a musical
instrument, or sight reading music may be able to perform simultaneous

tasks with amazingly little or no decrement (Allport, Antonis, & Reynolds, 1972; Shaffer, 1974). Usually the extent of interference between tasks will lessen with practice, but it may take a very long time indeed to reduce the interference to near zero.

These findings suggest that human subjects can time-share between two tasks and that the extent of the time-sharing is related to the overall difficulty of the two tasks. Many other studies confirm this basic result (see Kahneman, 1973, for an extensive review). However, there are some exceptions. In some studies, increasing the difficulty of one of the two tasks either does not affect the degree of overlap between the two or actually *increases* it (see Keele, 1973, for an extensive review). These exceptions suggest that a more careful look at the fine structure of tasks might aid us in finding out which aspects of a task can overlap without causing interference and which cannot.

MENTAL OPERATIONS AND CONSCIOUSNESS

Sometimes operations can be carried out with little evidence of interference. We can walk and talk without one seeming to interfere with the other. Many of us prefer to walk around when we are thinking, as though the stimulation from the motor movement might come to aid the difficult processes of thought. Careful analysis suggests that there are important limitations to this kind of time-sharing. If the path is strewn with unpredictable objects, walking may well prevent us from talking or thinking fluently. On some occasions, we slow down or stop moving when we are engaged in a particularly difficult mental operation (Kahneman, 1970). The analysis of divided attention made in the last section fits this introspective data quite well.

However, a much finer analysis of mental operations must be made if we are to understand the role which limited capacity has in the solution of problems. What mental operations in one task are likely to cause problems in processing other information? Some experiments provide a start to answering this question.

First, consider the letter-matching task which we discussed in the last chapter. The sequence of events is arranged as follows: There is a long wait during which the subject relaxes. Then a warning signal appears for a brief period. Next a single letter comes on which he must identify. After sufficient time is allowed for him to process the letter, a second letter appears. If the two letters have the same name, he must press a key marked "same." What are the mental operations involved in this simple task? First, when the warning signal appears the subject must become alert to process the first letter or, if it appears only briefly, he will miss it. When the first letter does appear, it must make contact with visual memory and produce a representation of the letter name. This involves what we have defined as the process of effortless retrieval. Finally, the

subject must rehearse the letter name, match it against the new letter, and select the appropriate response. At what point does the limited-capacity conscious system of the subject become involved?

The outline of an extensive series of experiments (Posner & Boies, 1971; Posner & Klein, 1973) is presented in Figure 28. The idea of these experiments is simple. Any event which requires the central capacity will interfere somewhat with the processing of any other event using that central capacity, even if that event involves another sensory modality. At crucial places in the sequence of processing the letters, an auditory probe tone is inserted. The subject is instructed to tap a key whenever he hears that tone. The reaction time to the probe serves as a measure of how deeply the processing system is involved in handling the letter task. In order to make sure that the subject places primary attention upon the letter task, the probes are presented on only half the trials and are rarely in any one position. Presenting probes has little or no effect on letter-match reaction times. These controls provide evidence which indicates that the reaction times to the probes do reflect the central-processing requirements of the main letter-matching task.

The results of one experiment indicating the probe reaction times are illustrated in Figure 29. The first finding is that during the interval following the warning signal, the reaction time to the probes improves. This reflects the general character of alertness. Alertness for letters actually reduces the reaction time to the probes as well. When the subject

FIGURE 28   SCHEMATIC DIAGRAM OF A SEQUENCE OF EVENTS IN A LETTER-MATCHING TASK IN WHICH A SERIES OF AUDITORY PROBES ARE PLACED AT EACH OF THE INDICATED PROBE POSITIONS

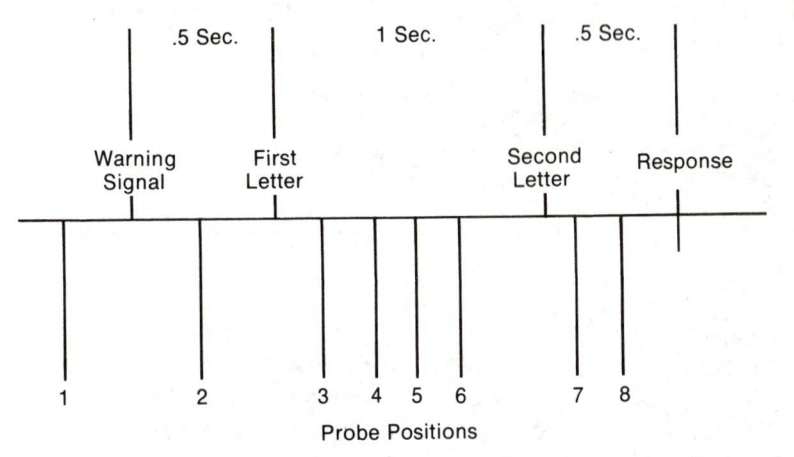

Adapted from Posner, M. I., and Boies, S. W. Components of attention. *Psychological Review*, 1971, *78*(5), 391–408.

FIGURE 29   RESULTS OF THE PROBE REACTION TIMES OBTAINED FROM ONE
LETTER-MATCHING STUDY

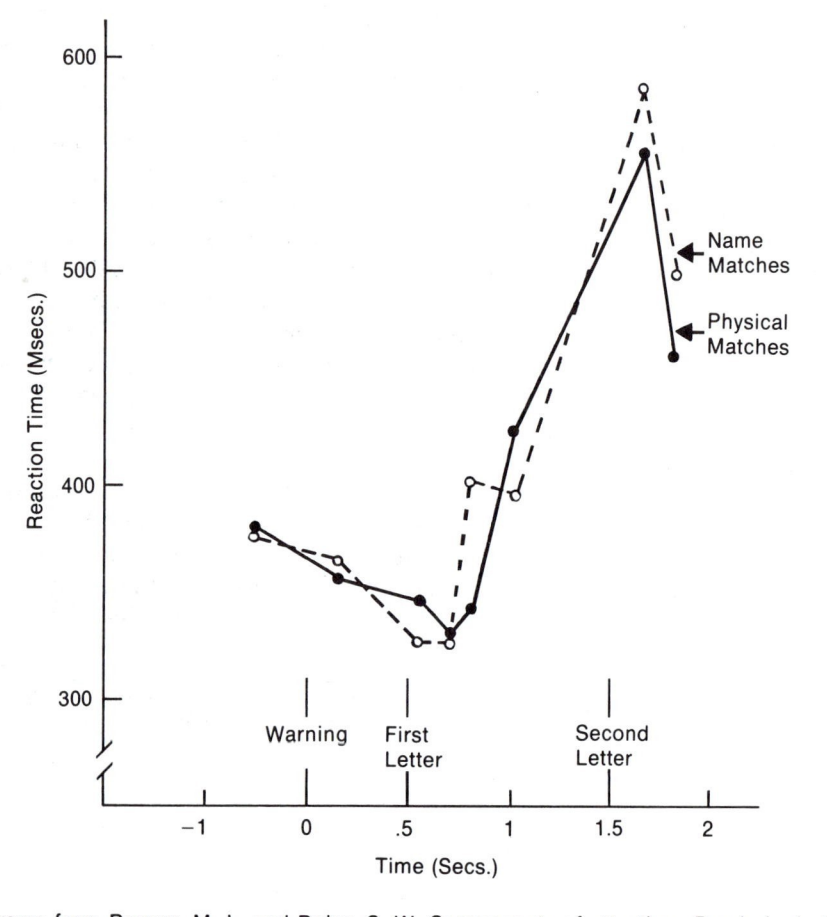

Redrawn from Posner, M. I., and Boies, S. W. Components of attention. *Psychological Review*, 1971, *78*(5), 391–408. Copyright © 1971 by the American Psychological Association. Redrawn by permission.

prepares to deal with information, he seems to put himself in a condition which makes him more receptive to information from any source. This contrasts sharply with the view that preparation selectively enhances the processing of information from one source (e.g., vision) and reduces it for other sources (e.g., audition) (Hernandez-Peón, 1960). Perhaps the non-selective character of preparation helps explain why concentration is so difficult. When we alert ourselves to process some stimulus, we do not make our sensory systems less susceptible to irrelevant stimuli. Presum-

ably concentration must be maintained in the face of the continued possibility of disruption. This is not to imply that selectivity is impossible. Undoubtedly, at some level, we can select some signals and ignore others, but this appears to be only after considerable processing has taken place.

Even more striking is what happens following the presentation of the first letter. In Chapter 5 it was shown that the abstraction of a letter name was a process which required substantial time and involved complex suboperations. Nevertheless, this processing does not seem to require the conscious attention of the subject. If a probe is presented during the first 300 msec. after the first letter, it is processed as efficiently as when it occurs during the warning interval. Control studies in which the first letter was turned off after varying intervals have provided evidence that the subject was processing the letter during this interval. However, effortless retrieval of the letter name does not seem to require the operations of the central processor. These experiments suggest that the operations of pattern recognition and name retrieval may occur outside of the involvement of consciousness as defined here.

There are other reasons to suspect that conscious processing enters rather late in the sequence of dealing with external information. At several points it has been suggested that introspective accounts of events which happen rapidly are unreliable. This poses a considerable problem for any kind of psychology which seeks to use introspection as the means of discovering processing steps. Perhaps these accounts are unreliable because activities which last only a brief time do not involve consciousness.

It has also been shown that complex discriminations of the general type we have been discussing are possible even while the subject is asleep (Oswald, Taylor, & Treisman, 1960). In one study, subjects were played long series of proper names while they slept. Electrical activity from the brain was monitored, both to be certain that sleep was maintained and to record the activity which resulted from the presentation of the names. Significantly, more electrical activity was recorded when the subjects' own names were presented than for control names.

None of these findings are definitive. However, in conjunction with the probe experiments, they do suggest that consciousness is unnecessary for contact between the incoming message and specific information stored in long-term memory. They suggest that a basic property of effortless retrieval is that information can be retrieved without a conscious mental operation. Moreover, in split-brain patients we have learned that complex discriminations take place without the subject being able to report them.

A third point of interest from Figure 29 is what happens to a probe which occurs .5 sec. or more after the first letter, and before the second letter. Reaction time to the probe increases substantially. Why is this so? Presumably because the subject at this point is doing something which

involves his central capacity. One possibility is that he is rehearsing the first letter. We know that rehearsal demands conscious attention and may be necessary to keep the letter present in active memory while the second letter is processed. Another possibility is that the subject is generating information related to the second letter, that he is imagining the letter he expects to see.

The reaction times to these late probes can be accentuated if subjects are required to perform a mental operation, such as counting forward from the letter they receive. For example, in one study they were asked to respond "same" if the second letter was three letters beyond the first. In this case, reaction time to probes which occurred 300 to 500 msec. after the first letter were more than twice as long as they would have been during a regular name match. However, probes which occurred 50 to 100 msec. after the first letter were barely affected. Probe times are extremely sensitive to mental operations, such as counting forward, which are effortful.

The tenor of the analysis so far has been to suggest that effortless retrieval does not require a conscious search, but rather that consciousness is the product of such retrieval. The same conclusion has been reached from studies using auditory speech stimuli (Liberman et al., 1967). These studies investigated the ability of subjects to discriminate small differences in speech sounds. In some cases the two sounds represented the same phoneme in the English language. That is, speakers of English had learned to interpret the two sounds as carrying the same significance in the language. In other cases, the sounds belonged to different phonemes. That is, they had different significance in English. These experiments indicated that the same degree of physical change would be heard as "different" if the two stimuli were from different phonemes, and as "same" if they were from the same phoneme.

The ability to make a perceptual discrimination appears to be influenced by concepts which are either innate or built on past experience. Thus, the investigators argued, we are conscious not of the sounds themselves, but of the results of the classifications of these sounds which are made by reference to learned concepts. This view has sometimes been called the *motor theory of speech perception,* because it argues that what becomes conscious is influenced by the sounds we have learned to make. This view emphasizes the importance of motor codes in what becomes conscious. However, the more general point which can be made from the foregoing data is that the organization of enactive, iconic, and symbolic codes in long-term memory all influence what becomes conscious.

Flexibility of Conscious Questions

It is important to consider the opposite side of this question. If consciousness is unnecessary for effortless retrieval, how early in the sequence of processing *may* consciousness intervene? Are we stuck only

with the classified results of past experience, or can we become conscious of data earlier in the processing sequence, perhaps before memory has made contact with input information?

This question has been of considerable importance in the history of speculations concerning thought. As mentioned before (see p. 104), some writers (Whorf, 1956) believe that the way we become conscious of the world is greatly influenced by the language we use in describing the world. In Chapter 5 we saw that visual perception involves mental operations which are often independent of verbal processing. However, there is a more general form of this question. Can we become conscious of information in a way which is free from the organizations imposed by memory codes? This is a difficult question to answer because certain types of organization of information are clearly imposed by the nature of our sensory apparatus. For example, we can see only those electromagnetic radiations which are within the visible spectrum. Our view of the world would be quite different if our visual apparatus did not have this limitation, and it is hard to separate such built-in limitations from learned ones.

With respect to learned classifications, however, data are not completely clear. You will remember that studies in the motor theory of speech perception (p. 136) suggested that we could not bring speech sounds to consciousness without influence from learned phonemic boundaries. Moreover, it is often difficult to see a picture in the same way we did before knowing what it represented. In most domains, classifications which we have learned do not prevent us from making normal discriminations within a class boundary (Lenneberg, 1967; Parks, Wall, & Bastian, 1969; Posner, Lewis, & Conrad, 1972). It is perfectly possible to identify "A" and "a" as physically different despite the identity of their names. The class boundaries do tend to govern what we will remember or how we will describe the experience.

The probe studies indicate that we have a good deal of flexibility in deciding when to give conscious attention to an input item. If unhurried, it is possible to attend to codes based upon the output of effortless retrieval. If time is important, however, probe interference appears at an earlier stage, presumably before activation of memory structures is complete. Thus the problem of the relation of our conscious perception to raw input is extremely complex. What does become conscious involves both input and effortless retrieval. Presumably this balance between perception of input and perception of activated structures is influenced by many factors, including the type of stored structures, the speed of analysis, and the level of alertness at which we are working.

Other Definitions

There are many definitions of consciousness to which our analysis does not apply. For example, the term is sometimes taken to mean having an

attitude or opinion toward something. We intend a much more restricted definition.

In this chapter we have proposed that consciousness is associated with a specific limited-capacity coordinating mechanism in the nervous system. Our experience of a signal depends upon the signal currently occupying this limited-capacity system. This view is consonant with the finding that some mental operations occur simultaneously without interference (see Chapter 5) and others seem to occur only in serial order. The probe technique uses delays in processing the probe to measure the conscious demands of other tasks. Another way of stating our proposed view of consciousness is to say that the primary and probe tasks represent different overall TOTE units (see p. 116) and that humans are unable to maintain such separate activities as efficiently as a single activity (Shallice, 1972).

How does this way of dealing with the problem of consciousness relate to other ways? According to one view, consciousness is identical with awareness. Awareness, however, is usually ascertained by a verbal report following some event. If the request is made soon after the signal, for example, subjects might become aware of the signal only after being asked to report it. The signal may be present in active memory and be examined only after the request. If the request is delayed, some signals which have been conscious at one time may be forgotten before the report is made, since active memories tend to be lost fairly rapidly. Despite these difficulties, there is substantial correspondence between awareness and the limited-capacity mechanism. In those cases in which a task produces very clear probe interference, subjects are able to report its presence.

Conscious operations are often thought to be those which are remembered. Since rehearsal requires processing capacity in the sense of probe interference and is also necessary for long-term retention, it follows that these two senses of consciousness are also closely related.

Another way of viewing conscious activity is to say that operations performed without intention are automatic or unconscious. In the Warren study (p. 86), subjects appeared to activate the category name of a word without any desire to do so. Such an operation seems to be automatic both because it is done without intention and because it does not require the limited-capacity system. It is an automatic consequence of structures in our nervous system, not the result of an effortful process.

In general, consciousness, as defined by interference within a limited-capacity processing system, corresponds moderately well with the ideas of awareness, memory, and intention which are usually intimately connected with the concept. Thus the learning of mental structures requires the limited-capacity system, but their activation, once learned, does not. This indicates that prior learning of mental structures may be used to reduce human limitations brought about by the central processing system. We shall now turn to some of the consequences of this fact.

Automatic Activation of Structures

It is now possible to understand in more detail the significance of the memory structures described in Chapter 4. A memory structure is a permanent organization of material in long-term memory. The items in it are bound together by a network of associations. The spread of activation among items in the structure is effortless. It requires time, but it does not require the capacity of the central processor.

What complexity of information can be represented by such structures? The answer depends upon the degree of development of the memory structures. Earlier we discussed how evidence using the probe technique indicated that names of visually presented letters could be retrieved without effort. In the adult it appears that visually presented words, at least simple ones, are read as efficiently as individual letters (Reicher, 1969). Moreover, we have seen that aurally presented words are classified by meaning even when subjects are engaged in shadowing material in the other ear (p. 129). The Stroop test has shown that word names are activated automatically in a color-naming task even when subjects attempt to avoid doing so.

There is reason to believe that complex semantic processing of sentences does not occur effortlessly in most adults. The processing of sentence meaning appears to interfere with probe reaction times (Foss, 1969). It seems that extraction of meaning from a sentence does require the central processor. The evidence is still somewhat fragmentary, but it agrees with the idea that sentences are rarely repeated and always represent something new, whereas words are relatively fixed elements of language.

Highly gifted individuals might possibly succeed in developing more complex effortless processing. Indeed, the existence of readers who claim to be able to obtain the meaning of written materials directly, without being aware of word names, appears to be one example. Surprisingly enough, there has been little study of speed readers by psychologists.

One high-level skill on which reasonably good data are available is the memory of chess players for positions on the board (deGroot, 1965). DeGroot studied the ability of chess masters, experts, and novices to reproduce actual chess positions. His subjects received a five-second look at a chessboard which contained pieces in positions occurring after the twentieth move in a masters-level game. There were approximately twenty men on the board at this time. He found two striking things. First, masters-level chess players made few errors. Most of these were corrected if they were given a single chance to guess again. Expert chess players did much worse. For example, masters had 85 percent correct on one trial, while experts had only 35 percent correct. Novices were even worse. Other studies have shown that the remarkable achievement of the chess masters was not due to any unusual general memory ability. When

required to produce chess pieces arranged at random, they were not much better than weak players; and the more removed the memory task was from similarity to chess, the more their memory performance resembled that of other subjects.

DeGroot suggested that the achievement of the master chess player is perceptual. It seems clear that a great deal of memory is involved. The input makes contact with a highly organized and efficient memory system. The chess master does not deal with individual men any more than the skilled reader deals with individual letters. He sees patterns in relation to the structures stored in his memory. He does not have to sample individual pieces and consciously relate them. Rather, groups of pieces are effortlessly related to familiar groupings in his past experience. The seven or eight items which represent the limits of active memory contain much more information for the master than for other players.

The chess master has automated the process of taking in chess information in much the same way as the skilled musician automates the operation of his instrument. Both can produce achievements of great complexity with relatively little cognitive strain. Do these habitual mental operations still require time? DeGroot reported that his subjects found it important to pause immediately following the stimulus exposure before beginning their reproduction. This pause may have allowed the new information to come in contact with the stored structures and given the subjects time to rehearse and attend to the organized information.

If this analysis of deGroot's striking results is correct, it indicates once again that the things which come to consciousness are heavily influenced by the structures we have stored in the past. This does not mean that the chess master is unable to examine the chessmen as individual perceptual objects, but it is most natural for him to examine them in the context of the information retrieved from his long-term memory. He "sees" them in terms of his past experience with chess.

The chess master is able to bypass the limited capacity for storing information because his long-term memory is able to repackage the information in meaningful units based upon long experience with the game. We are all familiar with less amazing accomplishments of memory along these same lines. The car buff is able to repeat the makes of a long series of cars he has just seen, while the psychologist is able to remember the details of an experimental graph after a brief glance. The relationship between what is presented to a subject and what he will remember depends heavily upon the way his past experience guides the process of effortless retrieval. For this reason, the professional may have different retention capabilities for information within his own domain.

Although the structures in long-term memory will differ among people, there still are many important common factors in dealing with less familiar input or memories. All of us face the difficult problem of holding things in active memory while trying to operate upon them. These common factors of memory and thought will be considered next.

MEMORY AND THOUGHT

There is an intimate relationship between the retention of information in active memory and the limited conscious capacity of the subject. Suppose you have just looked up a telephone number. If nothing interrupts you, there is a high probability that you will retain it long enough to dial. However, if you are first required to perform a conscious mental operation, this probability will drop.

Crowder (1967) had subjects retain strings of five unrelated nouns during a subsequent task of pressing keys to lights. The key-pressing task began immediately after the five nouns had been presented and continued for twenty-four seconds. Afterwards, the subjects attempted to recall the words in the order in which they had been presented. The results showed that the key-press task significantly reduced retention and that the more difficult the task, the greater the reduction of memory.

Another series of studies (Posner & Rossman, 1965) found essentially the same relationship. The stored material consisted of three letters. The interpolated tasks from easiest to most difficult were recording, adding, and classifying digits. Figure 30 shows that the amount of forgetting was related to the difficulty of the information-processing task which intervened in the thirty-second delay between the presentation of the three digits and their recall.

These experiments suggest that many types of mental operations place loads upon the same general capacity used to rehearse and keep information within active memory. If the mental operations involve the same code as the material to be retained, even greater losses result. The fact that symbolic and iconic codes require central-processing capacity in order to be retained has profound implications for many thinking tasks.

In Chapter 4 it was shown that the difficulty of concept learning was related to the kind of rule involved (see Figure 13). For example, rules involving only a single operation are simpler to learn than those involving more than one (e.g., exclusive disjunction). It is now possible to examine in more detail how limited capacity for mental operations affects the ability to solve such problems.

In concept-learning problems, subjects are repeatedly exposed to instances of information which they must classify on the basis of their current hypotheses and store as the basis for future hypotheses. It might be argued that any classification rule which requires more complex mental operations will also lead to reduced retention of information from previous instances.

In one study (Denny, 1969), the rules used were inclusive disjunction (red and/or triangle) and exclusive disjunction (red or triangle, but not both). The number of binary tests involved in exclusive disjunction are greater and thus more time and effort are required to execute the rule than is the case for inclusive disjunction (see Figure 23). Denny studied the learning of inclusive-disjunctive and exclusive-disjunctive rules. The

FIGURE 30   EFFECT OF MENTAL OPERATIONS OF VARYING DIFFICULTY UPON RETENTION OF A SHORT MESSAGE

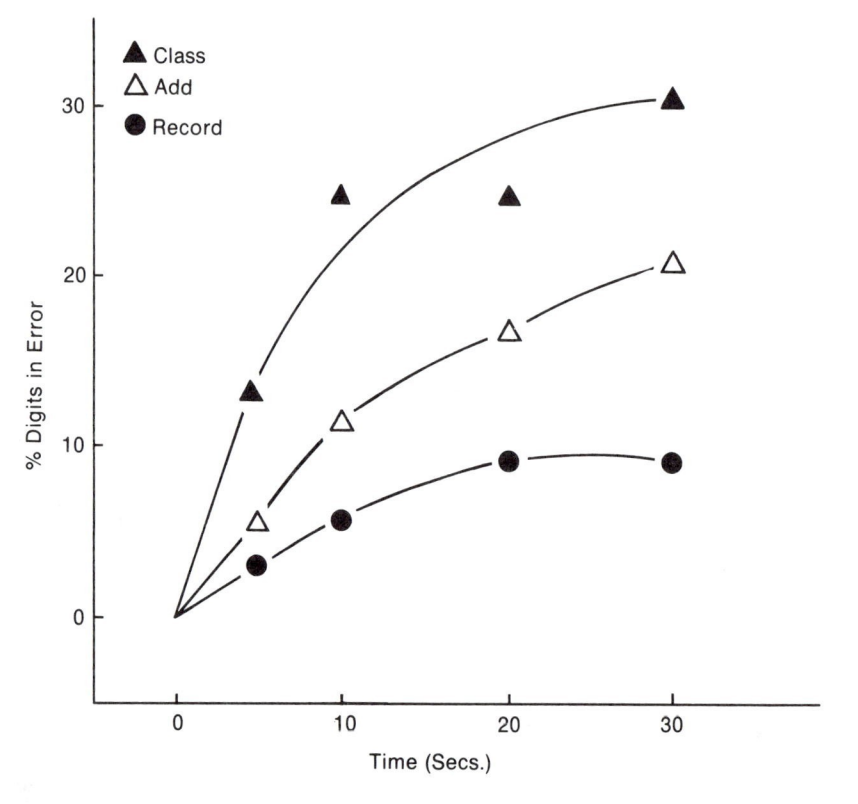

Adapted from Posner, M. I., and Rossman, E. Effect of size and location of informational transforms upon short-term retention. *Journal of Experimental Psychology*, 1965, *70*, 496–505. Copyright © 1965 by the American Psychological Association. Adapted by permission.

subjects knew which attributes were relevant, but not which rule was used to combine the attributes. They were shown a sequence of instances. After each instance appeared, they first reported whether or not they had seen it before in the list. Then they classified the card as to whether or not it was an instance of the concept, and were told whether or not they were correct. It took longer for subjects to learn the correct classifications with exclusive-disjunctive rules than with inclusive-disjunctive rules. Moreover, recognition memory for past instances was lower for subjects learning the exclusive disjunction than for those learning the inclusive disjunction. This led Denny to hypothesize that the reason exclusive disjunctions were harder to learn was that the mental operations involved

in classifying the stimuli were more difficult and led to increased forgetting of past instances.

In order to test this view, Denny set up a situation in which the subjects' memories were refreshed after seeing each instance. After each trial the subjects were shown a board upon which were hung all previous instances they had seen. This refresher eliminated the difference between recognition memory for the two concepts. Denny found that the difference in time to learn the rules was also eliminated under this procedure. This experiment suggests rather strongly that one major difference in the time needed to learn concepts results from the fact that more difficult mental operations produce more forgetting.

Indeed, much concept-learning literature has also suggested that the major problem in concept learning is due to memory (Hunt, 1962). Since we know that retention is related to the difficulty of the mental operations which intervene between an instance and its recollection, it seems reasonable to suppose that concept learning can be analyzed in terms of the relationship between mental operations and retrieval.

The concept-learning task requires the subject to store information in order to solve the problem. In many problem-solving tasks all the necessary information is presented to the subject simultaneously. The problem is written out in full and is in front of him for reference. Experiments suggest that many of the same principles which were apparent in concept studies apply in this case. Simon and Kotovsky (1963) investigated a number of serial-reasoning problems. These are problems in which the subject is presented with a gap which he must fill. Some examples are shown in Figure 31. The investigators found that the major variable contributing to task difficulty in such problems was the number of places in memory which had to be occupied simultaneously in order to derive the correct answer. They saw the subject as abstracting information from the series and holding the information in operational memory. They argued, "If a subject is able to extrapolate a sequence, he

FIGURE 31 SOME SIMPLE SERIAL-COMPLETION PROBLEMS

Test Problems

1. cdcdcd__	6. qxapxbqxa__	11. rscdstdetuef__
2. aaabbbcccdd__	7. aduacuaeuabuafua__	12. npaoqapraqsa__
3. atbataatbat__	8. mabmbcmcdm__	13. wxaxybyzczadab__
4. admcdmefmghm__	9. urtustuttu__	14. jkqrklrslmst__
5. defgefghfghi__	10. abyabxabwab__	15. pononmnmlmlk__

Reprinted from Simon, H. A., and Kotovsky, K. Human acquisition of concepts for sequential patterns. *Psychological Review*, 1963, *70*(6), 534–546.

holds in memory something very different from the bare sequence with which he was presented. The sequence, taken by itself, provides no basis for its own extrapolation [pp. 535–36]." The subject must then generate a pattern based upon transformed stimulus input.

In this view, such a problem represents exactly the combination of storage and mental operations which we have seen place a load on the central-processing mechanisms. The results of this study mean that, in the analysis of problem solving, active memory may be a limitation whenever items must be integrated in order to produce the correct solution. Merely having the items present on a page in front of the subject or in his own long-term memory does not eliminate the necessity for active memory during the act of transformation. Thus the analysis of problem solving as a sequential task involving active memory and mental operations may be extended to problems in which the subject has either continual display of the raw information or perfect long-term memory of the material.

GENERATION AND SPARE CAPACITY

A limited-capacity system may be either overloaded or underloaded. Overload leads not only to the performance problems we have been discussing, but also often to feelings of discomfort. Indeed, Milgram (1970) has argued that many of the problems of urban life arise from the continuous high level of information which people are required to process. A similar argument has reached the public in Toffler's book *Future Shock*. Feelings of boredom may also arise from a failure to have a sufficient variety of input to process. Psychologists have studied (Fiske & Maddi, 1961) extreme conditions of underload in experiments on sensory deprivation. Subjects were kept in soundproof, uniformly lit rooms for long periods with stimulation kept to a minimum. These conditions were found to be extremely unpleasant, with frequent complaints of boredom and sometimes extreme reactions such as hallucinations. Studies have indicated that such conditions are not conducive to clear thinking. After a day of sensory deprivation, subjects showed a general disruption in the quality of their perceptual and thought processes. Such findings are in accord with the idea that humans operate best at an intermediate, or medium, level of stimulation.

One set of studies (Antrobus et al., 1970) indicates how subjects attempt to keep themselves at or near their preferred level of stimulation in the absence of sufficient task input. In these studies, subjects were first instructed on how to give reports on their daydreaming. Daydreaming was defined as any conscious thought which was completely unrelated to the task or to their internal bodily state. Examples of daydreaming were: thinking about what they would do in the future, thinking about a girlfriend or boyfriend, or thinking about a paper they were writing. At varying points during a long session, subjects were shown an amber light

which meant they should report whether or not they had daydreamed in the time since the last report. Subjects in all conditions were required to make the same number of reports. However, they were assigned to different rates of task-relevant stimulation. The tasks were manipulated in two ways. First, the difficulty of the mental operations required to process each signal was varied, and second, the rate of signal presentation was varied.

The results are shown clearly in Figure 32. It was found that increases both in the complexity of a given mental operation and in the signal rate reduced the frequency of daydreaming reports. The two variables were additive, as might be expected, if the overall level of mental activity was the variable which governed the subjects' likelihood of daydreaming. This result agrees with findings in experiments on generation (see p. 108). The likelihood of the subjects' generating the opposite case of a letter depended upon the time they had to do so and upon the other information to which they had to attend during the delay interval. The same principles seem to apply to the generation of daydreams, although we are forced in

FIGURE 32   FREQUENCY OF DAYDREAMING REPORTS AS A FUNCTION OF THE TIME BETWEEN EVENTS AND THE DIFFICULTY OF TASK-RELATED MENTAL PROCESSING

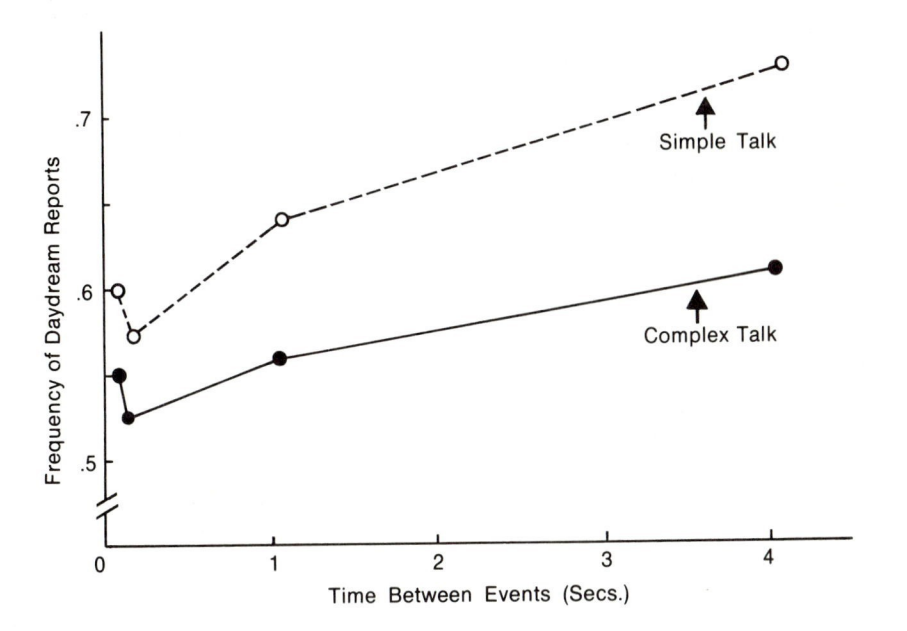

Adapted from Antrobus, J. S., Singer, J. L., Goldstein, S., and Fortgang, M. Mindwandering and cognitive structure. *Transactions of the New York Academy of Science*, 1970, *32*, 242–252.

this case to rely upon the subjects' own reports of their experience, rather than upon measurable aspects of their performance. The convergence of these studies extends the range of mental phenomena to which the analysis used in this chapter might apply.

SUMMARY

Consciousness is a varied subject, studied by many disciplines. The approach taken in this chapter has been narrower than the title implied. The chapter dealt not with the functions of consciousness, but rather with attempts to develop experimental indicants of consciousness as aids to its objective study. Consciousness has been identified with a limited-capacity mechanism for processing information. This capacity can be shared among mental operations, but the ultimate limitation remains.

Operations which may be performed without processing capacity are said not to be conscious. These include learned abstractions of considerable complexity. For example, effortless retrieval of the name of a stimulus does not appear to require consciousness for most adults, but rehearsal or transformation of the retrieved product does. It appears likely that in highly developed skills, complex abstractive processes such as relating current positions upon a chessboard to past experience may also become free of processing capacity. This suggests that the semantic structures built up from past experience exert considerable influence over the way we usually experience new input. However, conscious mechanisms often are directed toward codes which have not yet come in contact with long-term memory and thus are unbiased by past experience.

The importance of conscious rehearsal for the storage of information places humans in a difficult dilemma. The performance of transformations upon current input may preempt the processing capacity so that the storing of raw data is neglected. This leads to the biases in thinking outlined in earlier chapters. Nonetheless, such transformations are necessary if data are to be filed in a way which can lead to future effortless retrieval.

Processing capacity may be either overloaded or underloaded. In the absence of sufficient input from task-relevant stimuli, subjects will daydream, or process information stored in long-term memory.

7

Search Strategies and Problem Solving

Let no one say I have said nothing new. . . . The arrangement of the material is new.

Pascal

The evidence reviewed in the last five chapters has concerned performance in quite simple situations in which subjects rarely fail. Our goal has been to understand the organization of memory and human limitations in performing mental operations. We are now in a position to define the process of thinking in terms of our previous work. *Thought is the achievement of a new representation through the performance of mental operations.*

Thought occurs in a vast number of situations, which can be divided into three large categories, according to the motivation for thought. We may be led to think by some external event. Faced with the need to cross an unbridged river, we may invent a means of flotation. An external obstacle is the basis for most studies of problem solving. However, thought may be motivated by internal factors as well. Contradictory cognitions (Festinger, 1957) may motivate us to think, as, for example, when an old and respected friend adopts political views opposite to our own and causes reconsideration of our opinion of him or our political views. Finally, there is idle thought. In the absence of external stimulation, the mind may play with representations as a means of occupying itself. Such daydreaming can lead to creative innovation. Our general definition of thought includes all three of these major motivational categories. However, this chapter will concentrate upon situations in which a problem is posed externally. Many of our examples will come from puzzles which experimenters induce subjects to solve.

This chapter will also deal with creative or scientific thought. Hyman (1965) has defined creative thought as the achievement of a newer, more adaptive mental picture of some area of interest. This idea certainly fits our general definition of thought, but it raises the problem of how to determine when a thought is adaptive. One possibility is to define the success of the thought process in terms of the social utility of the product. Scientists or artists are often viewed as creative when they produce a socially useful product. To a psychologist, the success of thought must be determined by the utility of the new representation within the cognitive structure of the individual. Does the new representation help him reconcile conflicting cognitions, or grasp new problems which were inexplicable in terms of his older representations? When the child learns the conservation of quantity, his new representation is adaptive in the sense that he now can ignore the size and shape of the vessel in determining that the amount of water stays the same as it is poured from one beaker to another. Of course any representation may lead to error, as happens when the child applies his representation of the laws of English plurals to the word "mouse." Still, it is often possible to speak of a representation as having a higher level of generality and, in this sense, as being more adaptive. Occasionally, in the hands of an Einstein, Mozart, or Darwin, the restructuring plays a role not only for the individual, but for all people. In these cases what is creative in a psychological sense becomes creative in a social sense as well.

THE PREPARED MIND

Our definition of thought leads to stress upon the preconceptions or structures which are present at the start of a period of thought. Only in the light of the initial structures can the extent of restructuring be determined. Louis Pasteur said, "In the field of observation, chance favors only the prepared mind." The remark points out the frequency with which chance has been thought to lead to important discoveries. Much scientific work has begun with a chance or unplanned observation. Yet Pasteur was clearly right that the same observation made by someone unprepared to take advantage of it would not lead to the correct finding. The train of thought set up in the mind of a person whose memory is well stocked with concepts in a given field is utterly different from that which might occur to the novice. Moreover, the ability to follow a given line of thought and to make the needed transformation would not occur to the novice.

There is a mistake, however, in stressing only the advantages of the prepared mind. In one sense, the existence of a cognitive representation is a necessary prerequisite for the creation of a new one. Yet in another sense, the existence of a prior organization of information often limits or hinders the possibility of achieving a new representation. The experienced scientist has the advantage of treating new information within

already existing structures, but he also bears the burden of those structures. Some scientists have argued that fundamental changes in theory
can only really be incorporated into the thinking of the next generation,
since the minds of the current generation are not sufficiently adaptable to
make full use of the new organization.

TOPICS IN PROBLEM SOLVING

The processes of solving problems and of producing artistic or scientific
creations have been divided into stages by various authors (Polya, 1945;
Dewey, 1933; Wallas, 1926; Johnson, 1955). The exact stages differ, but
they usually include interpreting the problem, devising a plan, producing
solutions, and deciding among solutions. These stage models have
primarily been useful as a means of organizing discussions of problem
solving. The occurrence of such stages in actual problem solving seems
doubtful. Vast differences in types of problems make it unlikely that a set
of stages can be applicable in all situations.

We shall group the various aspects of problem solving into specific
topics. The first topic involves the interpretation of the problem. Stating a
problem forces some kind of representation. This representation will be
influenced not only by the problem statement, but also by things about the
problem solver, including his choice of a code or format for representing
the problem and the structures which are activated by it. The initial
representation of a problem may be the most crucial single factor
governing the likelihood of problem solution. What may appear as a
formidable problem in one representation may be solved immediately in
another format. A mere change of representation may by itself provide the
solution. Whether a problem is solved or not, and how long the solution
might take, depend a great deal upon the initial representation.

If a problem cannot be solved within its original representation or by a
reorganization of that same information, it may be necessary to collect
additional information. This involves a search either of memory or of the
external world for evidence to modify the representation. This search is
initiated by a plan about where to look for the needed information. The
development of a search strategy is a highly conscious and difficult aspect
of problem solving. The many factors which guide the direction of the
search will be discussed in the section on the development of search
strategies.

Many prominent scientists and artists report that the solution of a
problem frequently comes to mind only after a period of noninvolvement
with it. There is evidence that a delay or rest period may be helpful in
increasing the probability of solution, but the significance of this *incubation* period is greatly disputed. Some believe that unconscious mental
operations may be capable of solving problems which cannot be handled
by conscious operations. On the other hand, there are similarities between

incubation and the active reorganization of long-term memory which was considered in Chapter 2 (pp. 37–40). It was explained in Chapter 2 how a memory system might appear capable of spontaneous reorganization even if reorganizations occurred only when information was brought into active memory. The phenomenon of incubation forces another examination of the unconscious processing capability present within long-term memory.

When a clear goal is provided by an experimenter, there is relatively little question about how the problem arises or when it is solved. The problem solver working on his own must decide what constitutes a solution. In more common situations, a person may have to decide when to drop a problem from consideration or when the solution he has reached is sufficient. The decisions to begin work on a problem and to terminate such work are important ones. The final section of this chapter will discuss the collection of evidence and decisions relating to acceptance of a solution as satisfactory.

INITIAL REPRESENTATION

Selection

The most crucial time for solving a problem is in the first few moments after it has been presented. The initial selection of the relevant representation is important for deciding how the problem is to be solved. Consider the problem shown in Figure 33. If the subject represents the problem in terms of finding the length (l) by manipulating the triangle (l, d, x), he will find the problem difficult. There are many things which might influence him to choose such a representation. If the problem is presented in a mathematics class, the subject might expect that his knowledge of trigonometric relations is being tested and he might then select the triangle as crucial. On the other hand, if the problem is represented as one of finding something equivalent in length to l, the answer appears immediately. The length l is the diagonal of a rectangle, but a rectangle has two diagonals. The other diagonal is the radius of the circle, and by symmetry the value of l must be equal to the radius.

The example given above is a problem presented in visual form. Consider the following verbal problem:

> Two train stations are fifty miles apart. At 2 P.M. one Saturday afternoon two trains start toward each other, one from each station. Just as the trains pull out of the stations, a bird springs into the air in front of the first train and flies ahead to the front of the second train. When the bird reaches the second train it turns back and flies toward the first train. The bird continues to do this until the trains meet.

FIGURE 33   PROBLEM ILLUSTRATING THE IMPORTANCE OF THE INITIAL REPRE-
SENTATION

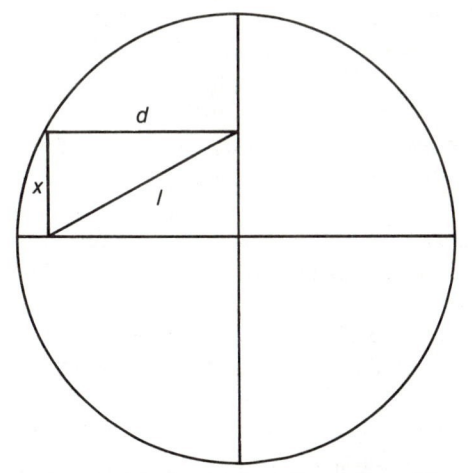

Determine the length of *l* given the radius of the circle

If both trains travel at the rate of twenty-five miles per hour and the bird flies at a hundred miles per hour, how many miles will the bird have flown before the trains meet?

If the problem is represented in terms of the bird's flight, it is necessary to calculate how far the bird goes on each trip between the trains. The problem is then very difficult. However, if the representation is focused upon the time which the bird has to fly, the problem becomes trivial. The trains must travel one hour before they meet (fifty miles at a closing speed of fifty miles per hour), and at the rate of a hundred miles per hour the bird will fly a hundred miles. The first paragraph of the problem serves mainly to distract us from the material which needs to be represented in the solution.

The format of a problem can suggest a particular representation to the subject. For example, the circle problem (Figure 33) becomes easy to solve if the second diagonal appears as part of the problem. In one experiment, subjects were asked to determine which one of four words was inappropriate (Cofer, 1954). A sample list was "skyscraper," "cathedral," "temple," and "prayer." These words could be seen as related to religion or to buildings. When the first item was "skyscraper," the building organization was dominant; when the first word was "prayer," the

religious organization dominated. This simple example illustrates the crucial importance of the initial organization. When people try to form an impression based upon lists of adjectives, the first items in the lists tend to structure their organization. Since a word (Warren, 1972) activates a whole network of associations, it is reasonable that the word "skyscraper" tends to structure the overall organization toward buildings.

Many books on problem solving emphasize that the initial representation should not be made too quickly (Polya, 1945). Instead, one is cautioned to view the problem from different directions before developing an opinion about what is asked. The tendency for early hypotheses to inhibit associations which might otherwise develop is a characteristic of thought which we have encountered before (pp. 73–76). Unfortunately, when the problem is presented quickly aloud, it is necessary to develop a representation while the problem is being presented. Careful notes and diagrams can serve to avoid too early a commitment to an initial representation.

The problem of early representation extends beyond the solution of simple puzzles. Charles Darwin, who spent a lifetime in the analysis of the phenomena discussed in *The Origin of Species,* wrote, "It occurred to me, in 1837, that something might perhaps be made out on this question by patiently accumulating and reflecting on all sorts of facts which could possibly have any bearing on it. After five years' work, I allowed myself to speculate on the subject [p. 21]."

Scientific analysis is often not so much a matter of finding hypotheses as of holding them in check (Caws, 1969). The choice of an initial representation may so structure the situation that new observations and changes of mind are difficult. Careful note-taking and full accounts of scientific experiments can often lead to a "discovery" in the sense of a reorganization of information which, when seen in a different light, has a new meaning. In 1885, a German psychologist, J. Merkel, discovered that the reaction time to a stimulus increased with the number of alternative events which might have been presented on a given trial. This fact was present in the literature for more than fifty years when, after the development of the mathematics of information theory, George Miller (1951) showed that it implied that the mind has a specific limit on the amount of stimulus information it can transmit. This same fact, when viewed in a new way, became the center of a powerful psychological theory. Our own memories play much the same role in individual thinking as the literature did in this example. They both provide a method for preserving information which can be used as raw material and worked into new points of view.

The initial representation of a problem is influenced both by what is in the problem and by what is in the problem solver. What comes to consciousness is influenced by the semantic structures to which the problem statement is referred. DeGroot (1965) studied the ability of chess

masters to determine what the next move should be after a brief exposure to a chess problem. He carefully recorded the subjects' ideas as they talked aloud. He found that the main difference between masters and less gifted players was the initial description of the problem. The masters tended to represent the problem at the very start in a way which was related to the move eventually selected as the best. In many cases the best move was the first one mentioned. Indeed, when deGroot investigated the rest of the protocols, he found that the reasoning of the masters after the initial representation did not differ from that of less gifted players. The advantage of the masters was in what first appeared in consciousness, not in their subsequent reasoning about what they should do.

Although one might push the importance of the initial representation too far, its role also appears in studies of the thought processes of artists and poets. Humphrey (1948) related that, as Beethoven composed, he pasted new versions over previous notes. After he submitted one final composition, an alert editor decided that he would trace the thoughts of the composer by looking at the successive versions. He found that when he at last uncovered the first version, it was identical to the final form. Regardless of the accuracy of this anecdote, the point reappears in experimental studies of the work of artists (Patrick, 1935, 1937). These studies suggest that the idea which is to serve as the final product tends to emerge very early as the artists think about a picture or a poem. It keeps returning in new forms and is elaborated upon at each successive occurrence. Sometimes an artist is unaware that an idea which delights him at a given time is a restatement of something proposed earlier.

The professional chess player or artist has prepared himself in a way which allows effortless retrieval of material crucial to the problem. Such preparation depends upon a long period of training and experience. Although no single method of training has shown universal superiority, it has been observed that when information is learned in the act of problem solving, it is more usable than the same information learned by rote (Anderson & Johnson, 1966; Szekely, 1950). Perhaps the best method is to provide the student with an increased understanding of the nature of thought itself, so that he might grasp the significance of the way he learns and relate it to his later experience.

Visual and Verbal Codes

In previous chapters evidence was presented concerning the importance of nonverbal associations. This emphasis has been reinforced by studies on nonverbal communication (Hall, 1959). The relationship between people in a given culture is often governed by information conveyed in glances, smiles, gestures, or accents not translated into verbal form. The cues of pleasure and displeasure introduced by facial expressions need not be translated into language to be effective.

In the study of problem solving and thinking, there has always been interest in the importance of nonverbal factors. For example, there have been many anecdotes concerning the importance of visualization in problem solving and scientific discovery (McKeller, 1957). The chemist Kekulé reported first conceiving of the structure of the benzene ring in a vivid dream in which he saw a series of linked atoms as a snake biting its tail. Many scientists have discussed the importance of transforming the facts of a scientific theory into a visual or mechanical model. The common term "seeing the answer" implies a visual analogy.

There are many difficulties with these accounts. First, there is a good deal of contradiction. Some authors have proposed that visual imagery is an important, if not necessary, condition for creativity in science (Walkup, 1965), while others have found that scientists tend to be unusually deficient in the vividness of their imagery (Galton, 1907). Remember also the case of Luria's mnemonist, who had fantastic powers of imagery, but was deficient in producing abstract representations. Secondly, anecdotes alone tell us little about how visualization is used in problem solving. What does it add to the process of problem solution? Some experimental work provides a start to answering this question.

One study (Maier, 1931) which provides evidence on the relationship of visual and verbal processes in problem solving uses the string problem. In this simple problem the subject's task is to tie together two strings which are hanging from the ceiling, but which are too far apart to be reached at the same time. There are several solutions to this problem, but the one of particular interest involves hanging a weight from one string and setting it in motion so that it can be reached from the other string. Maier studied the emergence of this solution in a group of subjects. For subjects who had not succeeded after ten minutes, he provided a hint by brushing against the string to get it moving. He found that many more of his subjects solved the problem following the hint than would be expected on the basis of the performance of a control group not given the hint.

The solutions appeared to be of two types. One group solved the problem with a mean latency of thirty seconds following the hint. The solution appeared to emerge at once for this group. They immediately tied an object to the string and began swinging it. These subjects uniformly failed to report the hint, even after extensive questioning. Another group averaged seventy seconds and appeared to grasp the solution in parts. They frequently verbalized that they were trying to find some way to get the string swinging far enough to reach. Finally, after some effort, they realized that they needed a weight. This group uniformly reported the hint. In a separate study of the same problem (Cofer, 1951), one group of subjects was taught the verbal sequence "rope-pendulum-swing" in a learning experiment which was divorced from the actual problem-solving sequence. This group showed a greater tendency to solve the problem than a group which had not learned the verbal sequence.

These results suggest two quite separate ways in which the hint can help in solving the problem. One involves a chain of verbal reasoning. Such a chain might occur to a subject if he sees the rope swinging and says to himself, "How can I get the rope to swing?" While attempting to discover those factors which might lead a rope to swing, he hits upon the idea of a weight. This chain of reasoning might also be set off by the learned associative sequence "rope-pendulum-swing." This hint would suggest to the subject a verbal association related to the action necessary to solve the problem. Solution by this method would rely upon verbal processes and would have a high probability of being reported to the experimenter after the study.

A second method of solving the problem might rely upon the association between the visual experience of a rope swinging and past visual experiences with swinging objects. A subject who sees the rope swinging might associate it with a clock-pendulum or some other visual association. He would solve the problem not by a chain of verbal associations, but by a chain of visual or motoric associations. In this case the process might not be available to verbal report, although it might well be conscious in the sense of that word as used in Chapter 6. This analysis is speculative since we have no direct way of knowing if it actually accounts for the subject's behavior. However, this kind of dual visual and verbal processing fits in well with what we found in Chapter 5, where we could infer more directly the operation of visual and verbal codes. It is worthwhile to inquire whether the analysis of separate levels of processing introduced in Chapter 5 can help us understand other phenomena in problem solving.

Functional Fixity.   Karl Duncker (1945) introduced the idea that if an object had one established use in a given situation, it was difficult to use the object in another way. Duncker studied a problem in which a cork had to be used as a wedge. In one case, the cork lay free in the center of the table. In the second case, the cork served as a stopper in a bottle of ink which was located in the center of the table. In the third case, the cork was in the ink bottle to the side of the table. When the cork lay free in the center of the table, 43 percent (three of seven) of the subjects were able to solve the problem. When it was a stopper in a bottle in the center of the table, 14 percent (one of seven) of the subjects solved the problem; and when it was a stopper in a bottle on the periphery of the table, none solved the problem. This tendency for a free object to be used in a flexible way, while an object which already had a function was not, was illustrated in a number of different experiments which Duncker performed and which have been repeated many times (Ray, 1967). Duncker called this phenomenon *functional fixity.*

One interesting aspect of this problem involves the difference between having the cork in the center of the table as opposed to on the periphery.

The subject is less likely to observe the cork when it is out of the main field of vision. Glucksburg (1964) examined a candle problem originally invented by Duncker. He seated subjects in front of a table on which were located three kitchen matches, a candle, and a small matchbox filled with thumbtacks. The problem was to affix the candle to a cardboard wall using any of the objects on the table. The problem was solved when the candle was affixed to the wall and burned properly. The correct solution involved using the tacks to fix the box to the wall, which then served as a platform for the candle.

Glucksburg observed the number of times subjects touched the box in the process of reaching for tacks or exploring the table. He found that seven of his eight subjects solved the problem immediately after having touched the box while reaching for tacks. These subjects were all in the process of tacking the candle to the wall and were repeatedly reaching to the box for more tacks. When asked when they thought of using the box, six of the seven subjects reported that the idea occurred to them when they happened to touch the box. The seventh subject could not say. The solution to the problem did not necessarily occur upon the first manual contact with the box, but it did occur in very close proximity to one manual contact with the box. Glucksburg suggests that the ability of subjects to overcome functional fixity depends upon the object being observed by them. Moving the object away from the center of the table reduces the likelihood of visual or manual contact and thus reduces the probability that the box will be observed. This fits in very well with the Duncker observation that a stopper is less used when it is on the periphery than when it is in the center of the table.

There remains a second question, however. Why is it that the cork is so much more frequently used when it is lying in the center of the table than when it is embedded as a stopper in the ink bottle? One possibility is that subjects see the cork but do not encode it as an independent item which can be used on its own. This suggests that if the subjects could get into their memory the name of the functionally fixed object, free from its particular function, they would then be free of functional fixity. That is, the block is between the visual item and its name.

Glucksburg and Weisburg (1966) studied the candle problem described previously with this idea in mind. This time the experiments were conducted with a picture of the situation rather than the actual objects. In several experiments the authors provided verbal labels for the candle, tacks, box, and/or matches, and compared the solution of the problem when these verbal labels were provided as against when no verbal labels were present. They found that the percent of subjects solving the problem was markedly greater when the box was labeled than when it was unlabeled. When the box was unlabeled and only the tacks were labeled, thus drawing the subjects' attention away from the box, a smaller number of subjects solved the problem than when the box itself was labeled. This

result confirms the view that functional fixity may prevent subjects from encoding an object by its own name. Once the word "box" is coded by the subjects, various uses of a box, such as a platform for objects, can be retrieved from memory and the problem can be solved. In very much the same way, the verbal sequence "rope-swing-pendulum" aided solution of the string problem. However, until the visual representation is separated so that the subjects give it the name "box," no such retrieval takes place and the subjects are unable to solve the problem.

There is still another way that functional fixity may operate. It may prevent a subject's getting from the name of an object to a particular use for the object. This may take place when the subject's search for the use of the object is guided along a particular direction by his immediate past experience. For example, in the pliers problem (Duncker, 1945) a board was to be made firm by two supports. The table contained, among other things, two iron joints, a wooden board, and the pliers. The two iron joints formed one support for the board and the solution of the problem was for the pliers to be utilized as the second support. In the neutral case, the pliers were simply lying upon the board. In an experimental condition, the subject had to use the pliers to free the board immediately before trying to solve the problem.

Duncker found that many more subjects were able to solve the problem using the pliers as a support when they were presented with the problem in a neutral way than in the experimental condition. In this problem the subjects in the functionally fixed condition probably were conscious of the word "pliers." Indeed, the very act of using the pliers in the standard way undoubtedly brought the visual experience into contact with the name "pliers" and their assorted usages (prying nails, etc.). Having developed this particular use of the pliers, the subjects were not able to use the pliers in a new way. Here it is unlikely that the fixity was between the visual pliers and the name "pliers," but rather between the name "pliers" and the various meanings or uses which might be made of that name. Subjects were simply led into the wrong pathway of associations by the use of the pliers to free the board. In this case the verbal label was a disadvantage.

Glucksburg and Danks (1968) studied the role of labels in fixity. They used a problem in which the subjects' task was to complete an electrical circuit. To do this they were given batteries, a bulb, and a switch, and were allowed to use any material on the table. The amount of wire supplied was insufficient to complete the circuit. Also among the materials was a screwdriver which was used to build the circuit, and which could be used to conduct electricity so as to finish the circuit. One group was not provided any verbal labels for the material, a second group was provided with the label "screwdriver," and the third group was provided with the label "screwdriver" and separate labels for the handle and the blade. The group which had separate labels for the handle and the blade

solved the problem significantly more rapidly. The name of the object, which had helped the subjects in solving the candle problem, did not facilitate performance in this problem. In order to facilitate performance it was necessary to call the subjects' attention to the blade, which had to be separated in their thinking from the usual function of the screwdriver. Once this was done, the subjects could connect the blade with conducting electricity and finish the circuit.

In another experiment in this paper, the authors showed that the use of the habitual name of a tool ("wrench") might actually reduce the probability of the subjects' using the wrench in a novel way (that is, as a conductor of electricity). It was found that significantly more subjects used the wrench to complete the problem when they were required to refer to the wrench by a nonsense name than when they referred to it by its usual name. The authors interpreted the results as suggesting that there is a rivalry between the visual perception of the ways in which a particular object can be used and the ways that are associated with the name. Once again we find that the perceptual code and the verbal code have their individual properties, and that much of our problem solving depends upon the uses to which these two codes are put.

These experiments in problem solving parallel some of the experiments discussed in Chapter 5. Mental operations may be performed upon the visual input, in relating the visual input to the name, and in relating the name to more complex associations. Functional fixity may arise based upon any of these codes. Each code becomes a possible basis for solving the problem. The names "box," "screwdriver," and "pliers" are closely associated with certain habitual uses. If these particular uses can solve the problem, a linguistic code will facilitate solution. If they cannot, the subjects might be better off using the visual information without reference to the name. Studies of functional fixity indicate that both visual and verbal codes play a role in problem solving, just as they do in the simple matching tasks. A further issue for experimental analysis is how they are coordinated and what role each plays.

Coordination of Codes.   In the study of memory some attention has been paid to the coordination of the visual and linguistic systems (Paivio, 1972), but there have been few such attempts to study the coordination of visual and verbal thought. Fortunately, however, separate groups of investigators (DeSoto, London, & Handel, 1965; Huttenlocher, 1968; Clark, 1969) have been trying to describe the solution of a type of problem in two different ways, the two ways corresponding to the distinction we have been making between mental operations on visual and on verbal codes. While the authors have tended to think of their experiments as conflicting, it may be more fruitful to view them as an opportunity to study the coordination of these codes.

The problems which have been studied are two- and three-term-series

reasoning problems. A number of examples of these problems are shown in Figure 34. It has long been known that certain wordings of these problems are more difficult than others (Hunter, 1957). For example, the problem "A is better than B and B is better than C. Who's best?" is easier than the opposite "A is worse than B and B is worse than C. Who's worst?" DeSoto et al. used this and other findings, including introspective reports of their subjects, to suggest a theory of how such problems were solved. They speculated that subjects used the verbal statements to construct a mental picture, and that they put the best thing on top and the worst on the bottom. Since, the experimenters argued, it is easier to scan from top to bottom than from bottom to top, we find solution times to be in accord with the example given above.

Huttenlocher (1968) studied such problems with children. She had some children construct piles of blocks in accordance with her instructions. She found that it was easiest for the children to have the blocks in their hands be the subject of the instructions. For example, if a child carried a red block, he was better off if told to put the red block under the car than if told to place the car above the red block. Thus, she reasoned that if subjects constructed a mental picture, they would do best if the subject of the final statement was one which they had not yet placed in the picture. This predicted that it would be easier to solve "B is better than C and A is better than B" than it would be to solve "A is better than B and B is better than C." In the first sentence A, which is not in the first

FIGURE 34 SOME TWO-TERM-SERIES PROBLEMS AND THE TIMES REQUIRED FOR THEIR SOLUTION

Mean Time to Solve Two-Term-Series Problems

Form of problem	Analysis	Form of question: Better?	Form of question: Worse?	M
I A better than B	A is good B is good	.61	.68	.64
II B worse than A	A is bad B is bad	1.00	.62	.81
I′ A not as bad as B	A is bad B is bad	1.73	1.58	1.66
II′ B not as good as A	A is good B is good	1.17	1.47	1.32

Note. Mean time is in seconds.

Adapted from Clark, H. H. Linguistic processes in deductive reasoning. *Psychological Review*, 1969, *76*, 387–404. Copyright © 1969 by the American Psychological Association. Adapted by permission.

proposition, is the subject of the second proposition, while in the second sentence B, which is already placed, is the subject of the second proposition. Huttenlocher found evidence in favor of the prediction for both children and adults.

These studies seem to support a theory of visual construction. However, Clark (1969) suggested that the data could be better handled by a theory which was concerned with the interpretation of the meaning of the propositions, rather than by one concerned with visual construction. His argument drew upon the ideas of comprehension which were introduced at the end of Chapter 5 (pp. 117–123). Clark suggested that each proposition has an underlying structure which serves as an interpretation. The basic problem is solved when the underlying interpretations produce an orderly set which allow a direct comparison. He relied upon a distinction between words like "good," "high," and "happy" (*unmarked* adjectives), which provide the positive end of scales, and those like "bad," "low," and "sad" *(marked)*, which are the negative ends. Marked adjectives, he argued, are more difficult to store and retrieve than unmarked ones. There is some evidence for this view. Moreover, Clark reasoned that it is easier to answer questions which use the same form that has been used in the proposition. Thus, if the propositions contain the word "high," the question will be easiest if it involves "highest" rather than "lowest" (principle of congruence).

These principles are applied to the analysis of the two-term problems shown in Figure 34. For example, the proposition that A is better than B is interpreted by the subject in terms of the "good" scale, with A higher than B on the scale. Any series interpreted in terms of "good" will be easier to deal with than any series interpreted in terms of "bad." For that reason Proposition I is easier than II and II′ is easier than I′. Note that DeSoto's theory would predict that I′ would be easier than II′ since I′ is solved from the top down and II′ from the bottom up. Moreover, Clark's principle of congruence better predicts the form of questions which will be easier. These predictions hold up well in the overall solution times.

The increase in difficulty between the first two rows and the second two is due to the "not" operation in the latter (see p. 113). Clark extended his analysis to three-term-series problems. Once again he found that the linguistic factors of his theory seemed to outweigh the visual factors. For example, Clark studied the following situation. Consider the use of the terms "deep" and "shallow." The term "deep" is an unmarked adjective (the "deep"-"shallow" dimension is known as the *scale of depth).* Thus, it would be expected from Clark's analysis that the term "shallow" would be more difficult to deal with than the term "deep." However, as far as a visual construction goes, subjects reported a tendency to put "shallow" on top of "deep." Thus DeSoto's prediction would be that "shallow" is easier to use. An analysis of the speed of solving problems using "deep" and "shallow" confirmed Clark's prediction.

Despite the success of many aspects of Clark's theory, it seems unlikely

that this problem can be explained entirely in linguistic terms. About half of Clark's subjects reported that they developed visual structures from the propositions. Moreover, in Clark's procedure the problem was presented visually and stress was placed on producing the solution as quickly as possible. Since it is known that visual codes are interfered with by new visual input (see Chapter 2) and that visual representations are relatively slow in being formed (see Chapter 5), these would seem to be techniques designed to minimize the use of visual codes. If reports of visual coding are taken seriously, along with the linguistic factors, these problems might be useful in learning more about the relative advantages of visual and verbal operations in problem solving. One possibility is that visual codes serve in part as storage devices to allow the subject to free as much as possible of his verbal capacity for interpretation of the propositions. If so, it is likely that the visual codes become more prominent if larger amounts of information and more than one dimension are used.

The study of the coordination of visual and verbal codes raises the question of individual differences in the efficiency with which people can use such codes. Anecdotal data certainly suggest that some people prefer to think in the linguistic mode while others prefer visual representations. There are also the "motor morons," that is, people who are terrible at performing operations which require coordinated movement, but who have no difficulty manipulating symbols. The relationship among these codes in different people is not entirely clear. There is evidence that enactive codes emerge first developmentally, with visual and linguistic operations following in that order (Bruner, Oliver, & Greenfield, 1966). All three codes are used by the normal adult (Chapter 2). Tests which are designed to measure the ability of individuals to manipulate things in each of the three codes (Guilford, 1967) suggest that the ability to use the three codes may be uncorrelated.

The analysis of individual differences in the manipulation of codes is still very incomplete, however. Neither linguistic nor visual representations necessarily dominate human thinking. Rather, we find in the solution of problems the same variety of forms of representation which have been outlined in Chapters 2, 3, and 4. Many problems can be solved by either linguistic or visual coding. Others perhaps can best be solved by a combination of codes. A problem which is difficult in linguistic form may be easy when viewed as a spatial structure. However, recoding alone cannot produce solutions if some element necessary for the solution is not available in the initial representation. In such a case, the subject must develop a search strategy for finding the needed information.

SEARCH STRATEGIES

A search strategy for solving a problem is a plan which directs the subject from the initial representation to a final goal state. The development of such a plan may come as a whole or, more likely, result from attempts to

test simpler plans. As the subject tries various approaches, he begins to understand the information he needs in order to move from his present representation to one which comes nearer to the solution of the problem. Such plans can be thought of as consisting of simpler TOTE units of the type discussed in Chapter 5. The subject formulates a subgoal which might move him closer to the solution, and then tries out various mental operations which may move him toward that goal.

Such plans are very much akin to retrieval cues (Chapter 2) or hypotheses (Chapter 4). They tell the subject where to look in memory or what to examine in the external world in order to advance toward a solution. To assemble a plan, the subject must take account of the initial representation, the likely organizing principles of his own long-term memory, and the mental operations he can perform. In some sense plans are the heart of problem solving and yet we know very little about their development. They appear to be a function of consciousness in that the subject can often report them verbally. If interrupted in the course of problem solving, he is likely to report the overall plan he is operating upon, rather than the specific operation occurring at the moment. Because of this ability, experimenters (Claparède, 1933; Duncker, 1945; Newell, Shaw, & Simon, 1958) have often found that having subjects talk aloud as they attempt to solve a problem helps the experimenter construct an account of the overall plan.

A plan, like anything else a person tries to retain, places a load upon memory. If the plan is well thought through, it might exist as a sequence in long-term memory, but the subject may still have trouble representing it in active memory. Indeed, investigators report many strategies which subjects use to overcome such difficulties. One is to use the current state as a starting place for the plan. For example, in chess (deGroot, 1965) it was found that players search through the sequence of possible moves which result from a given board position, returning frequently to the starting point as represented by the current position. In many problems the current state serves as a focus for each successive search, to be returned to when the search encounters the limits of memory. The use of plans is subject to the human tendency to deal with a relatively narrow focus at any given time. This should be kept in mind as we turn to evidence on the structure of plans.

Problem Solving

One of the fullest accounts of the development of a plan is given by Karl Duncker in his monograph *On Problem Solving* (1945). The primary problem which Duncker used was stated to the subjects as follows: "Given a human being with an inoperable stomach tumor, and rays which destroy organic tissue at sufficient intensity, by what procedure can one free him of the tumor and at the same time avoid destroying the healthy tissue which surrounds it?"

The subjects first came to an understanding of the requirement of the problem. In part this was a process of abstraction of the relevant information from the problem. First, the tumor must be eliminated, and second, no healthy tissue must be destroyed. In his analysis of one particular protocol, Duncker tried to reconstruct the search strategies of the subjects. One subject, for example, produced three possible guides (subgoals) for synthesizing information which could solve the problem. Each of these subgoals was a strategy for the search of memory for relevant solutions. First was to avoid contact between the rays and the healthy tissues. Second was to desensitize the healthy tissue. Third was to lower the intensity of the rays on the way through the healthy tissue. These three guiding tendencies then directed the development of the subject's search strategy. Figure 35 illustrates the plan employed by this subject. It can be seen, given each of the search strategies, that the subject was able to use past experience to generate a particular approach to the problem. Many of these led to blind alleys which were either dismissed by the subject himself or rejected by the experimenter.

Note that the tree diagram constructed from the protocol by Duncker is similar to the diagrams that were developed to deal with the organization of information in long-term memory. In a sense, the problem produced a new method of organizing information from various memory cells. Problem solving of this type can be seen as an elaboration of the methods by which we are continually reorganizing our long-term memory (pp. 37–40).

There is little in common between using the esophagus as a path to the tumor and displacing the tumor toward the surface except that both are means of getting at the tumor. The plan provides the dimensions along which ideas and experiences stored in long-term memory can be collected. In a real sense the plan provides the cues for retrieval from memory.

The essence of this kind of problem solving is to select items in memory which are alike in the particular way the subgoal requires. The plan becomes an executive or organizing scheme providing the key dimensions which relate possible solutions.

Innovations

The same principles of sorting on the basis of subgoals which apply in puzzle solving appear in science and, indeed, in innovations and inventions in general. For example, the mathematician Poincaré (1929) discussed the development of a mathematical proof as the result of a long period of conscious work:

> To invent, I have said, is to choose; but the word is perhaps not wholly exact. It makes one think of a purchaser before whom are displayed a large number of samples, and who examines them, one

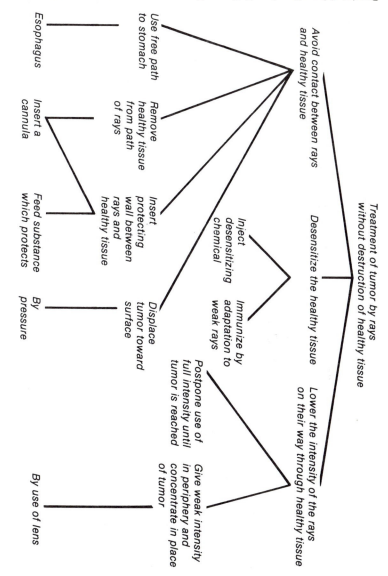

FIGURE 35   ANALYSIS OF THE PROTOCOL OF A SUBJECT WHO ATTEMPTED TO SOLVE THE X-RAY PROBLEM

after the other, to make a choice. Here the samples would be so numerous that a whole lifetime would not suffice to examine them. This is not the actual state of things. The sterile combinations do not even present themselves to the mind of the inventor. Never in the field of his consciousness do combinations appear that are not really useful, except some that he rejects, but which have to some extent the characteristics of useful combinations. All goes on as if the inventor were an examiner for the second degree who would only have to question the candidates who had passed a previous examination [pp. 386–87].

Of course the preliminary screening is not done magically; it is done by the strategy which has been set up by the conscious plan of the mathematician. The screening is successful because he has stored information during his lifetime in a way which is appropriate to the screening rules he develops in solving problems.

Barnett (1953), an anthropologist, attempted to formulate the general principles involved in creative innovation. His view was that a creation involves the synthesis of ideas from separate systems. Barnett's main point was that innovation demands that there be a representation which stands as a prototype. New information is combined with the prototype because the new input is seen to be identical to the prototype with respect to some relation or function. Thus, he argued, innovations are very similar to concepts in that two representations which actually differ are treated as identical. In some cases the resulting combination serves as a creative innovation, an invention, a new religion, philosophy, or scientific theory. This view regards analogy as the fundamental basis of innovation.

Guiding Search

There is plenty of evidence that a particular strategy, once chosen, may continue to direct search in ways which are not beneficial. An illustration of this is the water-jar problem (Luchins, 1942), in which subjects are told to obtain particular quantities of water by using three water jars. The first five problems can all be solved by the same equation $(X = B - A - 2C)$; that is, take bottle B, fill bottle A once, fill bottle C twice, and there will then remain in bottle B the proper amount. Problem 6, however, may be solved by a much simpler method; namely, spill from bottle A into bottle C and there will remain in bottle A the correct amount. In a number of studies Luchins showed that subjects who had been trained in the first five problems tended to solve the sixth problem by the same equation rather than by the simpler method. The application of the same formula saved the subject from having to think through the problem on each occasion. He could invest less processing capacity and still continue to

perform the task. A similar result has been obtained with training on a fixed rule for unscrambling letters in anagrams (Rees & Israel, 1935).

This tendency to repeat a solution once obtained has been called *Einstellung* (or *set*). It is like functional fixity in that a given direction is repeated. However, there may also be differences. In one functional-fixity problem (Adamson & Taylor, 1954), the likelihood of subjects' using either a switch or a relay as a paperweight was compared. It was found that if subjects had just used one of them to complete an electrical circuit, they tended to select the other item as the weight. This tendency declined markedly over time, as shown in Figure 36 (top panel). Sometime during the first day, the subjects showed a virtually complete loss of the tendency to select the item which they had not used previously. On the other hand, studies of the water-jar problem (Tresselt & Leeds, 1953) as a function of the delay between the inducing problems and the critical-test problem have shown no decline for delays as long as seven days.

It is not completely clear what the differences are between set induced by problem solving and functional fixity. Duncker's monograph suggests an important possibility. Duncker found that the likelihood of finding functional fixity depended on whether the fixity was introduced within the same setting as the problem to be solved. If an object was used in the same setting, it was very likely to prevent the subject from seeing a new solution, but if it was introduced in a different situation, there was very little reduction of the probability of a successful solution. Perhaps functional fixity and Einstellung are essentially similar phenomena and the differences in the effect of delay are due to the degree that the problem solution is associated with the context.

In the studies of Adamson and Taylor, the subjects participated in one experimental situation, and their susceptibility to the influence of that context was determined in a different problem-solving situation. When the period between the context and the solution was increased, it is likely that the problem-solving situation did not reinstate in active memory the old experience with the electric circuit. Therefore, the fixity was lost over time. However, in the Einstellung problem, the set was in exactly the same situation which had been used for the test. When the subjects were brought back to the laboratory and given the problem-solving situation with the water jars, this must have reinstated the same strategy which had been learned previously. Thus the period of time between the context and the solution made little difference in the influence of the context. If this explanation is correct, the two phenomena may be similar despite the reported difference in persistence.

Both functional fixity and Einstellung may be seen as experimental demonstrations of the important effect recently activated material has upon performance. The tendency of thought to follow paths similar to ones which have recently been activated is an important and pervasive one.

FIGURE 36   CHANGES OVER TIME IN THE TENDENCY TO AVOID A FUNCTIONALLY FIXED ITEM (a) AND TO SELECT THE PREVIOUSLY SET SOLUTION TO THE WATER-JAR PROBLEM (b)

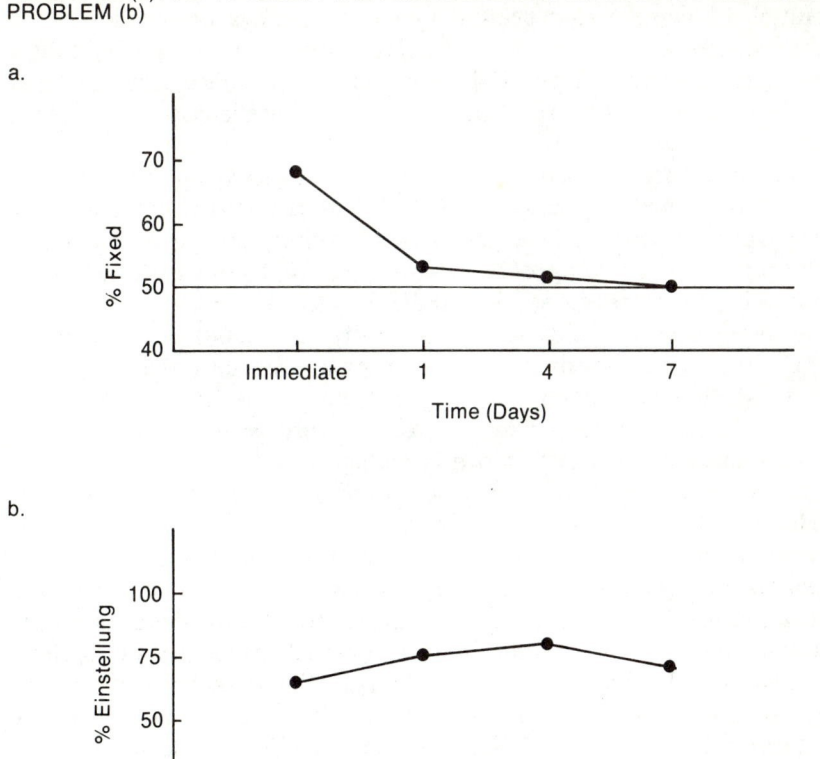

a. Adapted from Adamson, R. E., and Taylor, D. W. Functional fixedness as related to elapsed time and to set. *Journal of Experimental Psychology,* 1954, *47,* 122–126. Copyright © 1954 by the American Psychological Association. Adapted by permission. b. Redrawn from Tresselt, M. E., and Leeds, D. S. The Einstellung effect in immediate and delayed problem-solving. *Journal of General Psychology,* 1953, *49,* 87–95.

Redirecting Search

The experiments in set indicate that we often continue a given problem-solving method in a very rigid manner. Changing to a new representation or utilizing a new set of mental operations is very difficult, which is one reason why thinking is hard work. Once a particular direction has been taken in structuring a problem, it is difficult to rid

oneself of it and start fresh. Why should this be? Just about all of the principles which have been discussed in this book suggest that there are difficulties in reorganizing search. Once material is organized into a memory structure, it is hard to reconstruct the problem representation because each time one returns to the problem the same factors which have led to the original construction will be present. These factors resist a fresh approach.

Most books concerned with advice on how to think and solve problems effectively concentrate upon redirecting the approach to a problem. They suggest ways which will keep the person working on the problem and which will force him to approach it from different points of view. One method which was developed to aid original thinking involved training people to produce novel associations (Maltzman, 1960). Subjects were required to produce six different and atypical associations to the same word. In some experiments, subjects so trained showed increased originality on assessment tests which involved word associations or something similar, such as a test on which subjects had to produce as many uses for an item as possible and were scored for novel uses. Some other experiments have not shown benefits from originality training. This technique arises out of a theoretical orientation which emphasizes the importance of associations, but which does not give much consideration to the relationships between associations or to mental operations. It is somewhat questionable whether fluency in verbal associations is by itself very important for the solving of problems or the attainment of creative ideas. For this reason it is doubtful that this kind of originality training would transfer very far beyond assessment tests which are quite similar to the training situation.

A more elaborate proposal (DeBono, 1968) suggested the importance of what the author called *lateral thinking.* This technique, which was developed into a delightful five-day course in thinking, encouraged the students to look at a problem from many angles and not to be stuck with a rigid or single-minded view. In order to break away from the conventional way of looking at a problem, the students were encouraged to attempt exercises which would be seen differently when viewed from various standpoints. An analogy was made between thinking and viewing ambiguous figures from different perspectives.

Another popular and well-conceived book, *How to Solve It* (Polya, 1945), is designed primarily for mathematical problem solving. It advocates the use of general *plans* that might be helpful in directing a person to solutions in a variety of problems. Polya relates his plans to four stages of problem solving, which include: understanding the problem, devising a plan, carrying out the plan, and looking back. For each stage, certain general plans are provided to help the student avoid becoming stuck in a single view and continue to develop alternative conceptions of the problem. The plans include things like trying to work backward from the

goal, trying to formulate similar problems which have elements in common with the present problem, attempting to recode the problem in terms of a diagram, and many others. The main point, as with the other methods of aiding thinking, is to keep at the problem and to use every method possible to cut loose from too rigid an approach. Polya is particularly helpful in stressing the importance of storing past solutions as the best guides to developing general methods for solving new problems. He sees each problem solved as a basis for new solutions.

Another method which has been used to aid thinking of various sorts is the use of lists of action words which can be inserted into the problem to break old habits and produce new organizations (Crovitz, 1970). This method has been applied to many of the puzzles developed by Duncker. The use of small groups to foster original thinking has been advocated in the method called *brainstorming.* In this procedure the flow of ideas is supposedly enhanced by withholding all criticism in the early stage so that people will feel free to propose ideas which may be far off the subject. Another method, *synetics,* places emphasis on combining ideas by use of different types of analogy.

There have been a few attempts to evaluate or compare these methods. Since they are not mutually exclusive, but rather supplement each other and tend to be appropriate to different kinds of problems, perhaps there is little reason to compare them.

One effort to test a general method for improving problem solving has involved training subjects in criticizing or evaluating their own solutions and those of other people (Hyman, 1961). Separate groups first tried to solve a difficult practical problem, such as developing methods to improve tourism in the U.S. or developing a system which would automatically recognize boxes moving along a conveyor belt. After trying to solve the problem, different groups were required to criticize or constructively evaluate solutions. The evaluations did appear to have some effects on solutions to other problems of similar complexity but different content. Those who constructively evaluated the solutions of others and critically evaluated their own solutions seemed to improve the most. This finding confirms an idea which Hyman stressed and which seems to emerge from almost all work on thinking—that is, the overwhelming importance of proper analysis, sorting, and storage of information at the time it is learned so that it can be retrieved in a way which will allow it to be used in future problem solving.

INCUBATION

Psychologists have frequently distinguished between two different kinds of thinking (Neisser, 1967). The distinction has many names: *rational* vs. *intuitive, constrained* vs. *creative, logical* vs. *prelogical, primary* vs. *secondary,* and *spectator* vs. *participant.* One dimension of this distinc-

tion depends upon whether or not the process requires conscious attention. As we have seen, the setting up of a search plan appears to be a conscious effort. Subjects can speak aloud about it and give at least a rudimentary account of the factors which led them to take one path rather than another. However, many people who have written about thinking (Poincaré, 1929; Koestler, 1964) have proposed a process which does not require attention. Perhaps the most widely quoted account of this process is contained in the writing of Poincaré, who reported the events leading to one of his important discoveries:

> Then I turned my attention to the study of some arithmetical questions apparently without much success and without a suspicion of any connection with my preceding researches. Disgusted with my failure, I went to spend a few days at the seaside, and thought of something else. One morning, walking on the bluff, the idea came to me, with just the same characteristics of brevity, suddenness and immediate certainty, that the arithmetic transformations of indeterminate ternary quadratic forms were identical with those of non-Euclidean geometry [p. 388].

In commenting upon this kind of sudden importation into consciousness of a problem solution, Poincaré said:

> It never happens that the unconscious work gives us the result of a somewhat long calculation *all made,* where we have only to apply fixed rules. We might think the wholly automatic subliminal self particularly apt for this sort of work, which is in a way exclusively mechanical. It seems that thinking in the evening upon the factors of a multiplication we might hope to find the product ready made upon our awakening, or again that an algebraic calculation, for example a verification, would be made unconsciously. Nothing of the sort, as observation proves. All one may hope from these inspirations, fruits of unconscious work, is a point of departure for such calculations. As for the calculations themselves, they must be made in the second period of conscious work, that which follows the inspiration, that in which one verifies the results of this inspiration and deduces their consequences. The rules of these calculations are strict and complicated. They require discipline, attention, will, and therefore consciousness [p. 394].

The phenomenon reported by Poincaré has been confirmed by introspective reports from many scientists, mathematicians, and artists (Koestler, 1964). These reports usually emphasize a period of intense concentration on a problem, followed by a decision to put the problem aside. After a time the solution appears suddenly, often when the subject

is either asleep or engaged in idle thought. Some people can report a stimulus event which produced the solution; others are unable to do so or deny that any external stimulus was involved. Often the thinker reports a feeling of great certainty concerning the correctness of the solution or appropriateness of the idea, but, like Poincaré, may suggest that full development of it required a period of further conscious effort.

It is difficult to evaluate these reports. We do not know whether they describe a general or frequent aspect of thought, or whether they are quite rare, perhaps accidental, events which simply are very striking. Moreover, there are many possible mechanisms which could lead to improved problem solving as a consequence of a period of rest following intense concentration. The most interesting question is what role, if any, should be assigned to unconscious mental operations in the occurrence of this phenomenon? It should be no surprise, after reading the material in earlier chapters, that unconscious mental operations are possible and that they can be important in problem solving. The crux of the issue is whether they are capable of producing solutions which are more creative than can be produced by conscious operations, and whether this implies that unconscious operations are more complicated. Before examining some of the possible mechanisms, it will be useful to look at the few experimental studies which have tried to index the occurrence of incubation.

Incubation refers to an increase in the likelihood of successfully solving a problem that results from placing a delay between the period of intense work which initiates the problem solution and another period of conscious effort which finalizes the solution. What grounds are there for accepting incubation as a genuine empirical phenomenon? In addition to the introspective accounts of scientists, Patrick (1935, 1957) observed a number of creative artists and poets who talked aloud about the content of the material which they were creating. She took as an indication of incubation an idea which occurred early in the subject's report, reoccurred while the subject talked of other things, and finally appeared as the chief topic of the picture or poem the subject was creating. The percent of subjects who showed such evidence of incubation was between 80 and 90. This phenomenon occurred both with artists and with a control group of nonartistic people who were attempting to produce drawings. Thus, Patrick confirmed the introspective accounts of incubation in the sense that ideas did seem to keep coming back in various forms, separated by periods during which other ideas were prominent in the subjects' thoughts. Patrick's observations, however, did not provide any evidence that unconscious work was involved.

One of the few experimental studies on incubation was by Fulgosi and Guilford (1968). The subjects' task was to answer questions such as: "What would be the results if someone suddenly lost the ability to read and write?" or "What could be the results if none of us needed food anymore in order to live?" The subjects were directed to produce as many

answers to these questions as possible. The number and quality of the subjects' answers were scored. During incubation or rest intervals, the subjects were given a distracting task of working on numerical series. This presumably kept them from consciously considering new answers. It was demonstrated that the group with ten minutes of incubation yielded very little gain in production over the group with no rest interval, but the twenty-minute interval yielded a significant gain. In a similar study (Murray & Denny, 1969), subjects were given a complex problem-solving task to do. Half were interrupted after five minutes and half worked continually. The incubation period was five minutes long. The authors found that the incubation period was helpful for the subjects who were poorest in performance and harmful for those who were best.

The most convincing experimental evidence for the incubation concept was in a study of problem solving by Silveira (1971). The problem was as follows:

> A man had 4 chains, each 3 links long. He wanted to join the 4 chains into a single closed chain. Having a link opened cost 2¢ and having a link closed cost 3¢. The man had his chains joined into a closed chain for 15¢. How did he do it?

The problem required subjects to avoid the obvious solution of joining the chains end to end and instead take one chain completely apart and use its links to join the remaining three chains. The problem was surprisingly difficult. Of a control group allowed to work continuously for about one-half hour on the problem, only about half solved the problem. Four separate experimental groups were interrupted after either a brief time or a long time on the problem and allowed either a half-hour or four-hour break before resuming the problem. Silveira found that when interruption followed a longer period of effort, the probability of solving was dramatically increased over the control group's performance for both the short-interruption (.64) and long-interruption (.85) groups.

The subjects were all required to talk aloud as they solved the problem. This allowed Silveira to see how the interruption helped increase the number of solvers. She found that subjects did not return from the interruption with complete solutions in mind. They seemed to resume work pretty much as they had left off. This made the effect rather different from the spontaneous solution to which Poincaré referred. It also suggested that the subjects were honest in reporting that they did not work on the problem consciously during the delay. For the brief-interruption group, conscious effort on the problem during the delay had been partly controlled by requiring them to read a novel.

Silveira believed that the improvement could best be described in terms of the delay's increasing both the likelihood and the persistence of the subjects in following out the most promising direction. Subjects who hit

upon the right direction (disassembling links rather than joining them directly) after a long period of uninterrupted work tended not to work out the full implications of that direction (disassemble one whole chain), while the rested subjects did tend to do so.

The results were generally in agreement with a kind of fatigue hypothesis, according to which uninterrupted subjects were prevented from taking full advantage of their learning because of a lack of energy. However, the finding that the solution rate of subjects who returned to the experiment after a rest was higher than that of subjects during the initial stage of work suggested that the delay had a positive aspect, rather than merely allowing the reduction of fatigue.

There are a number of ways in which incubation could occur. First, it could be solely a matter of rest. It may well be that a subject who has been working on a problem is tired and is unable to continue a high level of productive activity for a long period of time. A rest gives a break and reduces fatigue. The earliest account of incubation (Helmholtz, as cited by Woodworth & Schlosberg, 1954) used this explanation. Silveira's results extended the analysis of how fatigue might reduce problem-solving performance. However, a fatigue theory taken alone does not account for Poincaré's observation or for the positive aspects of Silveira's findings.

A similar idea is that subjects forget inappropriate sets and directions formed at the time of development of the original search strategy (Woodworth & Schlosberg, 1954). The importance of this idea was seen in the discussion of the decay of functional fixity (see p. 166). Poincaré also considered this possibility as one aspect of his observation. It is easy to imagine that this simple mechanism accounts for most of the experimental evidence cited in the last section. It is more difficult to see how it could account for the occurrence of sudden insights which give the conviction of certitude, such as those reported by many scientists, mathematicians, and artists.

A third possibility is that rest provides the occasion for additional practice. Most introspective reports of incubation have claimed that the incubation period did not involve any active problem solving or thinking about the problem. However, it is difficult to know whether to fully trust such introspective accounts. It may well be that the material is consciously being analyzed (in the sense of Chapter 6), but the subject is unable to report that analysis at a later time. This particular problem is outlined in the following quotation from a chemist (cited by Woodworth & Schlosberg, 1954):

> I remember one morning I took my bath, shaved, took another bath, and in reaching out for a dry towel suddenly became aware that this was my second bath and that my mind had been deeply concentrated on a problem for half an hour. . . . I gave this as an example . . . because it gives a clear picture of what is going on.

> The mind is fresh; it is so full of the problem that there is no need to
> refer to anything and it is in deep concentration. . . . With a rested
> mind soaked full of data on a problem, and in deep concentration, I
> would expect a man to solve a problem if he could ever solve it
> [p. 839].

Thus, though we may attend at a given moment in time, we may forget
this attention after the solution of the problem. It is quite possible that the
incubation is due in part to our thinking about the problem but not
remembering that we had been working on it. The longer the period of
time for incubation, the greater the chance for this opportunity to take
place.

A closely related theory attributes the effectiveness of rest to the chance
occurrence of an external event which completes the solution. The
external event might retrieve the incomplete solution and provide the
missing association to complete it, leaving the subject aware only of the
solution and not of the event. Indeed, in discussing the Maier string
problem we found that many subjects who appeared to use the hint were
unable to report that there was a hint (see pp. 154–155).

Another possible mechanism was suggested by Poincaré, but was most
completely outlined by Campbell (1960). Campbell felt that unconscious
processes could result in random fusion of memory representations. He
called this process *blind variation.* There is a certain probability of
representations from different memory cells making contact with each
other and producing a combination which may on some occasions yield a
successful result. This notion is analogous to the Darwinian theory of
evolution in the sense that the mutations which produce genetic variation
are thought to be blind and undirected. The selective mechanism in
evolution is provided by the adaptability of the genetic variation to
survival in the world. Campbell argued that the selective factor in thought
was provided by a tendency to retain those solutions which were most
appropriate or best fit the problem, while forgetting or not retaining
others. Campbell did not provide much insight into the actual workings of
his mechanism. For example, how were the useful combinations retained? Did this require conscious rehearsal, and if so, how were the
mechanisms of consciousness summoned? However, Campbell's notion
is compatible with many of the known facts concerning incubation.

Incubation is also consistent with another view of unconscious processing. In Chapter 6 we argued that search of long-term memory could, under
some circumstances, take place without causing interference with another
task. For example, determining the name of a letter did not interfere with
processing an auditory stimulus. Suppose that conscious work laid down
a kind of retrieval plan which could then be carried out without
interfering with our ongoing activities. Provided that the retrieval plan
was explicit enough, it might eventuate in obtaining information which

would be imported into operational memory. Since memory cells are themselves organized structures, there is no reason to require that such a search be accidental or blind. After all, the search of memory for information which allows us to recognize a letter or face is organized sufficiently so that there is a high degree of consistency in the time relations, yet it does not require attention. Using the same principle, it might be possible that such searches go on even after the subject has laid aside conscious consideration of his plan. The importance of a period of planning in order for the unconscious to produce a solution might argue for such a mechanism as against a completely blind or accidental retrieval.

The empirical study of incubation has been far too primitive so far to allow us to determine which of these mechanisms are operative. Taken as a whole, these mechanisms would seem to account for the various introspective reports without requiring that unconscious operations have properties beyond those already established by experimentation discussed in earlier chapters. Perhaps if we come to understand the process of search and mental operations discussed in Chapter 5, we will have a more complete basis for explaining incubation.

TERMINATING PROBLEMS

When is a problem solved? In laboratory situations it is possible to specify an ideal solution. For example, most puzzles and mathematical and logical problems have only one solution. Many problems with which people actually deal have no optimal solutions or have solutions that are unknown. Even in a game such as chess, the optimal move at any point is impossible to calculate. It should not be surprising that people do not usually attempt an optimal solution, even in situations in which it can be computed. One writer (Simon, 1969) has termed human problem solving *satisficing,* that is, finding solutions short of optimality which will be good enough or acceptable.

We already know some of the constraints which the limitations of human capacity are likely to put upon obtaining solutions. People tend to avoid complex calculations in favor of the use of simpler heuristics, each of which requires them to deal with only a small part of the data. Thus, except in the case of highly skilled people, the problem goal is generally reached through a long series of subgoals, each of which requires only relatively easy operations. However, the limitations of operational memory make it difficult to deal with a long series of interrelated steps. People often seek to develop solutions for relatively simple aspects of a problem, returning each time to a reference position so they can keep their place. The formulation and testing of hypotheses help perform this function. Memory constraints become very severe in complex problems like architectural design. This has led to computer programs which attempt to aid

the architect in cutting the requirements into a manageable number of relatively independent subgoals (Alexander, 1964).

There have been two areas of research dealing directly with what people consider constitutes a satisfactory solution. One of these deals with the relationship between the amount of information a subject has collected and his decision that he has completed the solution. The second area deals with the question of the form of representation of the problem solution which is deemed satisfactory. The former area has given rise to research on the factors which govern the accumulation of information. The second area has provided mostly theoretical speculations concerning the kind of representation which gives a subject a feeling of completion.

Accumulating Evidence

Many problems can be viewed as involving the collection and evaluation of evidence. Indeed, one prominent theorist of thinking (Bartlett, 1958) defines thought as the process of filling gaps in evidence. Suppose you were given a simple problem of deciding whether or not to carry an umbrella on a particular day. There would be many possible cues which might be used in making such a decision. If it were raining, that alone might settle the issue. If it were not raining, you would need to decide how likely it was to rain. What kinds of evidence might be employed? You might use the weather report, the amount of rain during the last days, the month, the condition of the wind, a barometer reading, etc. No one of these cues would provide sufficient evidence for a decision, but after considering some of them you might decide that you should or should not carry the umbrella.

This is a simple example of the general method of induction. Induction is appropriate when there are a number of hypotheses (it will rain or it won't rain) and it is necessary to decide which hypothesis is most likely. Some of the concept problems discussed earlier are also examples of induction (see pp. 69–74). Note that in the case of the umbrella there is no way to be certain which hypothesis is correct since no cue is completely reliable. The best one can do is become more and more certain of the correct hypothesis.

To study induction, psychologists (e.g., Edwards, 1962) have set up simple situations in which subjects are given a few alternative hypotheses, each of which specifies the likelihood of a number of different events. The subjects are then exposed to a series of events and have to determine which hypothesis is true. One interesting aspect of this kind of problem is that it is possible for the experimenter to calculate the exact probability that each hypothesis is true, given each event.

A few general facts have emerged from such studies (Edwards, 1962; Slovic & Lichtenstein, 1971). One is that people do not behave in an

optimal or even a completely consistent way. If an event occurs which strongly indicates one hypothesis, they tend to weigh it somewhat less than they should, while if an event occurs which weakly indicates one hypothesis, they tend to weigh it too heavily. Moreover, people tend to be willing to accept less convincing evidence as final, the more evidence they have been given. They seem to weigh evidence more strongly if it comes in slowly, while great masses of evidence introduced quickly may have relatively less impact. Moreover, evidence introduced early will have a greater impact than evidence introduced later (Peterson & DuCharme, 1967). This last finding is yet another example of the effectiveness of the earliest information in determining judgments.

These findings suggest that what is a "satisfactory" solution is heavily influenced by how it was produced. The solution is not independent of the process which produced it. In one sense this is irrational. In the experiments, the current probability summarizes the likelihood that a given hypothesis is true, regardless of the history of how that probability came about. But in a more general sense, people are always faced with a limited range of time, attention, and memory. In the face of such limitations, it may be sensible to consider a problem as solved on the basis of weak evidence if better evidence requires patience or memory beyond one's capacity or if repeated effort has not yielded more convincing evidence.

People probably differ in how much evidence they require in order to be satisfied. It has been proposed that the tendency to come to conclusions based on only a slight amount of evidence is a good measure of intuitive thinking (Westcott, 1968). The idea is that the intuitive thinker will tend to leap quickly to a conclusion from very fragmentary evidence. However, there is no strong evidence favoring the existence of a stable trait of intuitive thinking which is general across differing types of problems.

Insight

One way to judge the quality of a solution is to see how well it meets the goals set forth by the problem. There is, however, another dimension to the study of problem solutions. Psychologists have been interested in the degree to which a solution produces a mental reorganization which is satisfying to the problem solver. This subjective aspect of the quality of problem solutions has been called *insight.*

The famous Gestalt psychologist Köhler (1969) points out that insight must involve more than merely finding a solution to the problem. Consider the sets of numbers shown in Figure 37. One can see that the third list is the set of odd numbers and presumably fill in the blanks almost immediately. But such a solution might not appear very satisfactory to an individual who is interested in why subtracting each successive square produces the set of odd numbers. Only when he finds a general

FIGURE 37   SUBTRACTING EACH SUCCESSIVE PERFECT SQUARE FROM THE NEXT HIGHER ONE PRODUCES THE SET OF ODD DIGITS

1	4	9	16	25	36	49	64
0	1	4	9	16	25	36	49

1	3	5	7	9

This problem is used by Köhler to illustrate the importance of insight in problem solving. Adapted from Köhler, W. *The task of Gestalt psychology.* Princeton, N.J.: Princeton University Press, 1969. Copyright © 1969 by Princeton University Press. Adapted by permission of Princeton University Press.

reason which fits into his representation of mathematics will the solution really seem satisfactory.

The criteria for insight are both subjective and objective. Köhler stresses the importance of the feeling of comprehension or understanding which accompanies insight. This is sometimes called the "Eureka" experience, and involves a feeling of satisfaction that the problem is understood completely. One measure of insight is an ability to transfer the learning on a problem to new situations (Wertheimer, 1945). An insightful solution is supposed to produce the kind of memorial structure which can be brought to bear on other problems (Szekely, 1950).

What are the characteristics which lead a solution to produce insight? In the terms that have been developed in this book, one suggestion seems likely. Insight might depend upon the problem solution's ability to be represented in operational memory at one time. Thus, when a long mathematical proof has been made, the subject may not feel that he understands it until he is able to condense the steps in such a way that they are present at least implicitly in a representation that he can grasp all at once. Many scientists have stressed the importance of visualizations or working models of abstract equations as means of giving insight. These allow us to "see" the solution as an image or as something simultaneously present. The development of such simultaneous structures may be of more than aesthetic use, since it may be their simplicity that allows them to serve as parts of new structures.

SUMMARY

Thought is the process of achieving new representations through the performance of mental operations. When the operations are systematic

and under the general guidance of a conscious plan, the thought is organized. When the operations are unrelated and chosen without reference to a plan, the thought is idle and similar to daydreaming. While aspects of either kind of thought may be conscious, it is only the former which gives the subjective feeling of great effort and difficulty. It is this kind of thought which is prominent in problem solving.

The variety of problems which people may be called upon to solve is enormous. In most kinds of problem solving the crucial elements are the initial representation of the problem and the systematic use of mental operations under the influence of a plan. The kinds of plans which can be formulated and executed are subject to the limitations of consciousness and memory, which have been discussed previously. Plans often involve an updated record which can summarize the current state, and from which mental operations can be performed. In order to overcome the limitations of memory, people tend to return frequently to the starting position. In games like chess the board position serves as a permanent record of the current state, while in other problems people must attempt to retain or develop an artificial record of the current state.

The execution of the search phase of the mental operations may be effortless and unconscious. This characteristic gives rise to reports of incubation, or the solution of the problem during a period of rest. Incubation could be an example of the human capacity for effortless retrieval under special circumstances.

The termination of a problem is heavily influenced by the sequence of experiences which people have had in reaching the current state. The end state may be considered unsatisfactory after a brief try, but satisfactory after a long effort. In many cases a satisfactory solution involves more than a correct answer, but also a representation which allows the answer to fit within the limits of operational memory.

References

Aaron, R. I. *The theory of universals.* Oxford: Clarendon Press, 1952.

Aaronson, D. Temporal factors in perception and short-term memory. *Psychological Bulletin,* 1967, *67,* 130–144.

Adams, J. A. *Human memory.* New York: McGraw-Hill Book Co., 1967.

Adams, J. A., and Dijkstra, S. Short-term memory for motor responses. *Journal of Experimental Psychology,* 1966, *71,* 314–318.

Adamson, R. E., and Taylor, D. W. Functional fixedness as related to elapsed time and to set. *Journal of Experimental Psychology,* 1954, *47,* 122–126.

Alexander, C. *Notes on the synthesis of form.* Cambridge: Harvard University Press, 1964.

Alexander, C., and Carey, S. Subsymmetries. *Perception and Psychophysics,* 1968, *4,* 73–77.

Allport, D. A., Antonis, B., and Reynolds, P. On the division of attention. *Quarterly Journal of Experimental Psychology,* 1972, *24,* 225–235.

Anderson, B., and Johnson, W. Two methods of presenting information and their effects on problem solving. *Perceptual and Motor Skills,* 1966, *23,* 851–856.

Anderson, N. H. Primacy effects in personality impression formation using a generalized order effect paradigm. *Journal of Personality and Social Psychology,* 1965, *2,* 1–9.

Anderson, N. H. Information integration: A brief survey. Technical Report No. 24, Center for Human Information Processing, University of California, San Diego, 1972.

Anderson, N. H., and Jacobson, A. Effect of stimulus inconsistency and discounting instructions in personality impression formation. *Journal of Personality and Social Psychology,* 1965, *2,* 531–539.

Anisfeld, M., and Knapp, M. Association, synonymity, and directionality in false recognition. *Journal of Experimental Psychology,* 1968, *77,* 171–179.

Antrobus, J. S. (Ed.) *Cognition and affect.* Boston: Little, Brown and Co., 1970.

Antrobus, J. S., Singer, J. L., Goldstein, S., and Fortgang, M. Mind-wandering and cognitive structure. *Transactions of the New York Academy of Sciences,* 1970, *32,* 242–252.

Atkinson, R. C., and Joula, J. F. Factors influencing speed and accuracy of work recognition. In S. Kornblum (Ed.), *Attention and performance.* Vol. IV. New York: Academic Press, Inc., 1973.

Attneave, F. Transfer of experience with a class-schema to identification-learning of patterns and shapes. *Journal of Experimental Psychology,* 1957, *54,* 81–88.

Atwood, G. E. An experimental study of visual imagination and memory. *Cognitive Psychology,* 1971, *2,* 290–299.

Averbach, E. The span of apprehension as a function of exposure duration. *Journal of Verbal Learning and Verbal Behavior,* 1963, *2,* 60–64.

Baddeley, A. D., Scott, D., Drynan, R., and Smith, J. C. Short-term memory and the limited capacity hypothesis. *British Journal of Psychology,* 1969, *60,* 51–55.

Bahrick, H. P., and Boucher, B. Retention of visual and verbal codes of the same stimuli. *Journal of Experimental Psychology,* 1968, *78,* 417–422.

Barnett, H. G. *Innovation: The basis of cultural change.* New York: McGraw-Hill Book Co., 1953.

Bartlett, Sir F. C. *Remembering; A study in experimental and social psychology.* Cambridge, England: The University Press, 1932.

Bartlett, Sir F. C. *Thinking; An experimental and social study.* London: Allen & Unwin Ltd., 1958.

Baum, M. H. Simple concept learning as a function of intralist generalization. *Journal of Experimental Psychology,* 1954, *47,* 89–94.

Beare, J. I. *Greek theories of elementary cognition from Alcmaeon to Aristotle.* Oxford: Clarendon Press, 1906.

Beller, H. K. Parallel and serial stages in matching. *Journal of Experimental Psychology,* 1970, *84,* 213–219.

Berkeley, G. A treatise concerning the principles of human knowledge. In G. Sampson (Ed.), *The works of George Berkeley, D.D.* Vol. 1. London: G. Bell & Sons, Ltd., 1897.

Bertelson, P. Central intermittency twenty years later. *Quarterly Journal of Experimental Psychology,* 1966, *18,* 153–163.

Bertelson, P. The time course of preparation. *Quarterly Journal of Experimental Psychology,* 1967, *19,* 272–279.

Boole, G. *The laws of thought.* LaSalle, Ill.: Open Court Publishing Co., 1916.

Boring, E. G. *A history of experimental psychology.* (2nd ed.) New York: Appleton-Century-Crofts, 1950.

Bourne, L. E. *Human conceptual behavior.* Boston: Allyn & Bacon, Inc., 1966.

Bourne, L. E., Jr., Ekstrand, B. R., and Dominowski, R. L. *The psychology of thinking.* Englewood Cliffs, N.J.: Prentice-Hall, Inc., 1971.

Bouthilet, L. The measurement of intuitive thinking. Unpublished doctoral dissertation, University of Chicago, 1948.

Bower, G. Analysis of a mnemonic device. *American Scientist,* 1970, *58,* 496–510.

Bower, G., and Trabasso, T. Reversals prior to solution in concept identification. *Journal of Experimental Psychology,* 1963, *66,* 409–418.

Brand, J. Classification without identification in visual search. *The Quarterly Journal of Experimental Psychology,* 1971, *23,* 178–186.

Bransford, J. D., and Franks, J. J. Abstraction of linguistic ideas. *Cognitive Psychology,* 1971, *2,* 331–350.

Bregman, A. S., and Charness, N. "Schema plus transformations" in visual pattern recognition. Paper presented at Eastern Psychological Association, Atlantic City, New Jersey, April 1970.

Broadbent, D. E. *Perception and communication.* Elmsford, N.Y.: Pergamon Press, Inc., 1958.

Broadbent, D. E. *Decision and stress.* New York: Academic Press, Inc., 1971.

Broadbent, D. E., and Gregory, M. On the recall of stimuli presented alternately to two sense organs. *Quarterly Journal of Experimental Psychology,* 1961, *13,* 103–109.

Brooks, L. R. Spatial and verbal components of the act of recall. *Canadian Journal of Psychology,* 1968, *22,* 349–368.

Brown, I. D., and Poulton, E. C. Measuring the spare "mental capacity" of car drivers by a subsidiary task. *Ergonomics,* 1961, *4,* 35–40.

Brown, R., and McNeill, D. The "tip of the tongue" phenomenon. *Journal of Verbal Learning and Verbal Behavior,* 1966, *5,* 325–337.

Bruner, J. S. *Processes of cognitive growth: Infancy.* Worcester, Mass.: Clark University Press, 1968.

Bruner, J. S., Goodnow, J. J., and Austin, G. A. *A study of thinking.* New York: John Wiley & Sons, Inc., 1956.

Bruner, J. S., Oliver, R. R., Greenfield, P. M., et al. *Studies in cognitive growth.* New York: John Wiley & Sons, Inc., 1966.

Bruner, J. S., and Potter, M. C. Interference in visual recognition. *Science,* 1964, *144,* 424–425.

Bryden, M. P. Laterality effects in dichotic listening relations with handedness and reading ability in children. *Neuropsychologica,* 1970, *8,* 443–450.

Bugelski, B. R. Presentation time, total time and mediation in paired-associate learning. *Journal of Experimental Psychology,* 1962, *63,* 409–412.

Bugelski, B. R., Kidd, E., and Segmen, J. Image as a mediator in one-trial paired-associate learning. *Journal of Experimental Psychology,* 1968, *76,* 69–73.

Buggie, S. E. Stimulus preprocessing and abstraction in the recognition of disoriented forms. Unpublished masters thesis, University of Oregon, 1970.

Burtt, E. A. *The metaphysical foundations of modern science.* New York: Doubleday & Co., Inc., 1954.

Caldwell, E. C., and Hall, V. C. Distinctive-features versus prototype learning reexamined. *Journal of Experimental Psychology*, 1970, *83*, 7–12.

Calfee, R., Chapman, R., and Venezky, R. How a child needs to think to learn to read. In L. W. Gregg (Ed.), *Cognition in learning and memory.* New York: John Wiley & Sons, Inc., 1972. Pp. 139–182.

Campbell, D. T. Blind variation and selective retention in creative thought as in other knowledge processes. *Psychological Review,* 1960, *67*, 380–400.

Carmichael, L. C., Hogan, H. P., and Walter, A. A. An experimental study of the effect of language on the reproduction of visually perceived form. *Journal of Experimental Psychology,* 1932, *15*, 73–86.

Caws, P. The structure of discovery. *Science,* 1969, *166*, 1375–1380.

Ceraso, J., The interference theory of forgetting. *Scientific American,* 1967, *217*, 117–125.

Chase, W. G., and Posner, M. I. The effect of visual and auditory confusability on visual and memory search tasks. Paper presented at the meeting of the Midwestern Psychological Association, Chicago, 1965.

Cherry, E. C. Some experiments on the recognition of speech, with one and with two ears. *Journal of the Acoustical Society of America,* 1953, *25*, 975–979.

Chomsky, N. *Aspects of the theory of syntax.* Cambridge, Mass.: MIT Press, 1965.

Chomsky, N. *Language and mind.* New York: Harcourt Brace Jovanovich, Inc., 1968.

Claparède, E. La genèse de l'hypothèse. *Archives de psychologie,* 1933, *24*, 93–94.

Clark, H. H. Linguistic processes in deductive reasoning. *Psychological Review,* 1969, *76*, 387–404.

Clark, H. H., and Chase, W. G. On the process of comparing sentences against pictures. *Cognitive Psychology,* 1972, *3*, 472–517.

Cofer, C. N. Verbal behavior in relation to reasoning and values. In H. Guetzkow (Ed.), *Group leadership and men.* Pittsburgh: Carnegie Press, 1951.

Cofer, C. N. The role of language in human problem solving. Paper presented at Conference on Human Problem Solving Behavior, New York University, April 1954.

Cofer, C. N. On some factors in the organizational characteristics of free recall. *American Psychologist,* 1965, *20*, 261–272.

Cohen, B. H. Recall of categorized word lists. *Journal of Experimental Psychology,* 1963, *66*, 227–234.

Cohen, G. Pattern recognition: Differences between matching patterns to patterns and matching descriptions to patterns. *Journal of Experimental Psychology,* 1969, *82*, 427–434.

Cohen, G. Some evidence for parallel comparisons in a letter recognition task. *Quarterly Journal of Experimental Psychology,* 1969, *21,* 272–279.

Collins, A. M., and Quillian, M. R. Retrieval time from semantic memory. *Journal of Verbal Learning and Verbal Behavior,* 1969, *8,* 240–247.

Conrad, C. Cognitive economy in semantic memory. *Journal of Experimental Psychology,* 1972, *92,* 149–154.

Conrad, R. Acoustic confusions in immediate memory. *British Journal of Psychology,* 1964, *55,* 75–84.

Crombie, A. C. *Augustine to Galileo; The history of science.* London: Falcon Books, 1952.

Crombie, A. C. *Robert Grosseteste and the origins of experimental science, 1100–1700.* Oxford: Clarendon Press, 1953.

Crovitz, H. F. *Galton's walk.* New York: Harper & Row, Publishers, 1970.

Crowder, R. G. Short-term memory for words with a perceptual-motor interpolated activity. *Journal of Verbal Learning and Verbal Behavior,* 1967, *6,* 753–761.

Crowder, R. G., and Morton, J. Precategorical acoustic storage. *Perception and Psychophysics,* 1969, *5,* 365–373.

Dainoff, M. J., and Haber, R. N. Effect of acoustic confusability on levels of information processing. *Canadian Journal of Psychology,* 1970, *24,* 98–108.

Dansereau, D. F., and Gregg, L. W. An information processing analysis of mental multiplication. *Psychonomic Science,* 1966, *6,* 71–72.

Darwin, C. *The origin of the species.* New York: P. F. Collier & Son, Corp., 1909.

Dawes, R. M. Memory and distortion of meaningful written material. *British Journal of Psychology,* 1966, *57,* 77–86.

DeBono, E. *New think; The use of lateral thinking in the generation of new ideas.* New York: Basic Books, Inc., 1968.

Deese, J. *The structure of associations in language and thought.* Baltimore: Johns Hopkins Press, 1966.

Deese, J. *Psycholinguistics.* Boston: Allyn & Bacon, Inc., 1970.

DeGroot, A. D. *Thought and choice in chess.* The Hague: Mouton & Co., 1965.

Denny, N. R. Memory and transformations in concept learning. *Journal of Experimental Psychology,* 1969, *79,* 63–68.

DeSoto, C. B. The predilection for single orderings. *Journal of Abnormal and Social Psychology,* 1961, *62,* 16–23.

DeSoto, C. B., London, M., and Handel, S. Social reasoning and spatial paralogic. *Journal of Personality and Social Psychology,* 1965, *2,* 513–521.

Dewey, J. *How we think.* Boston: D. C. Heath and Co., 1933.

Donders, F. C. On the speed of mental processes. *Acta Psychologica,* 1969, *30,* 412–431.

DuCharme, W. M., and Peter, C. R. Proportion estimation as a function of proportion and sample size. *Journal of Experimental Psychology,* 1969, *81,* 536–541.

Dukes, W. F., and Bevan, W. Stimulus variation and repetition in the acquisition of naming responses. *Journal of Experimental Psychology,* 1967, *74,* 178–181.

Duncker, K. On problem solving. *Psychological Monographs,* 1945, *58* (5, Whole No. 270).

Ebbinghaus, H. *Memory; A contribution to experimental psychology.* Trans. H. A. Ruger and C. E. Bussenius. New York: Columbia University Press, 1913.

Eccles, J. C. (Ed.) *Brain and conscious experience.* New York: Springer-Verlag New York Inc., 1966.

Edwards, W. Dynamic decision theory and probabilistic information processing. *Human Factors,* 1962, *4,* 59–73.

Egeth, H. Selective attention. *Psychological Bulletin,* 1967, *67,* 41–57.

Eichelman, W. H. Familiarity effects in the simultaneous matching task. *Journal of Experimental Psychology,* 1970, *86,* 275–282.

Epstein, W., and Rock, I. Perceptual set as an artifact of recency. *American Journal of Psychology,* 1960, *73,* 214–228.

Evans, S. H. A brief statement of schema theory. *Psychonomic Science,* 1967, *8,* 87–88.

Fehrer, E., and Raab, D. Reaction time to stimuli masked by metacontrast. *Journal of Experimental Psychology,* 1962, *63,* 143–147.

Feldman, J. Simulation of behavior in the binary choice experiment. In E. Feigerbaum and J. Feldman (Eds.), *Computers and thought.* New York: McGraw-Hill Book Co., 1963.

Festinger, L. *A theory of cognitive dissonance.* Palo Alto, Calif.: Stanford University Press, 1957.

Fillenbaum, S., and Rapoport, A. *Structures in the subjective lexicon.* New York: Academic Press, Inc., 1971.

Fiske, D. W., and Maddi, S. R. *Functions of varied experience.* Homewood, Ill.: Dorsey Press, 1961.

Fitts, P. M. The information capacity of the human motor system in controlling the amplitude of movement. *Journal of Experimental Psychology,* 1954, *47,* 381–391.

Fitts, P. M. Perceptual-motor skill learning. In A. W. Melton (Ed.), *Categories of Human Learning.* New York: Academic Press, Inc., 1964. Pp. 243–283.

Fitts, P. M., and Posner, M. I. *Human performance.* Monterey, Calif.: Brooks Cole Publishing Co., 1967.

Foss, D. Decision processes during sentence comprehension: Effects of lexical item difficulty and position upon decision times. *Journal of Verbal Learning and Verbal Behavior,* 1969, *8,* 457–462.

Fraisse, P. Why is naming longer than reading? *Acta Psychologica,* 1969, *30,* 96–103.

Fraisse, P. Reconnaissance de l'identité physique et sémantique de dessins et de noms. *Psychologie: Schweizerische Zeitschrift für Psychologie ünd ihre Anwendungen / Revue Suisse de Psychologie pure et appliqué,* 1970, *29,* 76–84.

Franks, J. J., and Bransford, J. D. Abstraction of visual patterns. *Journal of Experimental Psychology,* 1971, *90,* 65–74.

Frost, N. Clustering by visual shape in the free recall of pictorial stimuli. *Journal of Experimental Psychology,* 1971, *88,* 409–413.

Frost, N. Encoding and retrieval in visual memory tasks. *Journal of Experimental Psychology,* 1972, *95,* 317–326.

Fulgosi, A., and Guilford, J. P. Short-term incubation in divergent production. *American Journal of Psychology,* 1968, *81,* 241–246.

Funkhouser, G. R. Effects of differential encoding on recall. *Journal of Verbal Learning and Verbal Behavior,* 1968, *7,* 1016–1023.

Galton, Sir F. *Inquiries into human faculty and its development.* London: J. M. Dent & Sons, Ltd., 1907.

Garner, W. R. To perceive is to know. *American Psychologist,* 1966, *21,* 11–19.

Garner, W. R. Good patterns have few alternatives. *American Scientist,* 1970, *58,* 34–42.

Gazzaniga, M. S. The split brain in man. *Scientific American,* 1967, *217,* 24–29.

Gazzaniga, M. *The bisected brain.* New York: Appleton-Century-Crofts, 1970.

Gibson, E. J. *Principles of perceptual learning and development.* New York: Appleton-Century-Crofts, 1969.

Glucksberg, S. Functional fixedness: Problem solution as a function of observing responses. *Psychonomic Science,* 1964, *1,* 117–118.

Glucksberg, S., and Danks, J. H. Effects of discriminative labels and of nonsense labels upon availability of novel function. *Journal of Verbal Learning and Verbal Behavior,* 1968, *7,* 72–76.

Glucksberg, S., and Weisberg, R. W. Verbal behavior and problem solving: Some effects of labeling in a functional fixedness problem. *Journal of Experimental Psychology,* 1966, *71*(5), 659–664.

Goldberg, L. R. Diagnosticians versus diagnostic signs: The diagnosis of psychosis versus neurosis from the MMPI. *Psychological Monographs,* 1965, *79* (9, Whole No. 602).

Goldberg, L. R. Simple models or simple processes? *American Psychologist,* 1968, *23* (7), 483–496.

Goldman-Eisler, F. *Psycholinguistics.* New York: Academic Press, Inc., 1968.

Gordon, W. J. J. *Synectics: The development of creative capacity.* New York: Harper & Row, Publishers, 1961.

Greenberg, J. H. *Language Universals.* The Hague: Mouton & Co., 1966.

Groen, G. J., and Parkman, J. M. A chronometric analysis of simple addition. *Psychological Review,* 1972, *79,* 329–343.

Guilford, J. P. *The nature of human intelligence.* New York: McGraw-Hill Book Co., 1967.

Hall, E. T. *The silent language.* New York: Doubleday & Co., Inc., 1959.

Hart, J. T. Memory and the memory-monitoring process. *Journal of Verbal Learning and Verbal Behavior,* 1967, *6,* 685–691.

Hanfmann, E., and Kasanin, J. Conceptual thinking in schizophrenia. *Nervous and Mental Disease Monographs,* 1942, Whole No. 67.

Hawkins, H. L. Parallel processing in complex visual displays. *Perception and Psychophysics,* 1969, *5,* 56–64.

Haygood, R. C., and Bourne, L. E., Jr. Attribute- and rule-learning aspects of conceptual behavior. *Psychological Review,* 1965, *72*(3), 175–195.

Hebb, D. O. *Organization of behavior.* New York: John Wiley & Sons, 1949.

Hebb, D. O. Concerning imagery. *Psychological Review,* 1968, *75,* 466–477.

Heidbreder, E. Toward a dynamic psychology of cognition. *Psychological Review,* 1945, *52,* 1–22.

Heidbreder, E. The attainment of concepts: I., Terminology and methodology. *Journal of General Psychology,* 1946, *35,* 173–189.

Heidbreder, E. The attainment of concepts: II., The problem. *Journal of General Psychology,* 1946, *35,* 191–223.

Helson, H. *Adaptation-level theory.* New York: Harper & Row, Publishers, 1964.

Hernandez-Peòn, R. Neurophysiological correlates of habituation and other manifestations of plastic inhibition (internal inhibition). In H. H. Jasper, and G. D. Smirnov (Eds.), The Moscow colloquium on electroencephalography of higher nervous activity. *Electroencephalography and Clinical Neurophysiology,* 1960 (Supplement No. 13), 101–114.

Hinsey, W. C. Identification-learning after pretraining on central and noncentral standards. Unpublished masters thesis, University of Oregon, 1963.

Hislop, M. W., and Brooks, L. R. Suppression of concept learning by verbal rules. Technical Report No. 28, Department of Psychology, McMasters University, December 1968.

Hochberg, J. E. *Perception.* Englewood Cliffs, N.J.: Prentice-Hall, Inc., 1964.

Hoffman, P. J. Cue-consistency and configurality in human judgment. In B. Kleinmuntz (Ed.), *Formal representation of human judgment.* New York: John Wiley & Sons, Inc., 1968.

Hoffman, P. J., Slovic, P., and Rorer, L. G. An analysis-of-variance model for the assessment of configural cue utilization in clinical judgment. *Psychological Bulletin,* 1968, *69,* 338–349.

Hull, C. L. Quantitative aspects of the evolution of concepts; An experimental study. *Psychological Monographs,* 1920, *28* (1, Whole No. 123).

Humphrey, B. *Directed thinking.* New York: Dodd, Mead & Co., 1948.

Hunt, E. B. *Concept learning: An information processing problem.* New York: John Wiley & Sons, Inc., 1962.

Hunter, I. M. L. The solving of three-term series problems. *British Journal of Psychology,* 1957, *48,* 286–298.

Hunter, I. M. L. *Memory.* Baltimore: Penguin Books, Inc., 1964.

Huttenlocher, J. Constructing spatial images: A strategy in reasoning. *Psychological Review,* 1968, *75*(6), 550–560.

Hyman, R. On prior information and creativity. *Psychological Reports,* 1961, *9,* 151–161.

Hyman, R. Creativity and the prepared mind. Research Monograph No. 1, The National Art Education Association, 1965.

Hyman, R., and Frost, N. Gradients and schema in pattern recognition. In P. M. A. Rabbitt (Ed.), *Attention and performance.* Vol. V. New York: Academic Press, Inc., 1974.

Hyman, R., and Well, A. Judgments of similarity and spatial models. *Perception and Psychophysics,* 1967, *2*(6), 233–248.

James, W. *Psychology.* New York: Holt, Rinehart & Winston, Inc., 1907.

Jensen, A. R., and Rohwer, W. D. The Stroop color-word test: A review. *Acta Psychologica,* 1966, *25,* 36–93.

Johnson, D. M. *The psychology of thought and judgment.* New York: Harper & Row, Publishers, 1955.

Jones, W. T. *A history of western philosophy.* (2nd ed.) New York: Harcourt Brace Jovanovich, Inc., 1969.

Judson, A. J., Cofer, C. N., and Gelfand, S. Reasoning as an associative process: II., "Direction" in problem solving as a function of prior reinforcement of relevant responses. *Psychological Reports,* 1956, *2,* 501–507.

Kahneman, D. Method, findings and theory in studies of visual masking. *Psychological Bulletin,* 1968, *70*(6), 404–425.

Kahneman, D. Remarks on attention control. *Acta Psychologica,* 1970, *33,* 118–131.

Kahneman, D. *Attention and effort.* Englewood Cliffs, N.J.: Prentice-Hall, Inc., 1973.

Kahneman, D., and Beatty, J. Pupil diameter and load on memory. *Science,* 1966, *154,* 1583–1585.

Kahneman, D., and Tversky, A. Subjective probability: A judgment of representativeness. *Cognitive Psychology,* 1972, *3,* 430–454.

Kant, I. *The critique of pure reason.* Trans. J. M. D. Meiklejohn. London: G. Bell & Sons, Ltd., 1910.

Karlin, L. Cognition, preparation, and sensory-evoked potentials. *Psychological Bulletin,* 1970, *73*(2), 122–136.

Karlin, L., and Kestenbaum, R. Effects of number of alternatives on the psychological refractory period. *Quarterly Journal of Experimental Psychology,* 1968, *20,* 167–178.

Karwoski, T. F., Gramlich, F. W., and Arnott, P. Psychological studies in semantics: I., Free association reactions to words, drawings and objects. *Journal of Social Psychology,* 1944, *20,* 233–247.

Keele, S. W. Compatibility and time sharing in serial reaction time. *Journal of Experimental Psychology,* 1967, *75,* 529–539.

Keele, S. W. Movement control in skilled motor performance. *Psychological Bulletin,* 1968, *70,* 387–403.

Keele, S. W. Repetition effect: A memory-dependent process. *Journal of Experimental Psychology,* 1969, *80,* 243–248.

Keele, S. W. *Attention and human performance.* Pacific Palisades, Calif.: Goodyear Publishing Co., Inc., 1973.

Kendler, H. H., and Kendler, T. S. Vertical and horizontal processes in problem solving. *Psychological Review,* 1962, *69*(1), 1–16.

Keppel, G., and Underwood, B. J. Proactive inhibition in short-term retention of single items. *Journal of Verbal Learning and Verbal Behavior,* 1962, *1,* 153–161.

Kimura, D. Functional asymmetry of the brain in dichotic listening. *Cortex,* 1967, *3,* 163–178.

Klatzky, R. L. Inter-hemispheric transfer of test stimulus representations in memory scanning. *Psychonomic Science,* 1970, *21,* 201–203.

Koestler, A. *The act of creation.* New York: The Macmillan Co., 1964.

Koffka, K. *Principles of Gestalt psychology.* New York: Harcourt Brace Jovanovich, Inc., 1935.

Köhler, W. *The task of Gestalt psychology.* Princeton, N.J.: Princeton University Press, 1969.

Kolers, P. A. Some formal characteristics of pictograms. *Scientific American,* 1969, *57*(3), 348–363.

Konorski, J. *Integrative activity of the brain; An interdisciplinary approach.* Chicago: The University of Chicago Press, 1967.

Krueger, L. E. Search time in a redundant visual display. *Journal of Experimental Psychology,* 1970, *83*(3), 391–399. (a)

Krueger, L. E. Effect of frequency of display on speed of visual search. *Journal of Experimental Psychology,* 1970, *84*(3), 495–498. (b)

Kuhn, T. S. *The structure of scientific revolutions.* Chicago: The University of Chicago Press, 1962.

Landauer, T. K. Rate of implicit speech. *Perceptual and Motor Skills,* 1962, *15,* 646.

Landauer, T. K., and Freedman, J. L. Inforamtion retrieval from long-term memory: Category size and recognition time. *Journal of Verbal Learning and Verbal Behavior,* 1968, *7,* 291–295.

Leask, J., Haber, R. N., and Haber, R. B. Eidetic imagery in children: II., Longitudinal and experimental results. *Psychonomic Monographs Supplement,* 1969, *3* (Whole No. 35), 25–48.

Leeper, R. W. A study of a neglected portion of the field of learning—The development of sensory organization. *Journal of Genetic Psychology,* 1935, *46,* 41–75.

Lenneberg, E. H. *Biological foundations of language.* New York: John Wiley & Sons, Inc., 1967.

Levine, M. Hypothesis behavior by humans during discrimination learning. *Journal of Experimental Psychology,* 1966, *71*(3), 331–338.

Levine, M. Neo-noncontinuity theory. In G. H. Bower and J. T. Spence (Eds.), *The psychology of learning and motivation.* Vol. 3. New York: Academic Press, Inc., 1969. Pp. 101–134.

Levine, M. Hypothesis theory and nonlearning despite ideal S-R reinforcement contingencies. *Psychological Review,* 1971, *78,* 130–140.

Lewis, J. L. Semantic processing of unattended messages using dichotic listening. *Journal of Experimental Psychology,* 1970, *85,* 225–228.

Liberman, A. M., Cooper, F. S., Shankweiler, D. P., and Studdert-Kennedy, M. Perception of the speech code. *Psychological Review,* 1967, *74*(6), 431–461.

Locke, J. *An essay concerning human understanding.* Ed. Pringle-Pattison. Oxford: Clarendon Press, 1924.

Loess, H. Short-term memory, word class and sequence of items. *Journal of Experimental Psychology,* 1967, *74*(4), 556–561.

Loess, H., and Waugh, N. C. Short-term memory and intertrial interval. *Journal of Verbal Learning and Verbal Behavior,* 1967, *6,* 455–560.

Luce, R. D., Bush, R. R., and Galanter, E. *Handbook of mathematical psychology.* Vol. 1, Chapters 1–8. New York: John Wiley & Sons, Inc., 1963.

Luchins, A. S. Mechanization in problem solving: The effect of "Einstellung." *Psychometric Monographs,* 1942, *54*(6), 95.

Luria, A. *The mind of a mnemonist.* New York: Basic Books, Inc., 1968.

Luria. A., and Vinogradova, O. S. An objective investigation of the dynamics of semantic systems. *British Journal of Psychology,* 1959, *50,* 89–105.

MacKay, D. G. Mental dyplopia: Towards a model of speech perception at the semantic level. In D'Arcais and Levet (Eds.), *Recent advances in psycholinguistics.* Amsterdam: North-Holland Publishing Co., 1970. Pp. 76–100.

MacKay, D. G. Aspects of the theory of comprehension, memory and attention. *Quarterly Journal of Experimental Psychology,* 1973, *25,* 22–40.

Mackworth, J. F. Performance decrement in vigilance, threshold and high-speed perceptual motor tasks. *Canadian Journal of Psychology,* 1964, *18*(3), 209–223.

Maier, N. R. F. Reasoning in humans: II., The solution of a problem and its appearance in consciousness. *Journal of Comparative and Physiological Psychology,* 1931, *12,* 181–194.

Malpass, R. S., and Kravitz, J. Recognition for faces of own and other race. *Journal of Personality and Social Psychology,* 1969, *13*(4), 330–334.

Maltzman, I. On the training of originality. *Psychological Review,* 1960, *67,* 229–242.

Mandler, G. Organization and memory. In K. W. Spence and J. T. Spence (Eds.), *The psychology of learning and motivation.* Vol. 1. New York: Academic Press, Inc., 1967. Pp. 328–371.

Mandler, J. M., and Mandler, G. *Thinking: From association to Gestalt.* New York: John Wiley & Sons, Inc., 1964.

McKeller, P. *Imagination and thinking.* Oxford: Alden & Mowbray, Ltd., 1957.

McKeon, R. *Selections from medieval philosophers.* Vols. I and II. New York: Charles Scribner's Sons, 1929.

Mednick, S. The associative basis of the creative process. *Psychological Review,* 1962, *69,* 220–232.

Merkel, J. Die Zeitlichen Verhaltnisse der Willensthatigkeit. *Philosophische Studien,* 1885, *2,* 73–127.

Meyer, D. E. On the representation and retrieval of stored semantic information. *Cognitive Psychology,* 1970, *1*(3), 242–299.

Milgram, S. The experience of living in cities. *Science,* 1970, *167,* 1461–1468.

Mill, J. S. *A system of logic.* London: Longmans, Green & Co., Ltd., 1843. Republished 1956.

Miller, G. A. *Language and communication.* New York: McGraw-Hill Book Co., 1951.

Miller, G. A. The magical number seven, plus or minus two: Some limits on our capacity for processing information. *Psychological Review,* 1956, *63*(2), 81–97.

Miller, G. A. Some psychological studies of grammar. *American Psychologist,* 1962, *17,* 748–762.

Miller, G. A. Psycholinguistic approaches to the study of communication. In D. L. Arm (Ed.), *Journeys in science.* Albuquerque: The University of New Mexico Press, 1967.

Miller, G. A., Galanter, E., and Pribram, K. *Plans and the structure of behavior.* New York: Holt, Rinehart & Winston, Inc., 1960.

Milner, P. Brain disturbance after bilateral hippocampal lesions. In P. Milner and S. Glickman (Eds.), *Cognitive processes and the brain.* New York: D. Van Nostrand Co., Inc., 1965. Pp. 97–111.

Moore, T. V. The temporal relations of meaning and imagery. *Psychological Review,* 1915, *22,* 177–225.

Moray, N. Attention in dichotic listening: Affective cues and the influence of instructions. *Quarterly Journal of Experimental Psychology,* 1959, *11,* 56–60.

Morin, R. E., DeRosa, D. V., and Stultz, V. Recognition memory and reaction time. *Acta Psychologica,* 1967, *27,* 298–305.

Moyer, R. S., and Landauer, T. K. Time required for judgments of numerical inequality. *Nature,* 1967, *215,* 1519–1520.

Munsinger, H., and Kessen, W. Stimulus variability and cognitive change. *Psychological Review,* 1966, *73*(2), 164–178.

Murray, H. G., and Denny, J. P. Interaction of ability level and interpolated activity (opportunity for incubation) in human problem solving. *Psychological Reports,* 1969, *24,* 271–276.

Neisser, U. *Cognitive psychology.* New York: Appleton-Century-Crofts, 1967.

Neisser, U., and Weene, P. Hierarchies in concept attainment. *Journal of Experimental Psychology,* 1962, *64*(6), 640–645.

Newell, A., Shaw, J. C., and Simon, H. A. Elements of a theory of human problem solving. *Psychological Review,* 1958, *65,* 151–166.

Nickerson, R. S. "Same-different" response times with multi-attribute stimulus differences. *Perceptual and Motor Skills,* 1967, *24,* 543–554.

Norman, D. A. *Memory and attention.* New York: John Wiley & Sons, Inc., 1969.

Norman, D. A. (Ed.) *Models of human memory.* New York: Academic Press, Inc., 1970.

Oldfield, R. C. Memory mechanisms and the theory of schemata. *British Journal of Psychology,* 1954, *45,* 14–23.

Osborn, A. F. *Applied imagination.* (Rev. ed.) New York: Charles Scribner's Sons, 1957.

Osgood, C. E. *Method and theory in experimental psychology.* New York: Oxford University Press, 1953.

Osgood, C. E., Suci, G. J., and Tannenbaum, P. H. *The measurement of meaning.* Urbana: The University of Illinois Press, 1957.

Oswald, I., Taylor, A. M., and Treisman, M. Discriminative responses to stimulation during human sleep. *Brain,* 1960, *83,* 440–453.

Paivio, A. Mental imagery in associative learning and memory. *Psychological Review,* 1969, *76,* 241–263.

Paivio, A. *Imagery and verbal processes.* New York: Holt, Rinehart & Winston, Inc., 1971.

Parks, T., Wall, C., and Bastian, J. Intercategory and intra-category discrimination for one visual continuum, contributions of identification training and of individual differences. *Journal of Experimental Psychology,* 1969, *81,* 241–245.

Patrick, C. Creative thought in poets. *Archives of Psychology,* No. 178, April 1935.

Patrick, C. Creative thought in artists. *Journal of Psychology,* 1937, *4,* 35–73.

Pavlov, I. *Conditioned reflexes.* Trans. G. V. Anrep. London: Oxford University Press, 1927.

Perky, C. W. An experimental study of imagination. *American Journal of Psychology,* 1910, *21,* 422–452.

Peterson, L. R. Concurrent verbal activity. *Psychological Review*, 1969, *76*, 376–386.

Peterson, L. R., and DuCharme, W. M. A primacy effect in subjective probability revision. *Journal of Experimental Psychology*, 1967, *73*, 61–65.

Peterson, L. R., and Peterson, M. J. Short-term retention of individual verbal items. *Journal of Experimental Psychology*, 1959, *58*, 193–198.

Piaget, J. *Logic and psychology.* New York: Basic Books, Inc., 1957.

Piaget, J., and Inhelder, B. *The psychology of the child.* Trans. H. Weaver. New York: Basic Books, Inc., 1969.

Pick, A. D. Improvement of visual and tactual form discrimination. *Journal of Experimental Psychology*, 1965, *69*, 331–339.

Plato. *The collected dialogues of Plato.* Ed. E. Hamilton and H. Cairns. New York: Pantheon Books, Inc., 1963.

Poincaré, H. *The foundations of science.* New York: Science House, Inc., 1929.

Pollio, H. R. Composition of associative clusters. *Journal of Experimental Psychology*, 1964, *67*, 199–208.

Polya, G. *How to solve it.* Princeton, N.J.: Princeton University Press, 1945.

Posner, M. I. Abstraction and the process of recognition. In G. H. Bower and J. T. Spence (Eds.), *The psychology of learning motivation.* Vol. 3. New York: Academic Press, Inc., 1969. Pp. 44–96.

Posner, M. I. On the relationship between letter names and superordinate categories. *Quarterly Journal of Experimental Psychology*, 1970, *22*, 279–287.

Posner, M. I., Boies, S. J., Eichelman, W. H., and Taylor, L. Retention of visual and name codes of single letters. *Journal of Experimental Psychology*, 1969 , *7*(1), Part 2, 1–16.

Posner, M. I., and Boies, S. J. Components of attention. *Psychological Review*, 1971, *78*(5), 391–408.

Posner, M. I., and Keele, S. W. On the genesis of abstract ideas. *Journal of Experimental Psychology*, 1968, *77*, 353–363.

Posner, M. I., and Keele, S. W. Retention of abstract ideas. *Journal of Experimental Psychology*, 1970, *83*, 304–308.

Posner, M. I., and Klein, R. On the functions of consciousness. In S. Kornblum (Ed.), *Attention and performance.* Vol. IV. New York: Academic Press, Inc., 1973.

Posner, M. I., and Konick, A. F. Short-term retention of visual and kinesthetic information. *Organizational Behavior and Human Performance*, 1966, *1*, 71–86.

Posner, M. I., Lewis, J. L., and Conrad, C. H. Component processes in reading: A performance analysis. In J. Kavanaugh and I. Mattingly (Eds.), *Language by ear and by eye: The relationship between*

speech and reading. Cambridge, Mass.: MIT Press, 1972. Pp. 159–192.

Posner, M. I., and Mitchell, R. F. Chronometric analysis of classification. *Psychological Review,* 1967, *74,* 392–409.

Posner, M. I., and Rossman, E. Effect of size and location of informational transforms upon short-term retention. *Journal of Experimental Psychology,* 1965, *70,* 496–505.

Price, H. H. Thinking and representation. *Proceedings of the British Academy,* 1946, *32,* 83–122.

Quastler, H. (Ed.) *Information theory in psychology: Problems and methods.* New York: The Free Press, 1955.

Quillian, M. R. Semantic memory. In M. Minsky (Ed.), *Semantic information processing.* Cambridge, Mass.: MIT Press, 1968.

Ray, W. S. *The experimental psychology of original thinking.* New York: The Macmillan Co., 1967.

Reed, S. K. Pattern recognition and categorization. *Cognitive Psychology,* 1972, *3,* 382–407.

Rees, H. J., and Israel, H. E. An investigation of the establishment and operation of mental sets. *Psychometric Monographs,* 1935, *46,* No. 210.

Reese, H. W. *The perception of stimulus relations.* New York: Academic Press, Inc., 1968.

Reeves, J. W. *Thinking about thinking.* New York: George Braziller, Inc., 1965.

Reicher, G. M. Perceptual recognition as a function of meaningfulness of stimulus material. *Journal of Experimental Psychology,* 1969, *81*(2), 275–280.

Reicher, G. M., Ligon, E. J., and Conrad, C. H. Interference in short-term memory. *Journal of Experimental Psychology,* 1969, *80*(1), 95–100.

Reitman, J. Short-term verbal retention with interpolated verbal and non-verbal signal detection. Communication No. 262, Mental Health Research Institute, University of Michigan, November 1969.

Reitman, W. R. *Cognition and thought.* New York: John Wiley & Sons, Inc., 1965.

Restle, F. Speed of adding and comparing numbers. *Journal of Experimental Psychology,* 1970, *83*(2), 274–278.

Restle, F., and Brown, E. R. Serial pattern learning. *Journal of Experimental Psychology,* 1970, *83*(1), 120–125.

Rock, I., and Englestein, P. A study of memory for visual form. *American Journal of Psychology,* 1959, *72,* 221–229.

Rommetveit, R. *Words, meanings and messages: Theory and experiments in psycholinguistics.* New York: Academic Press, Inc., 1968.

Romney, A. K., and D'Andrade, R. G. Cognitive aspects of English kin terms. In A. K. Romney and R. G. D'Andrade (Eds.), Transcultural studies in cognition. *American Anthropologist,* 1964, *66*(3), Part 2.

Ryle, G. *The concept of mind.* New York: Barnes & Noble, Inc., 1949.

Sanders, A. F., and Schroots, J. J. F. Cognitive categories and memory span: II, The effect of temporal vs. categorical recall. *Quarterly Journal of Experimental Psychology,* 1968, *20,* 373–379.

Savin, H. B. What the child knows about speech when he starts to learn to read. In J. F. Kavanaugh and I. G. Mattingly (Eds.), *Language by ear and by eye.* Cambridge, Mass.: MIT Press, 1972.

Schaeffer, B., and Beller, K. Unpublished experiments, University of Oregon, 1970.

Schaeffer, B., and Wallace, R. Semantic similarity and the comparison of word meanings. *Journal of Experimental Psychology,* 1969, *82*(2), 343–346.

Schvaneveldt, R. W., and Staudenmayer, H. Mental arithmetic and the uncertainty effect in choice R. T. *Journal of Experimental Psychology,* 1970, *85,* 111–117.

Segal, S. J., and Fusella, V. Influence of imaged pictures and sounds on detection of visual and auditory signals. *Journal of Experimental Psychology,* 1970, *83*(3), 458–464.

Segal, S. J., and Gordon, P. E. The Perky effect revisited: Blocking of visual signals by imagery. *Perceptual and Motor Skills,* 1969, *28,* 791–797.

Shaffer, L. H. Multiple attention in transcription. In P. M. A. Rabbitt (Ed.), *Attention and performance.* Vol. V. New York: Academic Press, Inc., 1974.

Shallice, T. On the dual functions of consciousness. *Psychological Review,* 1972, *79,* 383–396.

Shepard, R. N. Attention and the metric structure of the stimulus space. *Journal of Mathematical Psychology,* 1964, *1,* 54–87.

Shepard, R. N. Recognition memory for words, sentences and pictures. *Journal of Verbal Learning and Verbal Behavior,* 1967, *6,* 156–163.

Shepard, R. N., and Chipman, S. Second-order isomorphism of internal representations: Shapes of states. *Cognitive Psychology,* 1970, *1,* 1–17.

Shepard, R. N., and Metzler, J. Mental rotation of three-dimensional objects. *Science,* 1971, *171,* 701–703.

Shiffrin, R. M., and Atkinson, R. C. Storage and retrieval processes in long-term memory. *Psychological Review,* 1969, *76*(2), 179–193.

Shulman, H. G. Encoding and retention of semantic and phonemic information in short-term memory. *Journal of Verbal Learning and Verbal Behavior,* 1970, *9,* 499–508.

Silveira, J. Incubation: The effect of interruption timing and length on problem solution and quality of problem processing. Unpublished doctoral dissertation, University of Oregon, 1971.

Simon, H. A. *The sciences of the artificial.* Cambridge, Mass.: MIT Press, 1969.

Simon, H. A., and Kotovsky, K. Human acquisition of concepts for sequential patterns. *Psychological Review,* 1963, *70*(6), 534–546.

Slamecka, N. J. Differentiation versus unlearning of verbal associations. *Journal of Experimental Psychology,* 1966, *71*(6), 822–828.

Slobin, D. *Psycholinguistics.* Glenview, Illinois: Scott, Foresman and Co., 1971.

Slovic, P. Cue-consistency and cue-utilization in judgment. *American Journal of Psychology,* 1966, *79*(3), 427–434.

Slovic, P. Analyzing the expert judge: A descriptive study of a stock-broker's decision process. *Journal of Applied Psychology,* 1969, *53,* 255–263.

Slovic, P., and Lichtenstein, S. Relative importance of probabilities and payoffs in risk taking. *Journal of Experimental Psychology, Monograph Supplement,* 1968, *78*(3, pt. 2), 1–18.

Slovic, P., and Lichtenstein, S. Comparison of Bayesian and regression approaches to the study of information processing in judgment. *Organic Behavior and Human Performance,* 1971, *6,* 649–744.

Smith, F., Lott, D., and Cronnell, B. The effect of type size and case alternation on word identification. *American Journal of Psychology,* 1969, *82,* 248–253.

Staats, A. W., and Staats, C. K. Meaning established by classical conditioning. *Journal of Experimental Psychology,* 1957, *54,* 74–80.

Starr, A., and Phillips, L. Verbal and motor memory in the amnestic syndrome. *Neuropsychologia,* 1970, *8,* 75–88.

Sternberg, S. High-speed scanning in human memory. *Science,* 1966, *153,* 652–654.

Sternberg, S. Memory-scanning: Mental processes revealed by reaction-time experiments. *American Scientist,* 1969, *57,* 421–457.

Stevens, S. S. On the operation known as judgment. *American Scientist,* 1966, *54,* 385–401.

Stratton, G. M. *Theophrastus and Greek physiological psychology before Aristotle,* New York: The Macmillan Co., 1917.

Stromeyer, C. F. III, and Psotka, J. The detailed texture of eidetic images. *Nature,* 1970, *225,* 346–349.

Studdert-Kennedy, M., and Shankweiler, D. Hemispheric specialization for speech perception. *Journal of the Acoustical Society of America,* 1970, *48,* 279–294.

Szekely, L. Productive processes in learning and thinking. *Acta Psychologica,* 1950, *7,* 388–407.

Taylor, D. H. Latency components in two-choice responding. *Journal of Experimental Psychology,* 1966, *72,* 481–487.

Thomas, H. B. G. Communication theory and the constellation hypotheses of calculation. *Quarterly Journal of Experimental Psychology,* 1963, *15*(3), 173–191.

Tighe, T. J., and Tighe, L. S. Differentiation theory and concept-shift behavior. *Psychological Bulletin,* 1968, *70,* 756–761.

Toffler, A. *Future shock.* New York: Bantam Books, Inc., 1970.

Trabasso, T., Rollins, H., and Shaughnessy, E. Storage and verification stages in processing concepts. *Cognitive Psychology,* 1971, *2,* 239–289.

Tresselt, M. E., and Leeds, D. S. The einstellung effect in immediate and delayed problem-solving. *Journal of General Psychology,* 1953, *49,* 87–95.

Tulving, E. Episodic and semantic memory. In E. Tulving and W. Donaldson (Eds.), *Organization of memory.* New York: Academic Press, Inc., 1972. Pp. 282–402.

Tversky, A. Intransitivity of preferences. *Psychological Review,* 1969, *76,* 31–48.

Tversky, A. Pictorial and verbal encoding in a short-term memory task. *Perception and Psychophysics,* 1969, *6,* 225–233.

Tversky, A., and Kahneman, D. Availability: A heuristic for judging frequency and probability. *Cognitive Psychology,* in press.

Uhr, L. *Pattern recognition.* New York: John Wiley & Sons, Inc., 1966.

Underwood, B. J. False recognition produced by implicit verbal responses. *Journal of Experimental Psychology,* 1965, *70,* 122–129.

Underwood, B. J., and Schultz, R. W. *Meaningfulness and verbal learning.* New York: J. B. Lippincott Co., 1960.

Vygotsky, L. S. *Thought and language.* Trans. E. Hanfmann and G. Vakar. Cambridge, Mass.: MIT Press, 1962.

Walkup, L. E. Creativity in science through visualization. *Perceptual and Motor Skills,* 1965, *21,* 35–41.

Wallace, A. F. C., and Atkins, J. The meaning of kinship terms. *American Anthropologist,* 1960, *62,* 58–79.

Wallas, G. *The art of thought.* New York: Harcourt Brace Jovanovich, Inc., 1926.

Walter, W. G., Cooper, R., Aldridge, V. J., McCallum, W. C., and Winter, A. L. Contingent negative variation: An electric sign of sensorimotor association and expectancy in the human brain. *Nature,* 1964, *203,* 380–384.

Warren, R. E. Stimulus encoding and memory. *Journal of Experimental Psychology,* 1972, *94,* 90–100.

Wason, P. C. The processing of positive and negative information. *Quarterly Journal of Experimental Psychology,* 1959, *11,* 92–107.

Weber, R. J., and Bach, M. Visual and speech imagery. *British Journal of Psychology,* 1969, *60*(2), 199–202.

Weber, R. J., and Castleman, J. The time it takes to imagine. *Perception and Psychophysics,* 1970, *8,* 165–168.

Welch, J. C. On the measurement of mental activity through muscular activity and the determination of a constant of attention. *American Journal of Physiology,* 1898, *1,* 283–306.

Wertheimer, M. *Productive thinking.* New York: Harper & Row, Publishers, 1945.

Westcott, M. R. *Toward a contemporary psychology of intuition: A historical, theoretical and empirical inquiry.* New York: Holt, Rinehart & Winston, Inc., 1968.

White, B. W. Recognition of familiar characters under an unfamiliar transformation. *Perceptual and Motor Skills,* 1962, *15,* 107–116.

Whitehead, A. N. *Science and the modern world.* New York: The Macmillan Co., 1948.

Whorf, B. L. *Language, thought and reality.* Cambridge, Mass.: MIT Press, 1956.

Wickens, D. D. Encoding categories of words: An empirical approach to meaning. *Psychological Review,* 1970, *77,* 1–15.

Wickens, D. D., Born, D. G., and Allen, C. K. Proactive inhibition and item similarity in short-term memory. *Journal of Verbal Learning and Verbal Behavior,* 1963, *2,* 440–445.

Wingfield, A. The identification and naming of objects. Unpublished doctoral dissertation, Oxford University, 1966.

Winkelman, J., and Schmidt, J. Associative confusions in mental arithmetic. *Journal of Experimental Psychology,* in press.

Woodworth, R. S. *Experimental psychology.* New York: Holt, Rinehart & Winston, Inc., 1938.

Woodworth, R. S., and Schlosberg, H. *Experimental psychology.* New York: Holt, Rinehart & Winston, Inc., 1954.

Name Index

Subject Index

Abstraction, 5, 6-7, 10, 44-60, 94, 124; and consciousness, 135, 137, 143-144, 146; iconic, 46-60, 74, 90, 99-101; and problem solving, 163; and schema formation, 49-52, 82; from sensory form to semantic structure, 94, 96-107, 117, 122, 135, 137, 146; and symbolic concepts, 65, 66, 68-69, 74

Active memory, 16-18, 19, 27, 29, 39, 42, 73, 89, 91, 117, 123; and consciousness, 136, 138, 140, 141-144; and problem solving, 162; scanning for, 104-107; *see also* Operational memory *and* Short-term memory

Adaptation level, 45

Aesthetics, 59-60

Affirmation, 76-77

Alertness, 108, 128, 133-134, 137

Arithmetic operations, 94, 103, 112-113

Associations, 2, 4, 9, 13, 16-17, 27-30, 40, 139, 151-152; in abstraction, 48, 58, 85-86, 122; and problem solving, 151-152, 155, 157, 168, 174; visual, 101-103, 104, 155, 157

Attention: divided, 129-132; and hypotheses, 75-76, 90; and memory, 17, 37; and mental operations, 125-132, 137; and problem solving, 174, 175, 177; span, 125-127

Attributes: and abstraction, 55-56; and concept classification, 61, 62-65, 66, 67, 70, 76-77, 84, 90; and consciousness, 141-142; and judgment, 77-80; in mental operations, 114, 115; selection, 77-80, 83

Auditory images: *see* Echoic codes

Availability, 82

Automatic activation, 138, 139-140

Brain processes, 18, 24, 103-104, 108

Brainstorming, 169

Capacity: allocation of, 127-132; limited, 125-127, 139-140, 141, 146; spare, 144-146

Central processor and consciousness, 127, 133, 135-136, 138, 139, 141, 144

Chess, 139-140, 146, 152-153, 162, 179

Child development: and abstraction, 54-55, 102-103; and code coordination, 159-160; and concept formation, 62-64; and counting time, 112; and motor codes, 25; and thought processes, 10, 93

Choice, 77-80, 95

Classical conditioning, 27

Classification: and abstraction, 49, 56-57, 60; and concept formation, 61-91, 136; and consciousness, 136, 137, 141-143; of input, 30-32, 42, 96-107; limits of, 34-36

Coding, 18-27, 66, 86, 94, 117, 120, 122, 156-157

Comparison, 10, 93, 94

Complexes, 63

Comprehension, 117-122, 123, 160

Concentration, 126, 127, 128-129, 134, 170, 171, 174; *see also* Attention

Concepts, 6-7, 46, 60, 61-91, 113, 114, 141-144; iconic, 46-60, 61, 63, 86, 99-101, 116; symbolic, 61-91

Conceptualism, 5

Conditioned stimulus, 27

Conjunction, 76-77, 86-87, 93-94, 113-116, 119

Consciousness, 11-13, 14, 37, 42, 124-146; capacity of, 93, 125-132; generation and spare capacity in, 144-146; and initial representation, 139-140, 152-153; and mental operations, 93, 95, 132-140; and problem solving, 152-153, 163, 165, 169-171, 173, 175, 179; and thought, 140-144

Content addressable, 42

Creative thought, 147, 148, 149, 153, 154, 163-165, 168, 169-175

Daydreaming, 144-146, 147, 179

Decision making, 11, 79; *see also* Problem solving

Deduction, 4, 10

Dimensionalization, 61-66, 67, 84-85

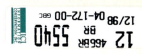